VIETNAM

Marxist Regimes Series

Series editor: Bogdan Szajkowski,
Department of Sociology,
University College, Cardiff

Further Titles

VIETNAM

Politics, Economics and Society

Melanie Beresford

 Pinter Publishers
London and New York

First published in Great Britain in 1988 and reprinted in 1989 by Pinter Publishers Limited
25 Floral Street, London WC2E 9DS

British Library Cataloguing in Publication Data

A CIP catalogue record for this book is available from the British Library.

Library of Congress Cataloging-in-Publication Data

Beresford, Melanie
   Vietnam: politics, economics, and society.
   (Marxist regimes series)
   Bibliography: p.
   Includes index.
   1. Vietnam—Politics and government—1975–
2. Vietnam—Economic conditions. 3. Vietnam—Social
conditions. I. Title. II. Series.
DS559.912.B47   1988   959.704   88-5859

ISBN 0-86187-448-X
ISBN 0-86187-449-8 (pbk.)

Typeset by Joshua Associates Limited, Oxford
Printed in Great Britain by SRP Ltd, Exeter

Editor's Preface

Vietnam occupies a unique position among the panoply of Marxist designs and experimentations. It is the only Marxist regime which after long and protracted war had to absorb a well-developed and ideologically hostile southern part of a previously divided country and consequently endure a complex process of reunification of social and political structures. This, the first comprehensive book on contemporary Vietnam's politics, economics and society provides the reader with an in-depth analysis of these processes as well as an evaluation of them. In addition it also gives a comprehensive background to the history of the country, the role played by Marxist groups in the development of Vietnam and Indochina, and Hanoi's relations with its neighbours as well as the wider communist movement. This work also raises a number of very important questions about the appraisal of Marxist adaptations in the developing countries.

The study of Marxist regimes has commonly been equated with the study of communist political systems. There were several historical and methodological reasons for this. For many years it was not difficult to distinguish the eight regimes in Eastern Europe and four in Asia which resoundingly claimed adherence to the tenets of Marxism and more particularly to their Soviet interpretation—Marxism-Leninism. These regimes, variously called 'People's Republic', 'People's Democratic Republic', or 'Democratic Republic', claimed to have derived their inspiration from the Soviet Union to which, indeed, in the overwhelming number of cases they owed their establishment.

To many scholars and analysts these regimes represented a multiplication of and geographical extension of the 'Soviet model' and consequently of the Soviet sphere of influence. Although there were clearly substantial similarities between the Soviet Union and the people's democracies, especially in the initial phases of their development, these were often overstressed at the expense of noticing the differences between these political systems.

It took a few years for scholars to realize that generalizing the particular, i.e., applying the Soviet experience to other states ruled by elites which claimed to be guided by 'scientific socialism', was not good enough. The relative simplicity of the assumption of a cohesive communist bloc was questioned after the expulsion of Yugoslavia from the Communist Information Bureau in 1948 and in particular after the workers' riots in Poznań in 1956 and the Hungarian revolution of the same year. By the mid-1960s, the totalitarian model of communist politics, which until then had been very much in force, began to crumble. As some of these regimes articulated demands for a distinctive path of socialist development, many specialists studying these systems began to notice that the cohesiveness of the communist bloc was less apparent than had been claimed before.

Also by the mid-1960s, in the newly independent African states 'democratic' multi-party states were turning into one-party states or military dictatorships, thus questioning the inherent superiority of liberal democracy, capitalism and the values that went with it. Scholars now began to ponder on the simple contrast between multi-party democracy and a one-party totalitarian rule that had satisfied an earlier generation.

More importantly, however, by the beginning of that decade Cuba had a revolution without Soviet help, a revolution which subsequently became to many political elites in the Third World not only an inspiration but a clear military, political and ideological example to follow. Apart from its romantic appeal, to many nationalist movements the Cuban revolution also demonstrated a novel way of conducting and winning a nationalist, anti-imperialist war and accepting Marxism as the state ideology without a vanguard communist party. The Cuban precedent was subsequently followed in one respect or another by scores of Third World regimes, which used the adoption of 'scientific socialism' tied to the tradition of Marxist thought as a form of mobilization, legitimation or association with the prestigious symbols and powerful high-status regimes such as the Soviet Union, China, Cuba and Vietnam.

Despite all these changes the study of Marxist regimes remains in its infancy and continues to be hampered by constant and not always pertinent comparison with the Soviet Union, thus somewhat blurring the important underlying common theme—the 'scientific theory' of the laws of development of human society and human history. This doctrine is claimed by the leadership of these regimes to consist of the discovery of objective causal relationships; it is used to analyse the contradictions which arise between goals and actuality in the pursuit of a common destiny. Thus the political elites of these countries have been and continue to be influenced in both their ideology and their political practice by Marxism more than any other current of social thought and political practice.

The growth in the number and global significance, as well as the ideological, political and economic impact, of Marxist regimes has presented scholars and students with an increasing challenge. In meeting this challenge, social scientists on both sides of the political divide have put forward a dazzling profusion of terms, models, programmes and varieties of interpretation. It is against the background of this profusion that the present comprehensive series on Marxist regimes is offered.

This collection of monographs is envisaged as a series of multi-disciplinary textbooks on the governments, politics, economics and society of these countries. Each of the monographs was prepared by a specialist on the country concerned. Thus, over fifty scholars from all over the world have contributed monographs which were based on first-hand knowledge. The geographical diversity of the authors, combined with the fact that as a group they represent many disciplines of social science, gives their individual analyses and the series as a whole an additional dimension.

Each of the scholars who contributed to this series was asked to analyse such topics as the political culture, the governmental structure, the ruling party, other mass organizations, party-state relations, the policy process, the economy, domestic and foreign relations together with any features peculiar to the country under discussion.

This series does not aim at assigning authenticity or authority to any single one of the political systems included in it. It shows that, depending on a variety of historical, cultural, ethnic and political factors, the pursuit of goals derived from the tenets of Marxism has produced different political forms at different times and in different places. It also illustrates the rich diversity among these societies, where attempts to achieve a synthesis between goals derived from Marxism on the one hand, and national realities on the other, have often meant distinctive approaches and solutions to the problems of social, political and economic development.

University College
Cardiff

Bogdan Szajkowski

Contents

List of Illustrations and Tables

Map

Figures

Tables

Acknowledgements

This book is the result of a long period of study of Vietnam, dating back to the 1960s. Over such a long gestation period I have acquired debts to many people both inside and outside Vietnam to whom I take this opportunity to express my gratitude for help given. I particularly wish to thank Bruce McFarlane who read this manuscript and made many helpful suggestions. None of the above are responsible for the final content. I would also like to thank the director and staff of Arbetslivscentrum, Stockholm, who provided excellent facilities and other forms of assistance while I was writing this book.

Basic Data

Official name	Socialist Republic of Vietnam (July 1976)
Population	60.1 million (1984)
Population density	181 persons per sq. km. (over 1,100 in parts of Red River delta)
Population growth (% p.a.)	2.6 (1979–84)
Urban population (%)	19.1 (1984)
Total labour force	23.1 million (1984)
Life expectancy	63 years (1986)
Infant death rate	49 per thousand under age of 1 year (1985)
Child death rate	4 per thousand under age of 4 (1985)
Ethnic groups	Viet (also known as Kinh) (88%); 60 minority nationalities (incl. Tay, Thai, Chinese, Khmer, Muong, Nung, Hmong)
Capital	Hanoi (population 2.9 million in 1984)
Land area	331,688 sq. km. of which 6 million ha. cultivated
Main language	Vietnamese
Administrative divisions	36 provinces, 3 municipalities (Hanoi, Haiphong, Ho Chi Minh City), 1 special zone (Vung Tau–Con Dao) 443 districts and town wards 9,504 communes and street blocks
Membership of international organizations	UN, IMF, World Bank, Asian Development Bank, Non-Aligned Movement
Political structure	
Constitution	December 1980
Highest legislative body	National Assembly (496 seats)
Highest executive body	Council of Ministers
President	Vo Chi Cong
Prime Minister	Pham Hung
Ruling party	Vietnamese Communist Party
Secretary-general	Nguyen Van Linh
Party membership	1.8 million (1986)

National income (UN method)
Per capita	US$189 (1982)
Growth rate	2.5% p.a. (1975–82)
Staple food production	c. 300 kg. paddy equivalent per capita (1984)
Energy consumption	76 kg. oil equivalent per capita (1985)
Structure of production	32.8% industry, 42.5% agriculture (1984)
Structure of workforce	11% industry, 71.3% agriculture (1984)

Trade and balance of payments
Exports coverage of imports	45% (1985)
Imports as % of GNP	13% (1984)
Main exports	Handicraft and light industrial products, fresh fruit and vegetables, coal, rubber, marine products, tea, wood, coffee
Main imports	Fertilizer, fuel, rice, cloth, machinery
Direction of exports	32% convertible area, 68% non-convertible area (1981)
External debt	US$5,339 million (1982)
debt service ratio	72% (1982)
Foreign aid	US$1.1 billion est. (1978), 70% CMEA
Foreign investment	n.a.

Armed forces   Approx. 1 million (Western estimates)

State budget (1983)
Wages, salaries and consumption subsidies	19%
Health, education, welfare	16%
Economic construction	31%
Other (incl. defence, admin., debt service	34%

Education (1980)
Pre-school enrolments	2.8 million
Primary school enrolments	7.89 million (in 1983 113% of age group)
Secondary school enrolments	3.16 million (in 1983 48% of age group)
Higher education enrolments	0.84 million
Adult literacy	95% (1978)

Religions   Buddhism, ancestor cult, Catholicism, Cao Dai, Hoa Hao

Women (1979)
    Labour force   53%
    University students   38%
    Technicians   42%
    Graduate cadres   26%
    National Assembly deputies   22%

Health (1984)
    Population per physician   4,310
    Population per trained nurse   1,040

Population Forecasting

The following data are projections produced by Poptran, University College Cardiff Population Centre, from United Nations Assessment Data published in 1980, and are reproduced here to provide some basis of comparison with other countries covered by the Marxist Regimes Series.

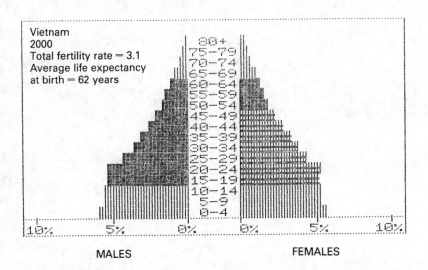

Vietnam
2000
Total fertility rate = 3.1
Average life expectancy at birth = 62 years

MALES   FEMALES

Projected Data for Vietnam 2000

Total population ('000)	78,894
Males ('000)	38,874
Females ('000)	40,020
Total fertility rate	3.08
Life expectancy (male)	60.0 years
Life expectancy (female)	63.6 years
Crude birth rate	25.9
Crude death rate	8.9
Annual growth rate	1.70%
Under 15s	33.30%
Over 65s	4.42%
Women aged 15–49	27.11%
Doubling time	41 years
Population density	237 per sq. km.
Urban population	36.4%

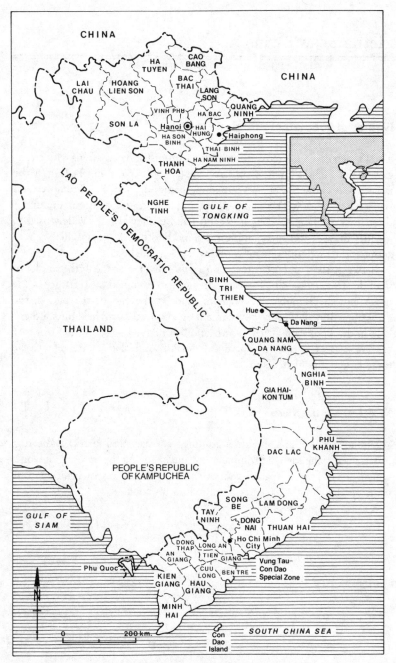

Vietnam: provincial boundaries and principal cities

Vietnamese Terms

Names of Vietnamese Regions

The French divided Vietnam into three administrative divisions which they called Cochinchina (in the south), Annam (central region) and Tonkin (in the north), also known by their Vietnamese names of Nam Ky, Trung Ky and Bac Ky respectively. These are no longer administrative divisions, but under the names of Nam Bo, Trung Bo and Bac Bo, they are still widely used to identify three distinct geographical regions. For the sake of simplicity I have adopted the modern nomenclature throughout the book.

Between 1954 and 1976 the country was divided at the 17th parallel of latitude. The Democratic Republic of Vietnam occupied the territory to the north and the Republic of Vietnam (and, at the end of the period, the Provisional Revolutionary Government of South Vietnam) held the southern half. In this book capitalized 'North' and 'South' refer to the former territory of these two regimes. Non-capitalized 'north', 'south' and 'centre' refer to the three regions designated above.

Written Vietnamese

Written Vietnamese contains a number of diacritical marks indicating differences in the tone of pronunciation and changing the meaning of words which are otherwise spelled the same way. For reasons of printing convenience these marks have been omitted in this book.

Abbreviations and Glossary

ARVN	Army of the Republic of Vietnam
ASEAN	Association of South East Asian Nations
CCP	Chinese Communist Party
CIP	Commercial Import Program (US aid program to South Vietnam)
CMEA	Council for Mutual Economic Assistance (COMECON)
CPSU	Communist Party of the Soviet Union
DK	Democratic Kampuchea
DMZ	De-Militarized Zone
DRV	Democratic Republic of Vietnam
FULRO	Front Unifié de Lutte des Races Opprimés
FYP	Five Year Plan
HES	Hamlet Evaluation System
ICP	Indochinese Communist Party
NEZ	New Economic Zone
NLF	National Liberation Front
OSS	US overseas intelligence agency
PAVN	People's Army of Vietnam
PRC	People's Republic of China
PRG	Provisional Revolutionary Government
PRK	People's Republic of Kampuchea
PRP	People's Revolutionary Party (southern wing of VWP, 1962–76)
RVN	Republic of Vietnam
SEATO	South East Asia Treaty Organization
SRV	Socialist Republic of Vietnam
USAID	US Agency for International Development
VCP	Vietnamese Communist Party
VCTU	Vietnam Confederation of Trade Unions
VNQDD	Viet Nam Quoc Dan Dang (Vietnamese Nationalist Party)
VWP	Vietnam Workers' Party (name of VCP, 1951–76)
VWU	Vietnam Women's Union
attentisme	non-commital or 'wait-and-see' attitude
colons	French colonial settlers

compradors   members of indigenous population who act as agents for
                      foreign capital
corvée   forced labour contribution
tram   species of Melaleuca from which oil is extracted for
                      pharmaceutical purposes

Part I
History and Political Traditions

In contrast to the experience of most other socialist countries, the establishment of a Marxist regime in Vietnam did not take place over a short period, by a single revolutionary upsurge or military coup. For thirty years after its establishment by the August Revolution in 1945, the regime led by the Vietnamese communists[1] held sway over only a part of the country. As early as three weeks after its establishment, parts of the southern region were seized by British and then French troops and from December 1946 the regime was forced to retreat to the rural areas of the north as well. Only in 1954 did the regime permanently regain full control over all of the territory north of the 17th parallel and it was not until 1975 that the whole country was restored to socialist rule. A history of the establishment of the Marxist regime in Vietnam is therefore very much a history of two successive wars, fought from 1945 to 1954 and from 1955 to 1975. These prolonged wars have to a great extent forged the style and outlook of the Vietnamese communists and have also wrought vast changes on Vietnamese society. It is impossible, therefore, to understand the nature of the Marxist regime in Vietnam without delving into this history to determine the forces that have shaped the attitudes and decisions of Vietnam's leaders today.

It is also important to note that the Vietnamese revolution, in 1945, was the first communist-led revolution to succeed, independently of external intervention, after the Bolshevik revolution of 1917. This fact has an important bearing on the nature of the Vietnamese regime today. Communist leaders in Vietnam are proud of the leading role of their movement in the struggle against colonialism and are careful to preserve the originality and independence of thinking which was established by Ho Chi Minh in the 1920s. While the existence of an international communist movement has been of some benefit to the Vietnamese, it has not been an unmitigated blessing and has not, on the whole, interfered with the ability of Vietnamese communists to act according to their own perceptions. In reality, the foundation of the success of the Vietnamese Communist Party has been its ability to relate closely to the demands of an insurgent population and to channel and organize these demands in an effective way. The main elements of popular consciousness which the communists were able to draw upon were a strong sense of national identity of the Vietnamese, based not so much on a modern geographically defined idea of the nation, but on a common historical and cultural tradition, and the demand for a more equitable system of land distribution.

In this part of the book, then, we will look at the roots of the Vietnamese revolution, the origins of communist leadership of it and the forging of a close relationship between the Communist Party and the majority of Vietnamese people over five decades. In so doing we will establish the basis for understanding the implications of this relationship for the structure, organization and policies of the Socialist Republic of Vietnam since 1975.

1 Geographical and Historical Setting

Vietnam lies within the tropical zone. It stretches over 1,600 kilometres in length from 8°30′ N to 23°22′ N, widening out at the northern and southern ends to encompass the main cultivated areas of the Red River and Mekong River deltas. A mountain chain (Truong Son) runs almost the full length of the country, dividing it from Laos and Cambodia in the west while, in the narrow central region of the country, it forms a series of small coastal plains cut off from each other by spurs reaching down to the South China Sea.

Although it is in a tropical region, the northern part of the country is affected by Siberian weather patterns in winter, causing mean January temperatures as low as 16 °C at Hanoi, but with hot summers. In the far south, on the other hand, there is less variation in temperature, the annual average being 27 °C at Ho Chi Minh City. Rainfall is high (1,678 mm. at Hanoi, 2,890 mm. at Hue in the centre and 1,979 mm. at Ho Chi Minh City), mainly brought by the southwest monsoon in June to September. The centre also gets rain from the northeast monsoon (December to February) but elsewhere this leads to mostly dry weather. Rainfall is fairly erratic in the northern and central regions which are also subject to frequent typhoons during the wet season. These factors combine to make the Mekong River delta in the south the most favourable region for wet rice agriculture.

Earliest human habitation of northern Vietnam has been traced to approximately 500,000 years ago, according to recent archaeological finds. But the first clear links with present inhabitants indicate the existence of Mesolithic and Neolithic cultures up to 10,000 years old, with primitive settled agriculture possibly as early as 9,000 years ago. A sophisticated Bronze Age culture (known as the Dong Son culture after the location of the main archaeological site) seems to have emerged by about the thirteenth century BC. When the Chinese conquered the Red River delta region in the late second century BC, they found a society apparently organized along feudal lines (Coedes, 1966) practising wet rice agriculture and engaging in foreign trade. When they subsequently attempted to impose a centralized state system and to Sinicize the culture, they encountered stiff resistance from local rulers—the most famous event being the rebellion of the Trung sisters (AD 40–42). Further serious rebellions broke out in the third and sixth centuries and there were many minor ones, but it was not until 938 that Ngo

Quyen managed to defeat the Chinese army and re-establish Vietnamese rule over the northern part of present-day Vietnam.

In the southern part of what we now know as Vietnam, an important Indianized kingdom based on the lower Mekong delta dominated an area as far afield as the Malay peninsula from the first to sixth centuries AD. Known to historians by its Chinese name of Fu-nan, this civilization was based on wet rice agriculture and carried out large-scale hydraulic works in the Mekong delta. From the late second century, the Hindu kingdom of Champa appeared in the central Vietnamese region (around present-day Hue and Da Nang). This kingdom gradually expanded southwards to occupy the Phan Rang–Nha Trang area by the eighth century while the territory of Fu-nan was absorbed in the seventh century by the pre-Angkor kingdom of Kambuja.

The eleventh to thirteenth centuries saw consolidation of Vietnamese independence from China under the Ly dynasty (1010–1225). Dai Viet (as the kingdom was known) was able to treat on equal terms with China and repelled several attacks from the latter (especially under the renowned general Ly Thuong Kiet). It also began to assert pressure on Champa to the south, forcing it to cede three provinces in 1069. During this dynasty the administrative system was extensively reorganized to provide the basis for taxation, the first flood control embankments along the Red River were constructed (in 1108) and a national university was created (1076).

The Ly dynasty was followed by that of the Tran (1225–1400), towards the end of which time the Red River delta came under attack from Champa. When the last Tran ruler was overthrown by Ho Quy Ly, both the Chams and the Tran loyalists encouraged renewed Chinese interest in conquest. There followed a period of Chinese occupation (1407–28) until a ten-year campaign by Le Loi, a peasant leader from Thanh Hoa, finally succeeded. Le Loi founded the Le dynasty (1418–1786, though in fact from 1524 onwards power was held by rival families, the Mac and later on the Trinh in the north and the Nguyen in the south). The fifteenth century saw the kingdom of Champa reduced to a rump by the Vietnamese under Le Nhan Tong and Le Thanh Tong. Vietnamese rulers now occupied the territory as far south as present-day Phu Khanh province. Another major achievement of this period was the attempt to break free of the cultural and intellectual influence of China in the fields of law and religion as well as literature, where institutions and themes from a more indigenous Vietnamese tradition came to the fore. The early years of the Le dynasty were also a period of great achievement in Vietnamese literary and historical writing. It is worth noting, however, that popular culture had never been greatly affected by Chinese influence and, within the sphere of elite culture, Chinese language and traditions remained strong.

With the rise of the Trinh and Nguyen families, internal fighting broke out which ended with the effective division of the country into independent kingdoms during the seventeenth and eighteenth centuries. But this period was also one of literary accomplishment—the great Vietnamese classic work of fiction, *Kim Van Kieu*, was written at this time and a famous woman poet wrote bitter, ironic poetry on the Confucian patriarchy of the upper classes (Marr, 1981). Throughout the period, the Nguyen in the south extended their domination into the former Khmer territories of the Mekong delta. Laos and much of Cambodia also were forced to recognize the suzerainty of Vietnamese rulers in the fifteenth and seventeenth centuries respectively.

In 1765 a serious rebellion broke out in the area of Tay Son in central Vietnam and by 1773 the Tay Son rebels controlled the whole central area of the country. The successor of the defeated Nguyen (Nguyen Anh) took refuge with the French bishop Pigneau de Behaine at Ha Tien in the far south, which later led to French involvement in his campaign to regain control over the country. It was not until 1801 that the Tay Son rebels were finally defeated and, in the following year, Nguyen Anh was able to pronounce himself emperor (taking the reign name Gia Long) of the whole territory from the Chinese to the Cambodian borders and the country was given the name of Viet Nam.

Gia Long's successors in the Nguyen dynasty failed to perceive the nature of the growing European presence in Southeast Asia. They repudiated Gia Long's policy of granting trade concessions and rights to missionaries and instead tried to exclude foreign influence from the country. However, the French were anxious about growing British influence in the region and demanded access to Vietnamese ports, chiefly as a means of facilitating entry into the China trade. The French navy seized Saigon and three surrounding provinces in 1861 and in 1867 took the rest of the Mekong delta, creating the colony of Cochinchina. During the remainder of the nineteenth century France forced central and northern Vietnam into submission (creating the Protectorates of Annam and Tonkin by 1883) as well as Cambodia and Laos.

French colonialism began a process of fundamental social change in Indochina. This change was most thoroughgoing in Cochinchina where French rule was direct and established early. But it was no less important in the north where Vietnamese resistance took longer to quell and where traditional rulers continued to exercise some influence. It was this fundamental social change, this destruction of the economic basis on which traditional Vietnamese social organization had stood, which gave rise to a new form of resistance in the 1920s and 1930s under the leadership of communists.

The social structure prior to the French takeover comprised three main classes, the imperial court, village notables and patriarchal families. Land was communally owned, in the sense that individual households had access to it only by virtue of their membership of a village community (though peasants, including women, held inherited tenure over much of this land as their 'patrimony' or ancestral land). All three classes retained some rights of control over the land and of surplus appropriation. Villages were collectively responsible for payment of taxes to the central government and for recruitment of soldiers and labourers for public works construction and maintenance. The chief form of surplus extraction by the central government was the poll tax, levied on all registered adult male residents who were also allocated land by the village. Taxes were collected and communal land periodically redistributed by the village notables according to their own practices. Notables were chosen by a village's registered males according to wealth, age and mandarin status, though there was some tension between the Confucian system of honouring age and education, on the one hand, and economic power on the other (Wiegersma, 1982). The notables had a certain amount of independent power to control land and labour in the village and could exercise the collective responsibility to their own advantage.

The central government controlled external trade, financed the construction and maintenance of hydraulic works (for transport purposes to aid tax collection and for irrigation) and provided security from external threats as well as conquering new lands. Migrants from more densely populated areas of the Red River delta were allocated these new lands, given a protective spirit by the emperor and established new villages on the same model as in their previous home. From time to time the emperor also allocated estates to important officials of the court as a reward for services rendered. During the course of a dynastic period, the fiefdoms established by these officials could become an important alternative source of political and economic power. The existence of decentralized power would weaken the dynasty and excessive burdens of taxation, corvée labour and rents on the peasantry would lead to economic stagnation and lack of popular support for the dynasty (loss of the 'Mandate of Heaven'). At times like these, the dynasty would become vulnerable to attack from outside or to rebellion from within. The establishment of a new dynasty, however, would result in renewed centralization of political power with the estates of the former officials being returned to communal ownership. Then the process would begin again: new estates would be offered to victorious generals and successful ministers. This cycle of centralization, which was normally associated with economic prosperity, cultural and political achievement, and decentralization, associated with gradual stagnation and dynastic weakness, explains both the major events of Vietnamese history up to the French invasion and the reason why Vietnamese society changed only very slowly during this period of its history.

At the time of the French invasion in the latter part of the nineteenth century, the Nguyen dynasty was in a phase of stagnation and internal weakness. The social tensions which had given rise to the Tay Son rebellion had not been resolved before Gia Long's death put an end to his program of reform (Marr, 1971). Corruption and opportunism among the mandarin officials of the court were prevalent (Woodside, 1976). The conservative Confucian restoration that followed under Emperor Minh Mang (1820–41) was accompanied by a number of serious uprisings which worsened in the two decades before 1860. In spite of this weakness, which resulted in the French gaining their initial foothold with ridiculous ease,[2] there was considerable resistance, drawing on a long Vietnamese tradition of opposition to foreign occupation. The Can Vuong (Aid the King) movement which reached its peak in the 1880s was led by mandarins who left the court rather than collaborate with the French. This movement represented an attempt, albeit belated, by the traditional Vietnamese rulers to rebuild the foundations of the monarchy in the countryside and forced the occupying power to intervene directly in village affairs, undermining in the process the real power of traditional village elites. Even though the French retained the institutions of the monarchial system, their content began to be thoroughly transformed by the requirements of the colonial economy.

2 The Colonial Regime and the Origins of Vietnamese Communism

In spite of the difficulties in maintaining social order of the Nguyen dynasty, resistance to French colonization of Vietnam was intense from the beginning. Admiral Rigault de Genouilly managed to capture the harbour and town of present-day Da Nang in 1858, but could not proceed any further. Attention was switched to Saigon in early 1859, but the French hold on the town and its surrounding provinces could not be consolidated until two and a half years later. Meanwhile, Da Nang had had to be abandoned in 1860. It was 1867 before the French could hold sway over the whole of Nam Bo (which they called Cochinchina). Sixteen more years of diplomatic manœuvring and two major military campaigns were required to gain control over Trung Bo (Annam to the French) and Bac Bo (Tonkin).

Even so, general uprisings in Nam Bo (1863) and Trung Bo (1885–8 and 1893–5) had to be suppressed as well as numerous local rebellions in Bac Bo. In some provinces prior to 1897, French control was relinquished for years at a time (Buttinger, 1972, p. 63).

From the beginning, Nam Bo was ruled as a direct French colony, while Trung Bo and Bac Bo as well as Cambodia (from 1863) and Laos (from 1893) received the status of protectorate. Although the four protectorates retained their traditional government structures (including the Vietnamese monarchy and mandarin hierarchy centred in Hue), real power lay with the French Residents and, after the creation of the Indochinese Union in 1887, the French Governor-General in Hanoi.

By 1897 the resistance to foreign occupation based on a desire to restore the old imperial system had been exhausted. The defeat of the traditional elite was followed by the establishment of what was effectively direct French rule over all parts of the country under Governor-General Paul Doumer (1897–1902). Doumer commenced a transformation of Indochinese economy and society which, by completely disorganizing the foundations upon which power had traditionally rested, ensured that no further resistance of a 'backward looking' nature could be successful. Of the two major strands of opposition to French rule which emerged in the twentieth century—nationalism and communism—the ultimate success of one and failure of the other can only be understood by reference to the effects of this colonial transformation of the economy.

The changes wrought by the colonial administration had the aim of supporting capital accumulation of French investors in the colony and, in particular, of supplying the demands of metropolitan France with raw materials for its industries. At the same time, pressure from a strong anti-colonial lobby at home led to French government reluctance to finance the necessary infrastructure and administrative costs of remodelling Vietnamese society to suit these aims. A ruthless taxation policy was therefore implemented to support the colonial budget and to assist the construction of railways, roads, canals, ports and other public works to serve the export of rice, rubber, coal, maize and minerals.

The taxation policy never succeeded in making the colonial government financially self-sufficient, but it did have a devastating effect on the traditional peasant economy. The imposition of a steeply regressive head tax, a land tax (in theory based on quality of land) and taxes on tobacco, salt, alcohol and opium consumption helped to immiserate the peasantry, especially that of the densely populated northern and central deltas.[1] The other main source of tax revenue was from various customs imposts. Village councils were held collectively responsible for tax collection, as in the pre-colonial system, and these in turn distributed the burden among villagers. But increasing concentration of land ownership and wealth in the villages during the colonial period meant that these councils were dominated by the rich, at the expense of elders and mandarin scholars, who had traditionally held at least some share of local power.

Social polarization also increased through the private appropriation of land, including the appropriation of communal land by village notables for their own benefit, and the reduction of the vast majority of peasants to the status of sharecropper, turning over about half their crops to the landowners (Truong Chinh & Vo Nguyen Giap, 1974). Concentration of landownership was particularly evident in the Mekong delta where communal land all but disappeared and, by 1939, 2 per cent of the population owned 45 per cent of the land.

Many peasants were forced to borrow at usurious interest rates in order to meet tax obligations and this provided a further impetus for peasant discontent with the new system (Ngo Vinh Long, 1973; Truong Chinh & Vo Nguyen Giap, 1974). Because of the great poverty of the Vietnamese population, the colony never became an important market for French manufactured products. Nor was there any significant industrial development, the only really large factory in the country at the time of independence in 1945 being the Nam Dinh textile mill, which employed some 6,000 labourers working up imported cotton for the domestic market. There were a few other modern factories in the country engaged in brewing, distilling, tobacco manufacture, sugar refining, rice and paper milling, cement and glass manufacture and locomotive repair. The profits of these enterprises were rarely reinvested in Indochina (Buttinger, 1972, p. 65).

One other aspect of the colonial transformation of the economy deserves mention and this is the recruitment of labour for French-owned plantations and mines. Hundreds of thousands of labourers were recruited for these enterprises (often press-ganged by Vietnamese contractors (*cai*) in collaboration with village council members), where they worked for abysmal wages and in appalling conditions (Thompson, 1937; Murray, 1980). The death rate from malaria on the rubber plantations in Nam Bo was high and contract labourers who tried other forms of escape were dealt with by police methods. Many did escape, however, and few renewed their contracts for a second term. The stories of returnees contributed to an extreme reluctance on the part of most peasants to volunteer for this kind of work, in spite of acute poverty in the Trung Bo and Bac Bo deltas.

Apart from fuelling Vietnamese hatred of the French occupation, this trade in human flesh had a number of important side-effects. One was that it greatly increased the mobility of peasants and their knowledge of the world outside the village boundaries.[2] In the employ of colonial export enterprises, Vietnamese workers travelled to the cities of Hanoi, Haiphong and Saigon; the mines of Hon Gai, upper Tonkin and Laos; the plantations of Cambodia and Cochinchina and to other French colonies in the South Pacific. Over a hundred thousand went to France as soldiers in the First World War. Here they also learned new forms of organization and new ideas. Vietnamese sailors were involved in the Black Sea Mutiny, when ships carrying arms to the White Russian armies were prevented from delivering their cargo after the Bolshevik revolution. A few years later, a series of major strikes in the southern rubber plantations in 1928–30 as well as strikes by factory workers at Vinh and Nam Dinh and dock workers in Saigon and Haiphong were early signs of successful communist-led organization in opposition to the French.

The uprooting of the traditional Vietnamese social order and the failure of the early resistance to the French, led Vietnamese intellectuals to search for a new rallying point around which a unified national movement could be organized. Prior to 1925, the most influential figures were nationalists like Phan Chu Trinh and Phan Boi Chau. Another, who came to prominence after 1925, was Ho Chi Minh.[3] These were the leaders of two divergent trends in the Vietnamese movement for national independence arising out of a common recognition of the need to challenge French colonialism with ideas and organizational forms belonging to the modern era rather than those of a society that no longer existed. At the same time, it must be said that part of the success of Vietnamese communism came through its ability to harness traditional ideas and beliefs to these new forms in a way that increased its appeal to the masses (Nguyen Khac Vien, 1974).

After the demise of the 'Aid the King' movement which had inspired the first wave of anti-colonial revolt, the focus of protest and rebellion shifted to the burdens and injustices of French rule, rather than the restoration of the monarchy and driving out the invader. The next wave of rebelliousness broke out in 1907-8 and took the form of demonstrations against taxes and, particularly, the corvée being levied by the French to construct public works. In this movement, the scholars tended to take the back-seat, although many of them were subsequently rounded up and imprisoned (Marr, 1971). Other intellectual opponents of the regime were involved in establishing the Dong Kinh Nghia Thuc (Tonkin Free School) in Hanoi or in a movement led by Phan Boi Chau to seek a pan-Asian response to Western imperialism by going to Japan. The point here is that a gap had opened up between the goals and activities of the intellectuals, on the one hand, and those of the masses, on the other. Followers of major dissident figures like Phan Chu Trinh and Phan Boi Chau either advocated reformism (in the face of violent French repression of reformist demands) in the first case, or concentrated on 'putschism', advocating the violent overthrow of the regime, without either the serious analysis of conditions in the country of the reformists or attention to mobilization of mass support in the second case. While these intellectual leaders did address the problems of modernization and the impact of the West on Vietnamese society, a number of millenarian movements began to appear among the peasantry which, though they were sometimes able to be a serious thorn in the French side, lacked a coherent political program capable of challenging the French state.[4]

Meanwhile, the reluctance of the reformists to challenge the violence of colonial repression led to the development of the Constitutionalist Party and increasingly collaborationist tendencies (mainly in the South). This tendency was in no small part due to the rise of a new type of Vietnamese upper class—made up of landowners and speculators, bankers, doctors, engineers and other professionals, who had benefited economically from French rule and whose demands for reform were correspondingly limited. At the other extreme, nationalist leaders in the north of the country, unable to develop strong organizational links with the peasantry, resorted to isolated attacks on the French administration (assassination attempts, bomb throwing, a famous incident in which the revolutionaries tried to poison the French garrison at

Haiphong). The Viet Nam Quoc Dan Dang (VNQDD), founded in 1927, was a nationalist party modelled on the Chinese Guomindang, but it was virtually destroyed after an abortive uprising at Yen Bai early in 1930.

The key factor that differentiated these political groups from the communists and that allowed the latter to become the only serious challenger to colonial rule after 1930 was their essentially traditional and hierarchical view of society, their inability to place the mass of Vietnamese peasants and workers at the centre of their political strategy.[5]

Ho Chi Minh came from a relatively poor mandarin family in Nghe An, a province of central Vietnam with a strong history of peasant rebellion—the most recent at the time being the 'Aid the King' movement against the French in the 1880s. He left the country in 1911, working his way to Europe as a ship's cabin boy. During the First World War he settled in Paris and began to participate in political activities there. At the Versailles Conference in 1918 he tried unsuccessfully to present a plea for the same democratic rights for the people of the colonies as were enjoyed in Europe and America. This was a radicalizing experience, since it showed him the futility of expecting reform to come from the colonial powers themselves—even the more liberal Americans.

In 1920 Ho Chi Minh participated in the Congress of the French Socialist Party at Tours. He spoke on behalf of the oppressed peoples of all France's colonies and voted with the group that left the Party to join the Third International. He thus became a founding member of the French Communist Party and appears to have been strongly influenced in these decisions by the indifference of the French Socialists to the problems of colonized peoples (Huynh Kim Khanh, 1982, p. 61) and by reading Lenin's 'Theses on the National and Colonial Questions' (Duiker, 1981, p. 7; VCP, 1980, p. 19).

In 1923 or 1924 he travelled to Moscow where he studied at the University of the Toilers of the East and participated in the 5th Congress of the Comintern. His contributions stressed the common struggle of all colonized peoples and argued the need for communists to harness the revolutionary power of the peasantry in countries like Vietnam (Lacouture, 1968, pp. 33–4).

At the end of 1924 Ho was sent by the Comintern to Canton where, in 1925, he and a group of Vietnamese revolutionaries established the Viet Nam Thanh Nien Kach Menh Hoi (Association of Vietnamese Revolutionary Youth—usually known by its abbreviated name of Thanh Nien). Activists of the Thanh Nien were given training in political theory and organization before returning to set up cells in Vietnam itself.

The external leadership of Thanh Nien was scattered by the Guomindang attack on the Canton communists in early 1927 and Ho returned to Moscow, later moving to Siam. By 1929, a movement had developed among some of the revolutionaries within Vietnam (perhaps fired by a series of strikes which had been organized in 1928-9) to take a step beyond the Thanh Nien towards establishment of a communist party. Accordingly, at a Congress of Thanh Nien held in Hong Kong in May 1929, the delegation from Bac Bo proposed the immediate establishment of a communist party. While their move was rejected by the majority, they nevertheless went ahead and formed the Indochinese Communist Party (Dong Duong Cong San Dang) in June 1929. Under pressure from this new organization, the southern and central leadership of Thanh Nien decided to form a party called Annamese Communism (An Nam Cong San) in October 1929 and, at the same time the League of Indochinese Communists (Dong Duong Cong San Lien Doan), formed by members of an organization not affiliated to Thanh Nien, the New Vietnam Revolutionary Party (Tan Viet Cach Menh Dang), made its appearance.

Acting with the support of the Comintern, Ho Chi Minh met with leaders of the three parties in Hong Kong early in 1930 and persuaded them to unite. The newly emerged organization bore the name Dang Cong San Viet Nam (Vietnamese Communist Party) and the date of its formal establishment on 3 February 1930 is today celebrated as the founding date of the Party. Total membership at the time was 211 (VCP, 1980, p. 30). However, it appears that the Comintern, following the policy arrived at during its 6th Congress in 1928, was not happy with the 'national' flavour imparted by the name of the organization and, at a meeting of the Central Committee in October 1930, the Party became the Indochinese Communist Party (Dang Cong San Dong Duong (ICP)). Comintern policy at the time stressed the need for inter-nationalization of the class struggle, led by the proletariat, in the colonies and opposed the formation of broad cross-class alliances including 'progressive' or 'patriotic' elements of the bourgeoisie and petty bourgeoisie for the purpose of 'national liberation'. Indeed it would appear to be a result of the adoption of this Comintern policy by the Bac Bo revolutionaries that led to the initial break up of Thanh Nien.[6]

The year 1930 was also one of great revolutionary upsurge in Vietnam. The VNQDD had organized an uprising at Yen Bai on 9 February, but it failed, largely as a result of their putschist ideology and lack of solid grassroots organization. In spite of strong misgivings by the Party's central leadership, the movement led by local communist organizations was initally more successful. Beginning with a strike by 3,000 workers at Phu Rieng rubber plantation in February 1930, the movement spread rapidly to other plantations and factories and then into the villages. In March 4,000 workers of the Nam Dinh textile mill struck, in April 400 workers at Ben Thuy (near Vinh) match factory and sawmill joined in and by May the movement had spread to Hanoi, Haiphong, Hon Gai, Cam Pha, Vinh, Saigon and Cholon. In the rural areas, villages in Thai Binh, Ha Nam, Nghe An, Ha Tinh, Quang Ngai, Gia Dinh, Thu Dau Mot and seven provinces of the Mekong delta had risen. In a number of districts of Nghe An and Ha Tinh provinces the colonial administration was overthrown, colonial taxes were abolished, debts annulled, land redistributed and a literacy campaign was held by revolutionary governments which became known as the Nghe Tinh Soviets. The movement lasted for more than a year, a testament to the strong organizational roots which the ICP had already put down, but in the end the colonial government was able to crush the revolt by mid-1931.[7] Repression of communists and other participants in the uprising was savage, leading to a resurgence of anti-colonial feeling in France. But with most of its leadership either dead or imprisoned, the ICP was in no position to take advantage of this mood.

Instead, the focus of communist agitation in the 1930s switched to Saigon, where a peculiar alliance of French-educated Trotskyists and Stalinists (not previously associated with ICP activities within Vietnam) began to cooperate in the production of a newspaper (*La Lutte*), which called for democratic rights, and in running a slate of candidates for municipal elections—in which they were successful in 1933 (though the result was overturned on a technicality), 1935 and 1937 (Huynh Kim Khanh, 1982, p. 199). The La Lutte group was full of ideological tension, seemingly held together only by bonds of personal friendship (Huynh Kim Khanh, 1982, p. 199), and broke up soon after the advent of the leftist Popular Front government in France in 1936. In the more relaxed political climate between 1936 and 1939, when, in spite of an absence of real political and economic reforms, the colonial government seemed somewhat afraid to move against the communists, the frail bonds holding the La Lutte group together were destroyed. The sudden freedom of debate proved too much and the vilifications began to fly, with a splinter group of the Trotskyists, the 'Octobrists', fuelling the fire in particular. Bitterness was not reduced by the resumption of French repression in 1939 and a number of the Trotskyists were reportedly murdered by Viet Minh cadres during the Second World War. One of the La Lutte Trotskyists was posthumously rehabilitated by Ho Chi Minh after 1945—an early indication of what became a consistent Vietnamese Communist tendency not to 'unperson' political opponents within the movement. At least one Vietnamese Trotskyist leader retired from politics in the late 1940s to re-emerge as a critic of the SRV regime in the 1970s. Some others rallied to the Viet Minh and Communist Party (Huynh Kim Khanh, 1982, pp. 193–9 gives biographies of some of the leading figures of the La Lutte group).

The process of rebuilding the ICP was facilitated by the advent of the Popular Front government in France and the ability of communists to work legally.[8] Candidates won elections in Tonkin and Annam councils in 1937 and 1938 (VCP, 1980, p. 53). But the Party also maintained its clandestine organization and, in the north at least, anticipated the return of repressive policies by the colonial government in 1939, ordering its cadres to retreat to rural areas. In spite of this, the Party suffered further heavy losses to its organizational ability, especially after 1940 when the independent-minded southern regional committee organized another insurrection which was brutally suppressed. All the important Party leaders in the south (including Pham Van Dong and Le Duan) were interned or executed.

Even in prison, however, the rebuilding process went on. In spite of cruel treatment by their captors, the communists were able to organize education sessions in gaol, especially in the main prison on the island of Poulo Condore (Con Dao). Many commentators today attribute the high degree of unity and discipline of the Vietnamese Party leadership through the subsequent decades of struggle to the common bonds of solidarity and theoretical training forged in these prison 'universities' during the 1930s and 1940s.

Conclusion

Anti-colonial activity was a constant thorn in the side of French rule in Vietnam from the outset. But the most serious problem for those seeking to overturn the colonial regime was to find an ideological and organizational framework that would both have widespread appeal to the Vietnamese population and provide an effective threat to a modern colonial state. Early efforts to restore the traditional monarchy were adversely affected by internal dissension and corruption of the Nguyen dynasty and by deliberate French disorganization of traditional Vietnamese society and economy. Although later leaders like Phan Boi Chau and Phan Chu Trinh rejected a return to the status quo ex ante, they were unable to distance themselves from the more elitist aspects of Vietnamese tradition, unlike the communists who placed the organization of peasants and workers at the centre of their strategy. Nationalist parties arose with modernizing programs, but lacking the organizational means to carry them out. On the other hand, especially in the South, millenarian peasant movements also arose which lacked a coherent political program or the ability to analyse the strengths and weaknesses of their opponents. Only the Communist Party was able to provide both elements of a strong appeal to the Vietnamese masses and a political vision based on a clear understanding of the domestic and international forces affecting Vietnam.

This being said, there were also a number of other factors that assisted the growth of Vietnamese communism. One was the existence of support from the Comintern, which provided external sanctuaries in times of severe repression as well as intellectual and psychological support. Through their contacts with other communist parties, the Vietnamese communists were able to gain in theoretical sophistication (most importantly an understanding of the international context) and cohesion, as well as having the knowledge of not being alone in their struggle against superior economic and military power. However, these contacts were not all of one-sided benefit. The Comintern's 'left turn' between 1928 and 1935 led to precipitate actions and severe repression, while the Popular Front policies of 1936–9 often left the ICP open to criticism from the Trotskyists (especially over the Molotov-Ribbentrop pact and the failure of the Popular Front government to bring real reform). The strategic thinking of the Vietnamese communists was at its most successful later, during the period 1941–5, when the Party was largely cut off from its outside friends and when Ho Chi Minh was himself in charge. It has often been said (cf. VCP, 1980; Kolko, 1986) that the development of a distinctive Vietnamese communism after 1941 was the result of hard lessons learned from the mistakes of the 1930s, but it surely should be added that where many communist parties around the world failed to learn these lessons, the crucial factor for the Vietnamese was their very success once they had decided upon their own course.

3 The Establishment of the Democratic Republic of Vietnam, 1945–1954

The August Revolution

The fall of France in mid-1940 and the decision of the Indochinese government to collaborate with the Vichy regime led to an agreement that allowed the French to retain administrative control over the colony during the Second World War, although Japanese troops were stationed there and Japan exercised real power throughout the region. The real focus of Communist activity now switched to the North, especially the mountainous areas close to the Chinese border (known as the Viet Bac region). Ho Chi Minh had left Moscow during the late 1930s[1] and travelled via Yenan in China, where Mao Zedong now had his headquarters, arriving back in Vietnam in February 1941, after an absence of thirty years. In May 1941 the 8th Plenum of the ICP Central Committee was held at Pac Bo in the Viet Bac region and, under Ho's guidance, a number of important principles were laid down for the coming period.

Already in November 1939 there had been a shift in Party strategy as a result of the collapse of the Popular Front with its emphasis on the 'bourgeois democratic' revolution and on an alliance with all anti-fascist groups (including, for example, Constitutionalists). From this time on the Party adopted an anti-imperialist position, advocating 'national liberation' and the formation of alliances only with 'patriotic' elements in society (Duiker, 1981, pp. 55-60; Huynh Kim Khanh, 1982, pp. 256-60). The new strategy developed at Pac Bo also emphasized the need to conserve strength by fighting only one enemy at a time (i.e., the imperialists) and called off demands for an overthrow of the Vietnamese feudal classes. It was determined that the resolution of the national independence question would be carried out within the framework of each Indochinese country. Three national fronts were therefore to be established within a federal league for the independence of Indochina (Huynh Kim Khanh, 1982, p. 262). For Vietnam the new front created was called the Viet Nam Doc Lap Dong Minh Hoi or Vietnam Independence League (known as the Viet Minh). The strategy adopted for the 1940s was thus a return to Ho Chi Minh's earlier policy of 1925-9, which had been overturned by the leftward shift of the Comintern (1928) and the ICP (1930).

The May 1941 meeting also laid down the prerequisites for a successful anti-imperialist revolution. These were, firstly, the ability to control a revolutionary base area from which to carry out military and political operations over a wider area; secondly, a favourable domestic situation entailing political, economic and military disintegration of imperialist rule combined with popular unwillingness to tolerate it any further; thirdly, a favourable international situation, especially the ability to obtain outside support.

To begin with, a revolutionary base area was established in Cao Bang, an area where 80 per cent of the population came from Tay and Nung ethnic minorities. But the ICP also stressed the importance of urban revolution and the headquarters of the Central Committee, with Truong Chinh as Party Secretary, were moved to Hanoi (Duiker, 1981, p. 74). A 'cultural movement' was launched in order to bring literacy to the peasants in the base area, to revive Vietnamese traditions of resistance to foreign invaders, to teach communist ethics and organizational methods and give peasants a wider sense of territorial and cultural community (Woodside, 1976, p. 220). However, very little else was achieved until early 1943 after the German defeat at Stalingrad began to cause increased tension within the Vichy French administration in Hanoi. A number of military setbacks to Japan in China and the Pacific also began to make an eventual Japanese defeat seem possible. At this time, with disarray in imperialist ranks growing, the opportunities for revolutionary successes began to expand, particularly in the rural areas. In urban areas, the Party had decided in 1943 that, in spite of its efforts, its influence was still too weak. To try to overcome this, a number of sympathetic intellectuals established the Vietnam Democratic Party in June 1944 in order to rally the urban middle classes to the cause.

By late 1944 the guerrilla forces in Viet Bac were re-organized into Armed Propaganda brigades in order to establish a mass base in the frontier regions from which a general uprising could be launched. In that year the Viet Minh also began to receive some small amounts of assistance from the United States' OSS operating from Chinese nationalist-held territory. OSS interest in the Viet Minh stemmed from the fact that it was the only anti-Japanese organization capable of effectively gathering intelligence on Japanese movements in northern Indochina. But the forging of this link was also of significance to the Viet Minh who were able to use the international recognition it gave them to establish their legitimacy against potential domestic rivals. In addition, it offered the hope of eventual US recognition of an independent Vietnamese state.[2]

In March 1945, facing defeat and sensing that the French administrators and colonists were no longer so firmly committed to the ideals of fascism now that France itself had been liberated, the Japanese staged a *coup d'état*. French troops were disarmed and officials interned. French colonial power in Vietnam had been overthrown.

The Japanese then installed the last of the Nguyen emperors, Bao Dai, as head of an 'independent' Vietnamese government[3] and allowed him to revoke the treaty of 1884 with France which had formed the Protectorates of Annam and Tonkin. Cochinchina, however, was not included in the new state and the Japanese retained concessions in Hanoi, Haiphong and Da Nang as well. The new government had no armed forces (not daring to establish a ministry of defence in case the Japanese forced them into the war). Meanwhile, in April 1945, the revolutionary army had grown stronger and its various units were consolidated into the Vietnam Liberation Army.

Most of the prerequisites for a successful revolution set out by the Central Committee in May 1941 were now in existence. The French administration had disappeared; the Japanese, although still in occupation, were increasingly demoralized and unable to direct attention towards combating the Vietnamese Liberation Army; ruthless requisitioning of rice by the Japanese army and compulsory planting of industrial crops (jute, cotton and oil seed) on rice land to supply the Japanese war machine had generated a catastrophic famine in Bac Bo and intense popular resentment; political and diplomatic support for the Viet Minh from the United States seemed possible. It was the famine, however—the only element in this conjunction of events which the Party had not predicted or foreseen—which proved decisive in its impact on the mobilization of the urban and rural masses. The virtually universal and spontaneous uprisings throughout northern Vietnam in response to the Party's call to storm the granaries were the engine on which it eventually rode to power. As we have seen, it was precisely the Communists' commitment to organization of the masses that differentiated them from other nationalist tendencies. From now on this organizational capacity ensured that the Viet Minh was seen as the only party which could provide the basis for economic and social recovery after independence.

By the spring of 1945 all the provinces of the north had Viet Minh organizations, agitation was growing in the central provinces and the Party's youth organization in Saigon was expanding rapidly. Military successes had enabled the amalgamation of seven combat zones into a single Liberated Area covering all or part of ten northern provinces and the Liberation Army was able to extend its operations to the rural areas of the Red River delta. The Japanese defended only the towns and main communications routes. Meanwhile, rising popular support for the Viet Minh was ensured by its mobilization of armed demonstrations to attack the granaries and release rice for distribution. Attacks on the prisons were also organized to release political prisoners and replenish the stock of Party activists.

On 15 August 1945 Japan surrendered and turned over its Indochina command to the Bao Dai government. But by this time the revolutionary process was already far advanced. Following an earlier Party directive setting out the right conditions and instructing cadres to use their own judgement (a necessary step in view of the poor communications in rural areas and the need for rapid action when the time came), a number of local Viet Minh organizations had begun uprisings on the 14 August. On 16 August the Bac Bo regional committee called for uprisings in ten provinces of the Red River delta and for occupation of provincial capitals in preparation for the outbreak of revolution in Hanoi (Duiker, 1981, p. 92). Meanwhile the Central Committee of the Party had convened a Congress at Tan Trao in the Liberated Area for 13–15 August which decided to launch the general uprising. At a National People's Congress held on 16–17 August, a National Liberation Committee (provisional government) was elected, a flag chosen and a ten-point program issued including:

—establishment of a Democratic Republic of Vietnam over the whole territory of Vietnam;
—guarantee of basic freedoms for all Vietnamese;
—confiscation of the property of 'Vietnamese traitors';
—distribution of this and communal land to needy peasants;
—rent reductions by 25 per cent;
—abolition of colonial taxes and their replacement by a single progressive tax;
—introduction of an 8-hour day, minimum wage and social insurance for workers;
—introduction of compulsory primary education.

The timing of the uprising was extremely important. On the one hand, the Japanese surrender had left a political vacuum which the Bao Dai government, lacking widespread political support, was unable to fill. The rural insurgency was at its height following the success of Viet Minh measures to combat the famine (in which, none the less, an estimated 2 million persons died) and there was widespread sympathy for the revolution in urban areas. On the other hand, at Potsdam earlier in the year the Allied Powers had already decided the fate of Indochina without reference to the nationalist movement. De Gaulle's Free French government-in-exile had always insisted upon the return of Indochina to French rule after the War, but the French armed forces were not yet strong enough to re-occupy their former colony.

Accordingly, the Potsdam Conference had divided Vietnam at the 16th parallel, assigning British troops to occupy the southern half and nationalist Chinese to occupy the north. For the Vietnamese revolutionaries, then, it was imperative to seize power before the Allies could carry out this plan.

The insurrection spread to Hanoi on 19 August as large demonstrations marched on the offices of local representatives of the Bao Dai government. On the 23rd of the month Hue fell amid popular demonstrations and Bao Dai formally abdicated his thousand year-old throne to the revolutionaries. By the end of August the revolution had taken control over the whole country, barring a few northern towns occupied by Chiang Kai-shek's troops and some areas of the rural south where the Party had to contend with strong Hoa Hao and Cao Dai influence. The Liberation Army marched into Hanoi towards the end of August. On the 28th the provisional government was announced and on 2 September, at a huge rally in Hanoi's Ba Dinh square, Ho Chi Minh read the Vietnamese Declaration of Independence (part of it copied from the American Declaration of Independence) and formally announced the establishment of the Democratic Republic of Vietnam. Total Party membership was then about 5,000 (VCP, 1980, p. 72).

The major factor accounting for the successful revolution in Vietnam in 1945 was the conjunction of international and domestic events—the disarray of the Japanese and French occupation forces, the lapse of time before the arrival of British and Chinese troops and the popular revolutionary upsurge of anger against the famine-inducing policies of the occupying powers. These factors provided the conditions in which a party of only 5,000 members could organize a widespread insurrection of sufficient strength to be able to seize state power. But here again, it was the strategic and tactical ingenuity of the Party, especially of Ho Chi Minh, which tipped the balance. The ICP's grasp of geopolitics, its understanding of the conflicts between the imperialist powers as well their common interests and its ability to link popular anger to concrete policies appealing to the widest possible section of the community were what enabled it to seize the opportunities which arose.

The First Indochina War

The Viet Minh victory in August 1945 had not been a military victory but the result of careful organization, which enabled the channelling of a popular uprising towards the goals set by the ICP. The new regime was now faced with an extremely delicate problem. The French government and the colonial powers clearly did not intend to allow the situation to persist and, rather than face the superior military power of the allies, Ho Chi Minh's government chose to try to buy time through negotiation. In the short term all the tactical skill and ingenuity of the Party leadership would need to be applied to ensure the survival, not only of the DRV, but of the Party itself.

In the Nam Bo region, setbacks to the authority of the DRV came shortly after its establishment. Ever since the 1930s, the Party organization in the south had maintained a rather urban bias. After the smashing of the Nam Ky uprising in 1940 most activists were either executed or interned and not released until 1945. This made the process of rebuilding the Party's organiza- tion in the south doubly difficult and it was further hampered in the rural areas by Japanese encouragement of the Cao Dai and Hoa Hao movements, which had their own militia forces. During 1945 these had collaborated with the Viet Minh for a while, but their collaboration was always conditional and they soon chose an anti-communist path, which, by 1946, saw them collaborating with the French. Thus the overwhelming support for the Viet Minh in the countryside to the north was somewhat diluted in the southern region and consequently the ability to mobilize for resistance to the British occupation of Saigon was initially not as strong as in other areas of the country. Nevertheless, when British troops arrived to take the Japanese surrender, they found it necessary, in order to accomplish their main purpose of securing the former colony for an eventual French return, to re-arm the Japanese troops so that the resistance of the DRV administration could be quelled.

French troops disembarked at Saigon on 23 September 1945 and were able to take possession of the city in short time, in spite of intense fighting around several key points of the city. They also began to push back Viet Minh influence in the rural areas. From this time on, the French ability to maintain a strong position in Nam Bo was to prove a sticking point for any attempt by the DRV to negotiate a settlement with France. The administration in the south consistently refused to abide by agreements reached between Ho Chi Minh's government and J. Sainteny, the chief French negotiator, providing succour to the hard line colonial lobby within France and ultimately contributing to the outbreak of war in December 1946.

In the northern part of the country the situation developed in a much more complex way. Whereas in the south, the occupying British force had been small, in the north approximately 180,000 Nationalist Chinese troops entered the country and began looting and pillaging in the rural areas. On the other hand, a French contingent was expected to arrive soon. Ho Chi Minh felt that the Viet Minh which, in spite of its growth in size, was poorly equipped and trained, could not deal effectively with both the French and

Chinese at once. In the longer run he felt that the French would be easier to deal with: colonialism had been dealt a fatal blow by the Second World War and it seemed possible to reach a compromise with the French that would buy time for Vietnam and lead eventually to complete independence. Meanwhile the Chinese troops were creating havoc in the rural areas; they were close neighbours of Vietnam with a long history of territorial and hegemonic claims. In the eyes of the Viet Minh the Chinese nationalists constituted a greater short-term and long-term threat to the DRV. Ho therefore chose to try to negotiate a compromise with France that would allow for a continuation of France's economic activities and interests, but would at the same time recognize the sovereignty of the Vietnamese state. In the interim he set about consolidating support for his new government among the broadest possible segment of the Vietnamese population.

The policies introduced by the government in 1945 were moderate. Preliminary steps were taken to establish People's Councils at all levels from the villages up, with elections for a National Assembly to be held at the end of the year. Equality was guaranteed to all citizens regardless of age, sex, religion or ethnicity. There was to be free instruction in the national language for everyone over 8 years old, using students to teach basic literacy. In addition to rent reductions and distribution of land, the head tax was reduced by 20 per cent, salt, opium and alcohol taxes were abolished and all government officials were asked to fast for one day in ten and to donate the food saved to the poor. Public utilities and a few major industries were nationalized, but circulars were issued respecting private property in all other areas (Duiker, 1981, pp. 109-10).

Another step taken towards consolidating the legitimacy of the regime was the bringing into the government in October 1945 of a number of non-communist nationalist leaders who took over some ministerial posts previously held by communists. This was done partly in response to Chinese demands that their VNQDD supporters should be able to gain control over the government, but it was also a step towards defusing claims by the bourgeois nationalist parties that they were being excluded from the democratic process. Moreover, the Viet Minh had one eye on the intensifying Cold War atmosphere in international politics, particularly the response of the US government which, even if he did not hope to gain its recognition, Ho at least hoped to neutralize in his attempt to deal with the French.

The next step taken with these considerations in mind was the formal dissolution of the Indochinese Communist Party in November 1945. In fact the Party *in Vietnam* remained intact as a clandestine organization and the dissolution was on paper only. Moreover, its membership began to increase rapidly so that by mid-1946 the Party had expanded from 5,000 (in August 1945) to 20,000 members and by 1949, when it was still not apparently in existence, membership stood at 700,000 (VCP, 1980, pp. 95, 104). Nevertheless, the dissolution of the Party was a public gesture aimed at domestic conciliation to create a broad united front against the French and at achieving neutralization of potential US support for France.

The fourth step in this direction was the holding of national elections for the National Assembly in January 1946. These elections were carried out under extremely difficult conditions with harassment from both Chinese nationalist and French troops. In the south, forty-two cadres died during the campaign (VCP, 1980, p. 89). However, the elections did register the full extent of popular support for the Viet Minh throughout the country. It obtained 300 of the 350 seats with 97 per cent of the electorate voting in an election that most observers thought was as fair as could be under the circumstances (Duiker, 1981, p. 117).

At the end of February 1946 the French and Chinese signed a Treaty by which the Chinese side agreed to withdraw its troops from the country. Six days later Ho Chi Minh reached an agreement with Sainteny on the terms under which the French would return. The agreement was also initialled by VNQDD representatives and witnessed by American and British officials. Under its terms, Vietnam was recognized as a free state within the French Union and Indochinese Federation.[4] A referendum was to be held to determine the status of Cochinchina (Nam Bo) within the Federation.

This agreement encountered intense unpopularity among the Vietnamese people, but Ho Chi Minh thought that it was essential to facilitate the Chinese withdrawal and to avoid a war with France in which the Viet Minh would suffer from lack of training and equipment and which risked bringing a return of chaos and famine to the countryside. In mid-1946 VNQDD opposition to negotiation with the French in an attempt to cash in on the unpopularity of the policy, led to the government's decision to close the Nationalist Party's office and newspaper in Hanoi. Its leaders fled to China (Duiker, 1981, p. 121).

A more fundamental problem which soon arose, however, was that interpretations of the meaning of the agreement differed widely. While the Viet Minh, on the one hand, interpreted the agreement as a recognition of Vietnamese equality within the Union, the French were not at all inclined to see the relationship as anything other than a continuation of colonial control. When Ho Chi Minh travelled to France to try to get formal recognition of the agreement reached with Sainteny, the French government kept him waiting for six days at Bordeaux, refused to hold the negotiations at Paris, but kept them out of the public eye at Fontainebleau and finally refused to ratify the agreement. Moreover, in Ho's absence, the French High Commissioner to Cochinchina called a conference at Dalat to decide Cochinchina's role within the Indochinese Federation in an attempt to by-pass the referendum process. The gesture succeeded in galvanizing pro-colonial opinion both in France and among the *colons*, and prospects for a negotiated settlement diminished sharply. By September 1946, at the conclusion of the Fontainebleau talks, Ho was forced to make a number of concessions and left with only a *modus vivendi* and no formal recognition by France of his regime.

On his return to Vietnam, Ho encountered rising sentiment in favour of open confrontation with France and by late November preparations had been begun for what the Party leadership now regarded as inevitable.[5] Base areas were prepared once again in the Viet Bac region, communications lines constructed and the process of evacuating personnel and material to the countryside was carried out. The incident that directly contributed to this move was the decision of the Bidault government in France to establish a customs house at Haiphong, provoking resistance from the Viet Minh troops stationed there. In the ensuing fighting, the French succeeded in driving the Viet Minh forces out of the city. On 18 December 1946, Viet Minh forces under the command of General Vo Nguyen Giap, counter-attacked in Hanoi in order to cover the evacuation of the government to Ha Dong a few miles south of the capital. By the next day, the French government was once again in full control of all the major cities of Vietnam. However, the Viet Minh retained control over most of the countryside. Even in the south, the Viet Minh had begun to win back some of the area initially lost to the French during 1945 and by late 1946, according to one estimate, they again controlled three-quarters of the southern countryside.[6]

Vietnamese strategy in the ensuing war combined political and economic elements as well as military and diplomatic ones. The theory was set out in Truong Chinh's *The Resistance Will Win*, written in 1947, in which it was argued that the war would proceed in three stages. The first stage would be essentially defensive while the Viet Minh regrouped and conserved its forces. In the second stage there would be an equilibrium between the two sides, with the Viet Minh launching guerrilla forays into enemy-held territory, and in the third stage the revolutionaries would go over to the offensive. In this final stage, a combination of military, political and diplomatic factors would be decisive. The strategy combined elements of Chinese military theories[7] with the ICP's traditional reliance on political struggle and diplomatic initiatives. One of the key elements in the thinking of the Viet Minh was that a drawn-out war of resistance would eventually lead to opposition within France itself, forcing the colonial regime progressively to withdraw.

For their part, the French also tried a political strategy, offering to restore the throne of Bao Dai in late 1947. But the nationalists were divided, especially over the French refusal to offer any form of independence, and nothing came of it until 1949 when Bao Dai accepted an 'Associated State' within the French Union, this time including Cochinchina in the deal. Many of the anti-communist groups in Vietnam rallied to this government, including the Saigon bourgeoisie. The eventual inclusion of Cochinchina was both a reflection of the growing need to appeal to these groups and a response to American pressure to give recognition to anti-communist nationalism in Vietnam.

By 1949, with the declaration of the Democratic People's Republic of Korea the previous year and the success of the Chinese revolution in October, US worries about the rise of communism in Asia were growing. Whereas the United States had distanced itself at first from the efforts of the European powers to restore the pre-war colonial status quo in Asia, it now became increasingly supportive of French attempts to defeat the Viet Minh. By the end of the year, Washington had established a Military Assistance Program to support France and the 'Associated State' in their struggle against communism and from 1950 onwards, US aid became increasingly vital in sustaining the French war effort.

In fact the French had begun to suffer some reverses in 1948 when the Viet Minh had been able to expand their guerrilla activities outside the base areas of Viet Bac, the U Minh forest and Plain of Reeds (both large swampy areas in the south) and Tay Ninh rubber plantations. In January 1950 first China and then the Soviet Union accorded diplomatic recognition and General Giap travelled to China to request assistance. In the autumn of that year the Viet Minh launched a major drive to wipe out French control over the area along the Chinese border and for the first time gave the DRV a common border with a fraternal socialist country. By this stage, then, the whole nature of the conflict in Vietnam had begun to change. Just as Viet Minh predictions of a weakening of pro-war sentiment in France were coming true, the far more powerful United States stepped in to bolster the French effort and to make Vietnam a major theatre, along with Korea, of its struggle to hold the line against a rising tide of anti-imperialist feeling in the colonial countries of the Pacific rim.[8] At a time when military and political developments were turning in favour of the Viet Minh, the international balance of forces thus took a significant turn for the worse. US aid to France was partly offset by a growing quantity of aid from China, but the Chinese were also careful not to do anything which might provoke direct American intervention against themselves.

The Political Front

During the final stages of the war a marked shift in the political strategy of the DRV occurred, which had important ramifications for the subsequent development of the regime. As early as 1948 and 1949 some concern had been expressed in Party circles that land and rent policies promulgated by the government were not being observed. In its effort to encourage the widest possible national united front against the French, the Party had carried out a massive membership drive and accepted large numbers of members who were not always subjected to a rigorous political test. In consequence, in many areas of the country, local Party committees were dominated by landlords and rich peasants. Moreover, a survey carried out by the Party in 1949 suggested that rent reduction policies had not been implemented by two-thirds of the landlords in the DRV-controlled area. Large numbers of people had clearly joined the Party for opportunistic reasons and this became particularly evident after 1948 when new French military tactics resulted in reversion of some areas to French control. Former Party members often changed sides when this happened. In other areas, the uncertainties engendered by the new military developments led to increasing *attentisme* by the peasantry—a refusal to become involved on either side until the issue was resolved. But it was precisely at this time, as the war intensified, that the Party needed increased commitment from the peasants, both in terms of their willingness to contribute revenues to the government and in their willingness to commit manpower.

The inherent contradictions of the united front policy were therefore becoming increasingly apparent. The Vietnamese countryside had never been free of class conflict and, for the bulk of the peasantry, support for the Indochinese Communist Party had always been primarily a vehicle for social change and economic reconstruction. Independence from France would provide the framework within which this became possible. As the war against France progressed, then, it became increasingly necessary for the Party to provide something for the peasants in return for their support.

The initial steps towards this change in policy were taken with the official re-emergence of the Party at its Second National Congress in February 1951 under the new name of Vietnam Workers' Party (Dang Lao Dong Viet Nam). At this congress the decision taken in 1941, that the revolution of each of the three Indochinese countries should be carried out within its own national framework, was formalized. Henceforth there would be three separate parties: the Khmer People's Revolutionary Party was set up in June 1951[9] as a result of this decision and in March 1955 the Lao People's Party was established.

Within Vietnam, however, the Congress also signalled the beginning of a process of tightening up the criteria for Party membership. At the time the Party had 760,000 members, but over the next two years this number would be reduced to about half a million as efforts to change the class composition and political education level of Party cadres were stepped up. A fiscal crisis, caused by large budget deficits leading to high inflation, was used as the excuse to sack about a third of the membership between 1951 and 1953 (Kolko, 1986, p. 46).

In January 1953 the Party decided to implement stronger measures to bring about social and economic change in the areas it controlled. Some anti-landlord moves had been made as early as 1949 with the cancellation of all debts incurred before 1945 and preference to poor peasants and tenants in the distribution of land confiscated from collaborators. But the policy had been difficult to implement as most of the new lands for distribution arose by landlords changing sides when their area reverted to French control. The April 1953 rent reduction campaign and December 1953 land reform legislation represented a significant shift in that they were aimed at *all* landlords, including patriotic ones and those who were also loyal Viet Minh cadres. These moves constituted a more determined effort by the Party to win the active support of poor peasants and to break the political power of landlords and rich peasants at the village level.

The rent reduction campaign carried out in the spring and summer of 1953 in the DRV-controlled areas was a successful attempt to carry out the policies announced in 1945 and to bring about a dramatic change in the social composition of local Party structures. The same techniques were used in this campaign as later, in the much more radical land reform campaign which aimed at expropriating the property of the so-called 'feudal' class. Using a technique borrowed from China, Party cadres who were directly responsible to the Central Committee, rather than local organizations, moved into the villages, staying with poor peasants and learning their personal histories. These personal histories were then used to explain the concept of exploitation and help peasants overcome their sense of dependence upon landlords. Peasant Committees were established to distribute land and People's Tribunals set up to try cruel and oppressive landlords.

As the movement gained momentum during 1954 and 1955, control over it passed increasingly out of the Party's hands and into those of the local councils comprising largely poor peasants. These peasants often did not make the careful distinctions between different categories of landlord and between landlord and rich peasant which the Party wished to maintain in order to be able to sustain a broad united front. While the Party tried to preserve an alliance with 'productive' rich peasants and small capitalist farmers, for example, it favoured expropriation of the land belonging to 'unproductive' landlords. Peasants, on the other hand, often found the former to be the harshest exploiters and lacked the inclination to distinguish between exploitation based on extraction of excessive rents by landlords and that caused by failure of rich peasants to pay arrears of already low wages. Moreover, the class analysis of the Party did not always take into account the existence of significant non-class conflicts within the villages which had been utilized by the French and by landlords to strengthen their power—for example, the division between Catholics and non-Catholics, 'insiders' and 'outsiders' (important in villages where refugees from famine had recently settled on the fringes), Viet Minh and ex-puppet troops. After 1954, these antagonisms and the failure of peasant committees and tribunals to follow the Party line were the cause of many tragic conflicts and excesses in the Land Reform campaign (Moise, 1976; Gordon, 1981; White, 1983). The Party itself, whose members often suffered as a result, was severely traumatized. In fact the level of internal disagreement which arose during the land reform campaign was one reason why it could not be curbed until 1956.[10]

But before the middle of 1954 these excesses and the internal disagreements to which they gave rise had not arisen. The immediate impact of the Land Reform was very positive in terms of renewed peasant commitment to the Resistance. Party commentators argued that the agrarian campaign was a crucial element in the Party's ability to mobilize over 200,000 peasants and 16,000 troops to build roads and trenches, and carry food, ammunition and guns to the front in preparation for the attack on Dien Bien Phu in March–May 1954 (VCP, 1980, p. 120; Vo Nguyen Giap, 1964, p. 150).

The Military Front

During 1952 and 1953 the Viet Minh won ground on the battlefield, including a large area of northern Laos. In order to counter this, the French decided to reinforce Dien Bien Phu, an outpost situated in a wide valley in north-western Vietnam, astride the route into Laos. In February 1954 the Viet Minh captured Kon Tum province and the town of Pleiku in the highlands of central Vietnam, giving them control over southern Laos and easy access to the coastal plains of Trung Bo where the French were forced to give up their offensive. The battle for Dien Bien Phu, which began in March 1954, therefore assumed vital importance since it would determine whether the French could effectively control any territory outside the towns of the two main deltas of Vietnam.

The Viet Minh, having recognized the strategic importance of Dien Bien Phu in late 1953, threw all their resources into the planning and logistical support of the attack. French and US experts had argued that Dien Bien Phu was invulnerable to artillery attack because gun emplacements on the hills encircling the valley could be wiped out from the air (the Viet Minh had no air force). But the Viet Minh mobilized thousands of labourers to dig tunnels and trenches to conceal the (Chinese-supplied) heavy guns deep inside the mountain sides. Due to artillery fire, the base airstrip, which was vital for maintaining supplies, was rendered useless from the outset of the battle. After withstanding a seige of fifty-five days, the starving French garrison surrendered and with this catastrophic defeat the political will in France to continue the campaign evaporated. The French military command drew up a plan for a strategic withdrawal south of the 18th parallel.

The Diplomatic Front

As the war dragged on and the French grew increasingly anxious to reach a settlement, an international conference at Geneva took up the problem in May 1954. The participants at the conference included the United States, Britain, France, the Soviet Union and China as well as a DRV delegation led by Pham Van Dong. The main problem facing the DRV at this conference was that, in spite of its military victories (Dien Bien Phu fell on the eve of the conference), and control over the majority of Vietnamese territory, the other participating powers shared neither its perspective nor most of its goals.

In the end, the Chinese delegation, led by Zhou Enlai, played a decisive role in achieving a settlement, but it was a settlement that was highly unsatisfactory to both the DRV government and the United States, so it was hardly surprising that conflict in the Indochinese peninsula was renewed before long. The DRV did make some important gains from Geneva, not least of which was the ending of the war with France and the chance to consolidate and rebuild its economy. But it was only allowed control over the northern half of Vietnam, with an election to be held within two years to establish a unified government of the whole country. In the interim, the French-dominated 'Associated State' gained control over the South.

The main sticking point in the negotiations was over the division of the country. Such a division, according to the Korean model, had been proposed by the Soviet Union[11] and endorsed by China in 1953 when the war had reached a less conclusive stage. Its allies were clearly prepared to push for a diplomatic solution before the Vietnamese considered the military and political conditions were ripe. At Geneva it was the Chinese who played the most active role in negotiating a division of Vietnam into two 'regroupment zones' at the 17th parallel of latitude. Such a division involved the incorporation of a large area already controlled by the DRV into the French regroupment zone, so it is important to ask why China—purportedly a socialist ally of Vietnam—was so keen to pressure Vietnam to accept the division.

The answer lies in the Chinese preoccupation at the time, in the immediate aftermath of the Korean War, with maintaining peace on its borders in order to concentrate on domestic development.[12] In view of the anti-communist fever in the United States, China was particularly anxious to avoid another confrontation and to establish, if possible, buffer zones between itself and any areas of anti-imperialist conflict. It was well aware, at the same time, that the United States was strongly opposed to any attempt to cede territory to the Viet Minh and had already established independent links with the Bao Dai government. Whereas the French were exhausted and keen to terminate the hostilities, the United States seemed more inclined to continue and possibly to internationalize the war unless the position of its Vietnamese allies could be bolstered. Kolko (1986) argues, admittedly with hindsight, that the United States would almost certainly not have intervened in Indochina in 1954, but neither the DRV nor China and the Soviet Union could have been certain of this at the time and from the narrowly Chinese point of view, division of Vietnam made good sense.[13]

The DRV government itself had few choices in the face of pressure from its allies to accept the Chinese solution. On the one hand, Mendès-France, the French Premier, had set a deadline to achieve a settlement. Beyond this date there would be an election in France, possibly a more conservative government and a renewal of the war effort. The Viet Minh had thrown an enormous effort into the Dien Bien Phu campaign and the political risks involved in asking the peasantry for even greater sacrifices in an extended war were great, as were the military risks if Chinese aid were withdrawn as a result of refusal to cooperate. The temporary division of the country, on the other hand, offered the chance for economic development and further consolidation of the regime's domestic support. The Party was confident that it would win the proposed elections for a re-unified government and there would be a breathing space in which to gather strength for any future confrontation with the United States.

The Geneva Accords were signed on 20 July 1954. Neither the United States nor the Bao Dai government were signatories, though the US representative gave verbal assurances that the United States would 'refrain from the threat or use of force' to disturb the arrangements reached. The two combatant sides, France and the DRV, were to withdraw to their respective regroupment zones south and north of the 17th parallel. The border between the two zones was left open while the regroupment took place and over the next year approximately 1 million people followed the French south. Many of these were Catholic peasants, persuaded by their priests that the communists would seek vengeance for the provision of troops to the French army by the Catholic villages. During this period the French themselves were able to dismantle and remove or destroy much of the capital equipment they had previously established in the northern half of the country. By the time they finally departed, in May 1955, very little was left of the North's small industrial sector. A few hundred thousand Viet Minh troops and supporters travelled north after 1954, but a large group remained in the South to carry out the legal political activity envisaged in the Accords. The Viet Minh did not expect that any effective political opposition to its influence could be mounted in the rural areas of the South during the two years prior to the elections.

Nine years after the August Revolution, the DRV was firmly and permanently established, at least in the northern half of the country. Owing to American intervention, the establishment of control over the southern half would prove much more difficult than it seemed in July 1954 and ultimately far more difficult than wresting control from the French had been. In the meantime, the regime turned to the solution of domestic problems thrown up by the land reform and by inflationary financing of the war.

4   From the Democratic to the Socialist Republic, 1954–1976

By 1950 Vietnam had become one of several testing grounds around the globe of US imperial strategies. The United States had emerged from the Second World War as the only economically and militarily powerful capitalist nation. Its governments and foreign policy decision makers saw themselves as having inherited the European mantle and increasingly viewed their role as one of maintaining an economic and political order in the world which would be amenable to further expansion of the world capitalist economy; specifically this meant the US economy. Between 1945 and the 1960s there existed a fairly broad consensus within the US ruling class and among the population at large in favour of this view. Though the fundamentally economic rationale of the policy was not always visible, often being clouded by arguments about American prestige and credibility or defence of the 'Free World', it nevertheless remained at the root of American foreign policy throughout the post-War period. Ultimately, the attempt to police the entire globe to this end proved inherently impossible and the United States was forced, by the mounting world economic problems brought on by its massive spending in Vietnam and the need to find a more rational ordering of its priorities, to retreat from Vietnam. But this did not occur before it had become embroiled to an extent unprecedented in its history or before it had wreaked such havoc on Vietnam that it would take years to recover.

The United States had begun supplying Bao Dai's government with economic assistance during 1951. Using this as a lever the Americans were able, by July 1954 during the Geneva talks, to persuade the pro-French Bao Dai to appoint the anti-French Ngo Dinh Diem as his Prime Minister. In this way, and by helping Diem to consolidate his political control over the Saigon government apparatus, the United States pressured the French to leave the country by the middle of 1955, thereby abrogating their responsibility under the Geneva Accords to ensure that the elections scheduled for 1956 would be held.[1] With American assistance Diem was able to overcome the armed resistance of the Binh Xuyen crime syndicate (to whom Bao Dai had sold the job of Saigon police chief) and various private armies of the Hoa Hao and Cao Dai whom the French had been aiding. In October 1955 Diem was strong enough to be able to depose Bao Dai, who in any case preferred the life of the Riviera to the difficult problems of state in Vietnam, and declare the establishment of the Republic of Vietnam (RVN) with himself as President. He then set about destroying the Viet Minh apparatus, which had been left in the south to carry out legal political activities.

The leaders of the VWP in the North had, at first, paid little attention to the activities of Diem. They did not believe that it would be possible to create within the short time available before the elections a serious political force to rival their own dominance in the South. However, it soon became apparent that Diem had no intention of holding the elections and, moreover, while the social basis of his regime remained very narrow, he intended to achieve complete domination of South Vietnam by force of repression. He appointed his brother Ngo Dinh Nhu to head the internal security forces and, over the next few years, this organization, and Nhu in particular, acquired a reputation for secrecy, brutality and arbitrariness which effectively terrorized South Vietnamese society at all levels. Between 1956 and 1963, when Diem was deposed, the repression was extended from the communists to all other forms of opposition to Diem's highly personalized rule, including the Buddhist church to which the majority of Vietnamese belonged and the Chinese business community who resisted his attempts to impose Vietnamese laws and nationality on them (Tsai Maw Kuey, 1968, pp. 55–70).

Opposition to Diem in the rural areas was intensified by two factors. On the one hand, the repression carried out against Viet Minh cadres and sympathizers affected a large number of people whose connections to the people of the villages in which they operated were close. On the other hand, Diem attempted to carry out a land reform, which, although it may have been detrimental to a few remaining French or pro-French landlords, largely reversed the system of land distribution that had been implemented by the Viet Minh. Whereas most of the old landlords had been driven out of the countryside during the war against the French, some were able to return under the new law, which allowed very large maximum holdings of 115 hectares and provided a generous period during which land could be exempted by conversion to industrial crops. Diem's reform also resulted in the distribution of land to military officers and local administrators, who were personal appointees of the President. Other military officers were able to profit from the fact that landlords often preferred to avoid the risks of living in the countryside and paid high commissions to soldiers to collect their rents. The purpose of the land reform was thus to consolidate Diem's grip on power by destroying or diluting the economic power of those landlords who were influenced by the French and by creating a new class of rural rich who owed their land, and their allegiance, to him. At the same time, by reversing the reforms carried out by the Viet Minh during the war, Diem's reform greatly increased the economic vulnerability of the peasants and gave them good reason for strengthening their support for the revolution.

The rise of Diem, with his at that stage unlimited backing from the United States, presented a powerful dilemma for the leaders of the DRV. For some time they maintained the hope that he could be persuaded to hold the election, but, as President Eisenhower was to write in his memoirs: 'It was generally conceded that had an election been held, Ho Chi Minh would have been elected Premier' (Kolko, 1969, p. 108). The United States therefore actively encouraged Diem in his refusal.

Party leaders in the South, on the other hand, were pressing increasingly between 1956 and 1959 for recommencement of armed struggle to liberate the region and considered the conditions very favourable to success. In many cases they took matters into their own hands, responding to Diem's repression by a series of assassinations of his local officials and village headmen and other armed activities. The peasants themselves often took action independently of the Party in response to the land reform, thus drawing themselves into Diem's category of 'Viet Cong' and widening the repression. Before 1959, however, the Party in Hanoi maintained the line that, while it was all right for the southern cadres to use armed struggle as a purely defensive measure, the focus should be on political struggle. The majority of Party leaders felt that even if the elections would not be held, the DRV could not afford to provide assistance to the southern revolutionaries at this stage. The most important priority for the DRV must be, they thought, to consolidate its reconstruction and economic development.

By 1959, however, events had overtaken this policy. It had become clear that unless the Party responded in a more systematic and aggressive fashion to the Diemist regime, its skeleton infrastructure in the South was in danger of being totally destroyed. Local rebellions by southern peasants were frequent occurrences, but without coordination they might become exhausted or be more easily manipulated by anti-communist elements. The Central Committee therefore took the decision in January 1959 to sanction greater reliance on military activity in the South, although the main focus continued to be on political activity. As events escalated, the Party sought out non-communist sympathizers in the South to form a united front against Diem and in December 1960 the establishment of the National Front for the Liberation of South Vietnam (Mat Tran Dan Toc Giai Phong Mien Nam Viet Nam) was announced.[2]

After the formation of the NLF and the placing of greater emphasis on armed struggle, things began to unravel fairly rapidly for the RVN regime. As the NLF gained an increasing number of military victories using local guerrilla forces, usually armed with weapons taken from the enemy, it was able to enforce rent reductions and some land reform over large areas of the country. This gave the peasants a strong reason for continued support to the revolution. The RVN regime, on the other hand, adopted a strategy of attempting to control the population militarily and administratively, but without heeding the demands for an equitable agrarian reform. Instead, the regime adopted a policy of creating 'Strategic Hamlets' in 1962 and moved large numbers of peasants into these, usually by force and often to a considerable distance from their original homes. Ultimately, the RVN claimed to have moved over 8 million people (a majority of the population) by the time of Diem's overthrow in late 1963. The sheer brutality with which the program was carried out created yet new sources of support for the NLF and solidified this support by overcoming class distinctions between poor and middle peasants. Moreover, while the policy was designed to separate the people from the NLF, the hamlets were rapidly infiltrated. In early 1963 the NLF began a campaign to destroy the Strategic Hamlets—most often by getting the villagers themselves to tear down the surrounding barricades— further enhancing its popularity and, in the process, turning entire villages into outlaws in the eyes of the government.

In January 1963 the disintegration of Diem's regime was further accelerated by a massive military defeat suffered in the first large-scale engagement of the war at Ap Bac. In the summer of that year rioting broke out among Buddhists protesting against Diem's repressive policies. In a climate of growing social and political instability caused by the President's efforts to concentrate power in his own hands and those of his closest relatives and by the extreme pressure on the regime from the NLF, intriguing had already begun among a number of senior military officers. After Diem's brother Nhu had secretly used French contacts to explore the possibility of re-establishing trade and postal relations with the DRV, the US government decided to throw the full weight of its support behind the plotters (Kolko, 1986, p. 117; *Pentagon Papers*, 1971).

Diem and Nhu were assassinated on 1 November 1963, but the succession of military regimes which followed over the next two years did little to resolve the problems facing the regime. The major causes of political instability in Saigon were the unremitting pressure of NLF successes and the narrow social base of the regime, in which political power had become a prerequisite for economic power, while, under Diem, political power had become highly personalized. Moreover, the armed forces had been organized, not so much to achieve military prowess (in spite of American efforts to the contrary), but to secure Diem's political control. Military posts had become both the only avenue of mobility for politically ambitious Saigonese and a means of acquiring wealth through corruption. After Diem's death, a struggle ensued among the military elite for the control of political office and the access to wealth that this brought. It became progressively clear to the Americans that if they were to preserve their Vietnamese clients from the consequences of successive military failures, they would have to take on most of the fighting themselves. The military regime remained the only alternative to the NLF and unless it could be massively bolstered by US forces, it might sink beneath the combined weight of domestic opposition and its own venality.

American escalation could only be undertaken, however, with the approval of Congress. Some doubts about the wisdom of the Vietnam venture had already surfaced in US public opinion, especially after an horrific incident in mid-1963, involving the self-immolation of a Buddhist monk in protest at Diem's repression, had been seen on television news programs. The instability following Diem's assassination was itself a source of disquiet. In 1961, the Bay of Pigs débâcle in Cuba had also created distrust in too much freedom of the executive to determine foreign policy and military commitments. So in order to head off potential Congressional objections to the escalation of war which it now proposed to undertake in Vietnam and to solidify public opinion in an election year,the Johnson administration looked for a more convincing way of presenting the policy as a 'response' to 'aggression' from the DRV. In fact its own data showed the US government that few resources were reaching the NLF from the North—the war in the South was still very largely a local affair and the NLF was winning by its own efforts (Kolko, 1986, p. 123).

To win needed Congressional approval of its policy of escalation, the administration presented a resolution in August 1964 which became known as the Gulf of Tonkin Resolution. The resolution was in fact a rather cynical attempt by the US executive to manipulate Congress, but it was not until the publication of the *Pentagon Papers*, a secret Pentagon history of decision-making on the war, which was leaked to the New York Times, in 1971, that the full extent of this deception was revealed (*Pentagon Papers*, 1971). The 'Gulf of Tonkin Incident', to which the Resolution was supposedly a response, was presented to Congress as an unprovoked attack by a North Vietnamese patrol boat on the USS *Maddox*, on patrol in international waters in the Gulf of Tonkin. In reality, the *Maddox* had been part of a navy patrol collecting electronic intelligence as close as four miles off DRV territory in conjunction with a program designated OPLAN 34A in which US Special Forces and the CIA, using Vietnamese mercenaries, conducted raids on DRV territory. An OPLAN 34A raid took place on 2 August 1964 and the *Maddox* was ordered to draw DRV boats away from the operation (Kolko, 1986, pp. 123–4). DRV authorities drew the obvious, and correct, conclusion that the raids and the patrol were linked and attacked the *Maddox*. The American administration immediately retaliated by bombing DRV patrol boat sites and storage facilities and presented the Resolution, which had been prepared for such an eventuality five months earlier, to Congress.

For the next few years the passage of the Gulf of Tonkin Resolution gave the US administration a free hand to carry out its policy of escalation of the conflict in Vietnam, a policy that had already been decided upon months before the incident occurred. The longer-term importance of the Resolution stemmed not only from its immediate quieting of potential opposition to the policy, but in removing the war from too much Congressional scrutiny. Although Congress continued to share in the broad consensus of opinion about the need to 'contain communism' and preserve American credibility and power in the world, it may have been more attuned to domestic sectional pressures to achieve a different ordering of priorities. Such pressures would become increasingly important as the war progressed and first the US economy then the world economy began to suffer, large numbers of Americans were killed and wounded and a very diverse spectrum of public opinion against the war began to become vociferous. But it was only later, after the extent of the Administration's deception had been revealed, that the evident failure of the escalation policy caused Congress to try seriously to reassert its power over financing of the war.

The air war against North Vietnam began after the Gulf of Tonkin incident and was soon expanded to the main industrial areas and communications facilities of the DRV under the operation aptly named 'Rolling Thunder'. This was orginally intended to be a short-term campaign aimed at halting the flow of supplies from North to South via the Ho Chi Minh trail, but was eventually extended until 1968 without achieving any of its goals. Twice as much bomb tonnage was used in this three-year campaign against a technologically unsophisticated Asian country as was used during the whole of the Second World War. The effect on North Vietnam's fledgling industrial sector was devastating (see Chapter 9), although much industrial production did continue because industrial centres were dismantled and moved to remote rural areas, or re-established in mountain caves. This was possible because of the low capital-intensity of most manufacturing in the DRV, but it was the newly-established modern and capital-intensive sectors that were badly hit. There was also a considerable loss of external economies through this forced decentralization. But in a predominantly agrarian society, where even most manufacturing was not dependent upon advanced technology, bombed bridges and roads could be repaired during the night and the productive activities of the majority of the population were largely unaffected. Moreover the sporadic terror brought about by bombing of villages—4,000 of the North's 5,788 villages were hit during the war (*Vietnamese Studies*, 1976, p. 149)—only served to strengthen anti-American sentiment and increase popular commitment to the struggle to evict the foreign invader. The US government's own figures showed that the flow of supplies down the Ho Chi Minh trail not only did not falter, but increased between 1965 and 1968.

The air war was the first major American escalation. The second was the introduction of US combat troops to supplement the 23,000 military advisers and technicians already in the country (Figure 4.1). Troops were originally brought in to defend US installations in the South, especially air bases, which had proved vulnerable to NLF attacks earlier in the year. But they were soon switched to more offensive tactics when static defence proved inadequate and gradually their activities spread from the immediate perimeter area of the bases to cover the entire countryside. As the 'Search and Destroy' missions were extended, the number of troops thought necessary to keep the NLF at bay increased, until by 1968 the United States had over half a million soldiers in Vietnam. South Korean, Thai, Filipino, Australian and New Zealand forces also contributed about 90,000 under SEATO arrangements. Altogether, by 1968 the RVN and its allies could muster approximately 1.5 million troops

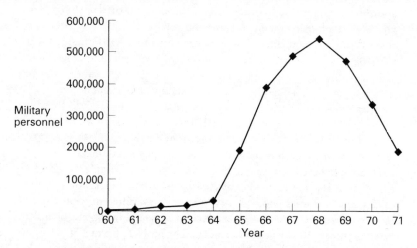

Figure 4.1 US troop build-up, 1960–71

to combat a combined NLF/PAVN army estimated at less than 400,000 (about a third of these were irregular forces). Not only did the RVN and allied troops vastly outnumber those of their opponents, but American military doctrine relied heavily on high technology and massive use of firepower. The United States set about defoliating large tracts of forest and agricultural land in order to deprive the NLF of cover and food and brought new, ugly weapons like napalm and fragmentation bombs to bear upon the civilian population. As the war dragged on and the RVN and Americans continued to use virtually indiscriminate firepower wherever the NLF was suspected of being, the civilian population of the South suffered from a far greater social upheaval than at any stage during the relatively localized and small-scale war against the French. This would have important consequences for the revolutionary forces in the longer run.

As the war dragged on, increasing numbers of Vietnamese peasants were turned into refugees, fleeing from both the destruction of war and the efforts of the government to move them into more easily controllable sites. Most of these went to the cities, especially to the central coastal towns like Da Nang and Nha Trang where the surrounding rural areas were most extensively devastated. Here they formed a large lumpenproletariat, living mostly off their wits from petty trading or from providing services to the foreign troops. Because of the uprooting of village communities caused by this process as well as the inherently individualistic, competitive lifestyle of the urban poor, these people became to some extent immune to Party attempts to organize them. A further problem was exhaustion, which often affected cadres as well as ordinary civilians, and a rising level of *attentisme* in rural as well as urban areas. Although many retained their sympathy for the NLF, the latter would find it more and more difficult to mobilize peasant action, the longer the war went on. There was less overt revolutionary fervour and more devotion to economic interests and to sheer physical survival—especially as the land question had, by the early-1970s, been mainly resolved. The question of agrarian reform remained on the agenda, particularly in areas still controlled by the RVN, until the Thieu regime largely defused the issue after 1970 by formally distributing titles to the occupants of the land in the Mekong Delta. Middle and rich peasants, now secure in their tenure, dominated the class structure of the rural areas in the Delta and these became progressively locked into the market economy, fed by plentiful imports of subsidized inputs and consumer goods. A new form of class differentiation based on private capital accumulation through commerce and hiring out of agricul-tural machinery slowly began to emerge. The problem for the United States, on the other hand, was that while people may have become privately sick of revolution and the Cold War retribution it had brought upon them, they did not become friendly to the RVN as a result—its plundering of the civilian population was still too great and Vietnamese antagonism to the foreign invader remained strong.

Under these circumstances, the flexibility and pragmatism of the Party in the South, made necessary by the wartime conditions and the need for the Party to survive and grow in influence, enabled it to retain a greater closeness to population than might have been expected. But a number of problems for future development were clearly inherent in the situation. One was that the Party's strategy of combining urban and rural struggle would become increasingly difficult to manage as time wore on. Another was that the Party's ability to balance the economic interests of the new large class of middle peasants with those of the much smaller group of poor peasants, as well as meeting the needs of the urban unemployed and the many other groups which it sought to bring under its united front, would require a different approach after the war from that taken in the North, where much of the land question had still been unresolved in 1954. In other words, the revolutionary goals of the Party, which had been its most profound basis of support during the war against the French, had by the 1970s themselves created a new set of social relations in the countryside which presented a challenge to the Party's traditional ways of thinking. Some of these problems emerged as early as the Tet Offensive of 1968, but others would not become apparent until after the war was over. After Tet the focus of revolutionary strategy shifted away from the essentially political struggle in the villages and cities towards much greater emphasis on diplomatic and military activity. While cadres at the local level no doubt remained in touch with the peasants, it is not evident that the Party leadership in Hanoi had a very clear understanding of the social transformation taking place at the grassroots in the South.[3] This shortcoming was, of course, exacerbated by the destruction of large parts of the Party's most experienced and skilled local southern cadre force under the CIA-inspired Phoenix program begun in 1967.

The Tet Offensive and its Aftermath

In late January 1968, during the Tet (Lunar New Year) holiday, the American military machine in Vietnam received an enormous shock. Although it had been watching the NLF/PAVN build up for some months and fully expected a major offensive, the US military command had not been able to predict the timing and was totally unprepared for its extent and its success. Perhaps most symbolic of the collapse of the American military strategy which the Tet offensive represented was the fact that the American Embassy itself, in the heart of Saigon, was temporarily captured.

The US strategy, because it concentrated on the physical control of population and territory, had ignored the main source of support and strength of the NLF which was its ability to retain the active cooperation of the bulk of the population in the rural areas precisely because it offered and implemented economic and social benefits. The United States, on the other hand, was associated with a repressive regime which had consistently refused to be interested in peasant demands for an equitable land system. Indeed the United States was dependent for the survival of its anti-communist project on a regime which was in turn dependent on maintaining an inequitable land system to ensure itself of a social base among landlords and the military officers who also profited from it. The class interests of the peasantry therefore coincided with the more abstract goals of the Party of national independence and freedom from foreign occupation through which it could also appeal to the long traditions and highly developed national consciousness of the Vietnamese (Chapters 1 and 2). For these reasons, the Party was always able to gain a commitment from enough peasants to be able to maintain its organizational structure, even in RVN-controlled zones. As far as the VWP was concerned, the only unknown quantity in its planning for the Tet offensive was its ability to gain a parallel commitment from the urban population in order to achieve a general uprising like the one which had carried it to power in 1945.

The objectives of the offensive in 1968 were flexible. The Party hoped that a general uprising in the cities of the South would lead to the collapse from within of the Thieu regime and leave the Americans with no option but to withdraw. Failing that, the offensive would, at the very least, show the Americans the utter failure of their escalation policy and might also galvanize many of the growing number of fence-sitters among the Vietnamese population into taking a more active role in the revolution. In the event, the cities did not rise. Though there was sustained fighting by NLF groups which had entered Saigon and the other cities and two northern provinces, including the city of Hue, were captured, the offensive was finally blunted by lavish use of American firepower. In retaking the town of Ben Tre, which had been captured by the NLF, the American officer in charge coined one of the most quoted quotes of the war: 'We had to destroy the town in order to save it'. Hue also, with its ancient royal citadel, was devastated.

Large areas of the countryside changed hands during the Tet offensive, returning to NLF hands the control of many villages where they had been forced into retreat since US escalation three years earlier. In the longer run, however, the tremendous effort expended on the offensive and its failure to achieve the primary goal of an early end to the war led to great difficulties for the NLF. Many of its local forces were killed and the let-down, when the expectation of success had been great, was to cause serious morale problems and resulted in the revolutionaries going on the defensive during an extended period of rebuilding between 1969 and 1972. During this time, the RVN was able gradually to encroach once more upon the areas it had lost during 1968. This period of relative calm was also a period of economic recovery, financed by massive injections of American aid, and of the final settling of the land question in the crucial Mekong delta by Thieu's *de jure* recognition of the land distribution system prevailing after successive Viet Minh and NLF reforms.

The most dramatic effect of the Tet offensive, and the one that in the end proved decisive, was on the United States. The possibility that it could persuade the United States of the folly of its Vietnam policy had always been in the calculations of the DRV leadership and, despite the enormous costs of staging the offensive and subsequent demoralization among cadres who had been expecting greater success, it was nevertheless a sufficient justification in·the longer run. US leaders had been lulled into a false sense of security by optimistic assessments, based on 'body counts' and the 'hamlet evaluation system',[4] of the progress of the war by Saigon-based military advisers. The dramatic impact of the Tet offensive on the military situation thus came as a complete surprise to President Johnson and his advisers. After three years of bombing the North and three years of rapid escalation in American troop numbers, the NLF remained no less capable than before of shaking the RVN regime to its foundations. Large numbers of American troops had been deliberately drawn into and tied down in one of the most intense battles of the war at Khe Sanh in the central highlands leaving the NLF and PAVN greater freedom of action in the southern part of the country. When the offensive subsided the PAVN units at Khe Sanh simply withdrew, leaving US generals to claim an empty victory, but leaving the strategic initiative firmly in the hands of the communists. The Tet offensive had shown not only the complete inability of the RVN to survive without US military assistance, but it had exposed the limits of that assistance. President Johnson was now faced with an insoluble dilemma: he could not persuade a growing and powerful section of American public opinion that further escalations would be justified in terms of the United States' overall global objectives, nor could he continue to promise the 'light at the end of the tunnel', which had been the subject of a major speech only a few months earlier.

The cost of the Vietnam war had, by 1967, become a major problem for the US economy. The American approach to fighting the war involved high levels of expenditure on technology and this was particularly true of the air war in which B52 strategic bombers, stationed as far away as Guam, had been used since June 1965. By 1972, the Pentagon had admitted to the loss of no less than 3,689 fixed wing aircraft and 4,857 helicopters, valued at over $10 billion (Kolko, 1986, p. 190); 15 million tons of munitions had been used and estimated military budgets had risen from $5.8 billion in 1965–6 to $26.5 billion in 1967–8 (Kolko, 1986, p. 189). In March 1965 the US Defense Secretary, Robert McNamara, had given the military virtual *carte blanche* for the war and, by 1966, this was already posing serious problems for President Johnson's Great Society program. In spite of cutbacks to the latter, budget deficits by 1968 had risen to 3 per cent of GNP (Kolko, 1986, p. 288). At the same time, capacity utilization of American industry had risen sharply and inflation thus became the inevitable result of further increases in expenditure. From an average of 1.3 per cent per annum in 1960–5, inflation reached 6.1 per cent in 1969. Full capacity utilization and expanding employment led to rising unit labour costs and this also greatly exacerbated the balance of payments problem of the American economy, which had been building since the end of the 1950s.

Throughout the 1960s rising inflation and its consequences for the US balance of payments increasingly threatened the international economic order which had been established by the Bretton Woods conference in 1944, during the final stages of the Second World War. At Bretton Woods, the strength of the US economy and its domination of world trade had made the US dollar an acceptable international reserve currency, convertible into gold at $35 an ounce, However, the recovery of the European and Japanese economies and their share of world trade after the War meant that the dollar soon became overvalued. American investment overseas was encouraged to accelerate and the post-war trade surplus turned into a deficit. The enormous structural problems of the US economy which now followed the expenditure on Vietnam only served to exacerbate this problem. Foreign governments began to lose confidence in the dollar and some began to switch their reserves into gold, causing a run on US gold holdings. Others, such as West Germany, held such large reserves in dollars that they needed to protect its value. American and European bankers alike now began to be very worried about the possible consequences of continued Vietnam expenditure for the US position in the world economy. Protecting their interests in Europe and the Middle East began to be more important than winning the war in a small Asian country, which, in itself, was of little economic interest to the United

States. From late-1967 onwards a steadily increasing amount of attention in Washington had to be devoted to the international economic ramifications of the war.

Even without the Tet offensive, it is certain that these problems would eventually have forced Washington to wind down its Vietnam involvement and the end result might have been substantially the same. What Tet did was to bring home, even to the most optimistic 'hawks' in the administration, the realization that the results of three years of continuous and massive escalation did not justify the costs to the US economy and to the government's overall project of structuring the world economy to promote the interests of US capital. The Tet offensive also provided a big fillip to the American anti-war movement, which included many far less powerful elements of society than the big financiers, being based on a broad coalition of humanitarian, religious, left-wing and other diverse opposition to the war. The growing strength and vociferousness of this movement was to assume some importance in an election year.

The DRV leadership had analysed the dollar crisis and it had formed a part of their calculations in planning the offensive. In this sense, then, they did achieve their objective and in this sense Tet 1968 was a turning point in the war. From 1968 onwards the United States began a search for a new and less costly way to achieve its goals, which it now phrased increasingly in terms of saving its 'credibility' or 'honour' rather than using the earlier terminology of the domino theory. And from 1968 onwards US administrations were increasingly constrained in their ability to achieve even this limited goal, not only by the resurgent strength of the NLF, but by global economic considerations and by the need to present at least the appearance of ending the war to an ever more critical domestic audience.

In the aftermath of the 1968 offensive President Johnson took steps to cut the cost of the war. He ordered a bombing halt and refused a military request for a further 206,000 troops (108,000 of whom were to be sent to Vietnam). Faced with budget cuts, the Pentagon itself now became worried that it could no longer sustain its global military commitments and, under its new Secretary, Clark Clifford, began to pressure for a reduced Vietnam involvement in order to replenish its armaments elsewhere. Seeing no way out of the impasse, Johnson resigned.

The new Republican President, Richard Nixon, came to office with a clearly defined strategy. On the one hand, he would continue the process, begun by Johnson, of reversing the American troop build-up and push more of the responsibility for the fighting on the RVN forces. This policy became known as Vietnamization. On the other hand, he would concentrate on diplomatic initiatives and his 'madman' theory to pressure the DRV into accepting a political resolution of the conflict on US terms: i.e., one which at least maintained the Thieu regime in office. The 'madman' theory consisted in trying to convince the Soviet Union, China and the DRV that Nixon was such a rabid anti-communist that he would be prepared even to press the nuclear button in order to end the war.

Peace negotiations were begun in Paris in 1969, but at this stage neither side carried them on very seriously. The DRV, pursuing its strategy of 'fighting and negotiating', needed to be able to negotiate from a more decisive military situation; the United States hoped to be able to buy time for its South Vietnamese allies to remedy their fatal political amd military weaknesses and to stand on their own. In the meantime Nixon and his National Security Advisor, Henry Kissinger, began to establish contacts within the Chinese and the Soviet Union in the hope of exploiting the antagonism between these two allies of the DRV to make gains for the United States. The Soviet Union, on the one hand, had a strong interest in achieving *détente* with the United States to be able to increase its imports of Western technology and relieve the pressure of high military expenditure on consumption standards at home. China, on the other hand, was interested both in preventing such a *détente*, which would leave it more isolated, and maintaining the status quo along its southern borders, where a divided Vietnam provided a buffer zone against possible US aggression. One faction with the Chinese Communist Party was also interested in achieving more positive links with the United States and Japan in order to gain access to Western technology. But offsetting these reasons for greater cooperation with the United States was the fact that both China and the Soviet Union needed to maintain their practical support for Vietnam as a means of gaining leverage in the Southeast Asian region, already a zone of growing strategic importance with the rise of Japan as a major economic power, and more generally as leaders of the 'Third World'. The conflicting objectives of both Soviet and Chinese policy served to ensure that Nixon's diplomatic strategy of isolating Vietnam did not work at all smoothly. Aid to the DRV remained sufficient for its needs, although China did try to exert some pressure on Vietnamese leaders to accept the continued existence of the Thieu regime.

While the American diplomatic offensive bore little real fruit by 1972, the military and political balance once again began to swing in favour of the communists and their allies. In 1969 Nixon and Kissinger had begun the illegal, and therefore secret, bombing of Cambodian territory in an effort to halt the flow of supplies along the Ho Chi Minh trail. Partly as a result of the destabilizing effect this had on the Cambodian ruling elite and partly due to the inherent contradictions of Cambodian society, Prince Sihanouk's neutral regime was overthrown by pro-American military officers and Cambodia was dragged inexorably into the war. In March 1970 the ARVN invaded Cambodia and, in April, the United States followed to rescue its ally from embarrassment once again. The net effect of these new escalations of the conflict was that US public opinion was further infuriated, the weakness of Vietnamization was exposed and Cambodian society began the process of polarization and brutalization which was eventually to lead to the rise to power of Pol Pot. As Kolko points out, the spread of the war to Cambodia diluted the concentration of ARVN forces and provided the NLF with new opportunities in South Vietnam itself.

This pattern continued over the next two years: as more US troops were withdrawn, the weakness of the RVN was more exposed. In 1971 the ARVN launched a major drive into southern Laos which was a total failure: having been warned in advance the PAVN prepared a trap and the ARVN was forced to retreat after suffering heavy losses. Encouraged, and convinced that the United States could not re-enter the ground war, the DRV launched another major offensive in the spring of 1972, during which it achieved the decisive change in the military balance that it sought in order to begin serious negotiations. Nixon and Kissinger, after the former's successful visits to Beijing and Moscow early in the year, also felt that their diplomatic strategy was beginning to work and, for good measure, they ordered the resumption of bombing of Hanoi and Haiphong and the mining of DRV ports to try to win more concessions. This was apparently a rehearsal of the 'madman' theory as Nixon now ran the risk of blowing up a Soviet freighter. By October 1972 agreement was reached which substantially fulfilled the immediate objectives of the two governments. It provided for a ceasefire in place followed by a complete withdrawal of American troops within two months and a political settlement to be worked out at a later date. This agreement proved utterly unacceptable to the South Vietnamese regime for the obvious reason that it would have forced them to accept the control of NLF/PAVN troops and the Provisional Revolutionary Government (which had been established in June 1969) over a large part of the South. As for the DRV and PRG delegations, although the continued existence of the Thieu regime was in principle unacceptable, their leaders were justifiably convinced that without the American prop, it could not last long. The main objective of the DRV and PRG in the negotiations had been to get the Americans to leave. For the Americans, the agreement was simply an attempt to buy time for the RVN while fulfilling the now pressing imperative that the United States wind down its commitments.

Nixon's diplomatic success in China and the seriousness with which negotiations were now proceeding gave him an overwhelming victory in the November 1972 election, in spite of his decision not to sign the October agreement. In December, with the election safely behind him, he decided to try to get new concessions from the DRV and ordered new bombing of Hanoi–Haiphong. The communists had themselves raised more demands after the American refusal to sign, but by January 1973 a new agreement had been reached which was, in its essentials, no different from the earlier one. The DRV had made concessions on their new demands which allowed Henry Kissinger to save face, but in fact the massive bombing of civilian targets in North Vietnam, which took place during the so-called 'Christmas bombing', had achieved nothing new. Instead the American public was outraged and this only added to Nixon's problems with the Watergate scandal, which began inexorably to destroy his presidency from now on. The last US combat troops were withdrawn from Vietnam in March 1973.

None of this meant that with the signing of a peace agreement the US administration had abandoned all of its objectives in Vietnam, and President Nixon continued to seek alternative ways to buy time for the RVN in the hope that it could establish itself. The chief means used after the Paris Accords were the intensive bombing of Laos and Cambodia, but by August 1973 an angry Congress had imposed a ban on all bombing of Indochina. Military aid to the South Vietnamese regime was progressively cut, with the Pentagon one of the most enthusiastic advocates of different priorities in American spending.

By late 1974, though the leadership in Hanoi was cautious on account of the massive technical resources which the United States had left behind in the hands of the ARVN, the southern-based revolutionaries clearly felt that a renewed offensive was called for.[5] Opposition to the Thieu regime within the South Vietnamese cities was reaching new heights as declining US dollar expenditures and the accompanying severe recession in the economy created a new round of speculation and competition among military officers for a diminishing pool of lucre. President Thieu, who had depended very much on his ability to distribute largess to maintain the loyalty of subordinates, had to spend much time concentrating on his own political survival rather than on the military situation in the country. Middle-class Saigonese, whose businesses were crumbling in the face of the recession, began to complain bitterly about the continued lavish lifestyles and corruption of the elite. Many students and intellectuals also began to feel that the only way to restore peace to the country and achieve some sort of political stability was for the NLF to take over power. Thus while much of this opposition to Thieu was not actively pro-NFL, large segments of hitherto apolitical southern society had begun to call for an end to the war. After the Tet offensive of 1968 had exposed its organizational weakness in the urban areas of the South, the Party had encouraged the growth of a 'Third Force', which came to include many non-communist intellectuals and some of the religious opposition to the American-backed regime. These people had acquired the expectation that they would be included in some form of power-sharing arrangement as a result of an eventual political settlement to the war. But for all these opposition groups, an end to the war was now predicated upon Thieu being removed from power. The situation in the South was such that, by early 1975, a concerted push would see the RVN crumble, both within and without.

On 6 January 1975 PAVN and NLF forces attacked Phuoc Long province not far north of Saigon and captured the provincial capital with little resistance. Pessimism and panic rapidly began to envelope the Saigon regime, while the revolutionaries received confirmation that a spring offensive would succeed. In mid-March, the strategic town of Ban Me Thuot in the central highlands was taken in the first thrust of the communist main offensive and the next day Thieu decided to order a strategic withdrawal from most of the central highlands, defending only the coastal cities and the southern part of the country. He also ordered the best troops to Saigon to defend his political position from the threat of a coup. Most of his troops in the northern part of the country had their families living with them and, when they were ordered to withdraw under attack from the PAVN, most of them simply deserted and tried to save their families. Scenes of great chaos followed, which were only increased over the next few weeks. Two weeks after the fall of Ban Me Thuot, the communist troops captured Hue and the Political Bureau of the Party then took the historic decision to abandon the more limited objectives of the offensive and to push for a complete victory. Pandemonium prevailed in Da Nang, as panic stricken soldiers and citizens attempted to grab transport to the south amid scenes of pillage and rape. Calm only returned on 30 March, when PAVN troops entered the city. The only significant resistance offered by Thieu's army was at Xuan Loc, less than 100 km. from Saigon, but this was soon overcome and, on 21 April, with the city surrounded by thirteen divisions, Thieu finally abandoned his office, leaving the country the next day. On 30 April, as the last Americans left by helicopter from the roof of their embassy, PAVN troops entered Saigon and the war was over.[6]

From the DRV to the SRV

Formal re-unification of the country was not undertaken until July 1976, more than a year after the end of the war. Until then the PRG continued to operate, at least nominally, as the government of the South and the DRV in the North. In many ways this was an absurd situation as most of the major decisions continued to be made as always by the leadership in Hanoi, but it also reflects an ongoing debate in Hanoi about how best to deal with the South.

For the most part, the DRV leaders had been caught unawares by the final collapse of the Saigon regime. In planning the 1975 offensive, they had calculated on the basis of a two-year campaign and no specific plans had been drawn up for the transition to a new social system in the South, nor, amid the general preoccupation with the war on the one hand and the economic problems of the DRV itself on the other, had a great deal of attention been devoted to analysing the southern economy and its potential or the way it might interact with the northern economy. The Party was, moreover, greatly hampered in developing such an analysis by several factors resulting from the war.

One obvious factor was the enormous loss of experienced and skilled cadres via the CIA's Phoenix program. In 1968 alone 13,000 were killed according to one source (Kolko, 1986, p. 330), although the CIA officially listed 'only' 20,000 dead under the entire eight-year program and 86,000 arrested. Phoenix was especially damaging to the NLF because it tended to eliminate those working closest to the grassroots in the NLF's highly decentralized organization and thus destroyed many with the best working knowledge of conditions and attitudes in the rural areas.

Another major factor was the fact that for a party that had successfully organized a revolution in 1945 in a very backward agricultural region, where (although the towns had played a significant role) the general uprising was based largely on peasant demands for food and land, the social transformation of the South was an unknown quantity. Urban dwellers of the South in 1975 constituted 35 per cent of the population, yet the Tet offensive of 1968 had revealed that the Party had not been able to put down deep roots in the cities as it had in the countryside. The widespread urban unrest during 1974 and early 1975 expressed inchoate points of view and lacked any coherent organizational base. While many people, especially intellectuals, were clearly sympathetic to the NLF, they had not joined it and they were disinclined to accept Party discipline with the sacrifices it imposed in everyday life. To overcome the problem that they did not really know or trust the urban intelligentsia in the South, the Party sent large numbers of cadres from the North to manage the transition. This was a sensible decision in so far as it replaced lost Party cadres with new ones and helped overcome the extreme urban bias of the southern intellectuals who had been effectively cut off from contact with the rural areas for years, but it also created resentment among those not given positions of responsibility commensurate with their skills or expectations and resulted in the 'Third Force' people largely being denied the important role they had come to expect. In the face of resistance by the dominant ethnic Chinese business establishment to its measures of economic control, the Party in Hanoi tended to respond by tightening its political control and, in 1976, those who wanted to embark upon a fairly rapid transition to socialism to bring the southern system into line with that prevailing in the North gained the upper hand. There was a considerable increase in tension in the South as this policy came into effect during 1977 and, for reasons which will be discussed in more detail in Chapter 10, the level of economic hardship also increased. The two processes were mutually reinforcing.

The changes that had been wrought in the rural areas of the South, partly by the war but largely by the revolutionary process itself, were also to create problems for the Party. By the early 1970s, the land question, which had provided most of the impetus to the revolution in the 1940s and 1950s, had been largely resolved—at least in the main rice bowl of the Mekong Delta. The dilemma for the Party now was whether to proceed directly to collectivization to bring the South into line with the North, or to allow individual farming to develop and to allow capitalist production relations to continue in the foreseeable future. This question too, tended to be resolved in favour of a more rapid transition to socialism after 1976 with consequences that were in the short run disastrous for the southern economy and contributed to the outflow of 'boat people' in 1978–80. Between 1965, when the Americans began their massive escalation to prop up the Thieu regime, and 1975 a gap had opened up between the ideological precepts of the Party and the needs of the peasantry, which only now, with the ending of the war, was to become apparent. As long as the war continued, the vast majority of peasants of the Mekong delta remained either passive or else active supporters of the NLF. Passivity was often a question of physical survival, but the Party had nevertheless been able to put down deep roots in the country-side and had avoided antagonizing any of the different rural social classes (even small landlords) by its flexibility and decentralized structure. Once the war was over, however, the economic interests of the peasantry became uppermost and, in the changed circumstances, the petty bourgeois aspirations of a large middle peasantry were at odds with the predominantly poor peasant orientation of Party policy. This is not to say that the peasantry would no longer accept any move towards socialism, but the situation required careful analysis and a more creative approach than was initially adopted.

The formation of the SRV would therefore create a new set of challenges for a party which has probably had to face more severe tests over a longer period than any other communist party. The enormous resilience of Vietnamese communism in three decades of almost continuous warfare has, however, been largely attributable to its ability to react flexibly and pragmatically in a crisis and ultimately to come up with a response based on a realistic appraisal of the political, economic, diplomatic and social parameters within which it needs to act. An awareness of the fundamental material constraints imposed on human activity is perhaps a lesson the United States may have learned from its involvement in Vietnam.

Part II
The Social System

5   Social Structure

Historical Development

Because of the way in which French colonial rule in Vietnam was organized, and because of the long period of separation after 1954, the social structures of North and South Vietnam have developed in quite different ways. As was noted in earlier chapters, the northern and central regions of the country were ruled as Protectorates under the French while the Nam Bo region was ruled as a direct colony. One result of this was that private property was established on a more widespread basis in the southern region, whereas in the north and centre it co-existed with more traditional forms of land ownership. In the Mekong River delta, which was then quite sparsely populated, the French continued the work begun by earlier Vietnamese settlers of draining and irrigation, and established rice plantations, usually farmed by tenant sharecroppers, for the export trade. In the northern, older settled areas, on the other hand, although large tracts were appropriated for private plantations, the traditional Vietnamese village institutions and forms of property ownership persisted, in particular communal ownership of land. The different patterns of settlement and social organization resulting from these variations in the method of colonial domination and penetration have had important ramifications for Vietnamese social structure in subsequent periods.

In South Vietnam, because of the importance to the economy of the region of the export trade in commodities like rice, rubber and maize, a capitalist market economy was established from the early days of French rule. The commerce of the colony was dominated by the French and by a substantial community of ethnic Chinese who were mostly concentrated in Cholon, a satellite city of Saigon. The French capitalists, the main owners of the land, did not invest large amounts of capital and create a modern agricultural economy; rather they relied on labour-intensive farming methods carried out by sharecroppers or plantation labour.[1] In rice production, neither the tenant nor the landowner had an interest in improving the productivity of the land—the tenant because he did not have security and feared that increases in output would be siphoned off in rent; the landlord because his interest lay in the appropriation of the surplus and not in the production side of the enterprise (many of them in fact lived in the cities and relied on agents to collect the rent). The system created intense class antagonisms in the southern countryside, especially during the last two or three decades before the Second World War, when, pushing against the natural productivity barriers of backward farming technology, the demands for an ever increasing rent by landlords caused peasant subsistence levels to fall (Norlund, 1986).

As in the northern areas, where French demands for taxation payments and corvée labour had led to immiseration of the majority of peasants, the class conflicts engendered by the agricultural system in the south provided fertile ground for the Viet Minh and the NLF with their program of land reform. The land reform process in South Vietnam was a gradual one extending over three decades from 1945 to the mid-1970s. When the communists finally took power in the South in 1975, the change that had taken place in the system of land tenure over these three decades was very large indeed. Whereas in 1955, the poor peasants had constituted over 70 per cent of the rural population and owned only 14 per cent of the land, by 1978, when the first post-war survey of land tenure in the Mekong delta was carried out, they were less than a quarter (and owned 8 per cent of the land). Instead the great bulk of peasants were classified as middle or rich and it was these peasants who produced the large marketed surplus of the delta.[2]

Under the American-backed regime in the South, the agricultural sector had also continued the trend to commercialization. Whereas in colonial times, however, this commercial development had left the peasants largely unaffected—since they retained no marketable surpluses for their own use—the gradual progress of the land reforms during the following two decades enabled more and more peasants to enter the market, not only for consumer goods, but for investment goods as well. Although by comparison with other countries in the Southeast Asian region, the extent of this capitalization and commercialization of agriculture remained low, largely because war conditions interfered with expansion of output, it was nevertheless a significant development within the Vietnamese context. It has meant that the problems of transforming the southern social structure and collectivizing agriculture have been very different in South Vietnam compared with the experience of the North twenty years earlier, as will be seen in Chapter 10.

The other major social change which took place in the South during the years of separation was the extremely rapid urbanization. Such urban growth was partly a result of the changes taking place in the southern economy—the stagnation of agricultural output prior to 1969–70 and the very rapid expansion of the service and commercial sectors. In 1960, 88 per cent of the work-force of the South had been employed in agriculture. (Le Khoa *et al.*, 1979, p. 110) But the huge quantities of American economic assistance to the

South Vietnamese regime gave rise to a flourishing commercial sector, chiefly based on import businesses. Although President Diem had made some efforts to encourage the growth of an indigenous Vietnamese bourgeoisie in the South, this commerce was still largely dominated by Chinese, the more so since Thieu abandoned Diem's discriminatory measures against them. But this period also saw the growth of a large Vietnamese middle class of people employed in the administration and various professions. By 1974 27 per cent of the work-force were employed in commerce, administration and services and 52 per cent of GDP came from this area. Altogether, 45 per cent of employed people worked outside agriculture in 1974 (including 15 per cent in the armed forces), but industry (including mining, construction, transport and public utilities) employed only 3 per cent (Le Khoa *et al.*, 1979, p. 110).

Urbanization was also the direct result of the enormous destruction wrought in the countryside by war. This was especially true of the coastal cities of Trung Bo where the hinterland was badly ravaged by American firepower. Cities like Da Nang, for example, grew from 50,000 before the war to over 500,000 by 1974 and other coastal cities experienced comparable rates of growth (Thrift & Forbes, 1986, p. 124). The result was that by 1975 around 35 per cent of the South Vietnamese population lived in urban areas (compared with only 11 per cent in the North). But the extraordinary rapidity of the urbanization process in South Vietnam meant that these cities suffered to an even greater extent than usual from the problems characterizing cities in underdeveloped capitalist countries all over the world. The South Vietnamese cities had expanded without adequate housing, water and sewage facilities or electric power and could not supply sufficient employment opportunities for the vast numbers of people pushed and pulled into them from the rural areas. Estimates of unemployment rates in Saigon towards the end of the war ranged from 20 per cent (the official figure) to nearly half. Large numbers of people had earned a living dependent upon continued high levels of American expenditure—sectors servicing US troop requirements, for example, ranged from major industries like the French-owned breweries and tobacco companies to prostitutes and drug pushers. When US troops were withdrawn and US aid levels began to wind down after 1972, the economy was plunged into a severe recession and unemployment rose. Demobilization of the Thieu regime's huge army at the end of the war added to the problems of finding productive employment for those dislocated by the war.

The Communists clearly hoped to alleviate this problem through voluntary movement by urban slum dwellers either back to their villages of origin or to the New Economic Zones which they were establishing in highland regions and in areas which had fallen out of use through war-time destruction. But the number of urban dwellers who were prepared to emigrate to the countryside proved much smaller than the government had estimated. By 1979 about three-quarters of a million had left permanently—only half the target number. Many who did leave the cities after the war returned again when they found the hardships of a pioneering lifestyle difficult to cope with. This was particularly true of former officials of the Thieu regime who had been pressured to take up farming, but who were often long-time urban residents with no previous experience of manual labour, let alone farming skills.

The peculiar nature of the urbanization process in South Vietnam created another set of social problems, which would absorb much of the limited resources of the state budget in the years after the war. This was the large number of people who required rehabilitation before they could re-enter the labour force. The regime's own estimates were that the South Vietnamese cities contained some 100,000 drug addicts, 500,000 prostitutes, 400,000 war invalids and about a million orphans. Five or six per cent of the population was thought to have venereal diseases. Orphanages and rehabilitation centres were established in 1975, but these were on too limited a scale to be able to deal with the problems quickly and outwardly the cities changed very little over the next few years. Nevertheless, the efforts made to deal with prostitution and drug addiction were imaginative and made good use of the few resources available.

The southern half of the country, then, was characterized by the development of bloated cities in which the opportunities for productive employment were limited and in which the problems of post-war adjustment would be very great. On the other side of the coin, rapid urbanization created rural labour shortages that encouraged mechanization of farming and, after the land reform, this also helped to create a large class of middle and rich peasants who benefited from the growing commercialization of agriculture and rising productivity. Although a renewed stratification had begun to take effect in the countryside after the land reforms, particularly through the accumulation of commerical capital (based on importing of aid-subsidized goods) and the concentration of ownership of machinery in the hands of a few wealthier peasants (Ngo Vinh Long, 1984), this had not undermined the effects of an overall rise in prosperity between 1970 and 1974. After that year, the recession induced by the US retreat was felt in the rural areas too and, when aid was cut off completely in 1975, dislocation of the rural economy was severe.

The historical development of the northern social structure was very different. To begin with, the distribution of landholdings had never been as unequal in the northern deltas as it was in the Nam Bo area. When it came to implementing land reform, the picture was therefore rather more confused, especially as the Viet Minh included many landlords in its broad united front against the French. In the 1940s the only targets of the land reform program were foreign land owners and those who collaborated with the colonial regime. But this did not involve distribution of very large tracts of land and could not satisfy poor peasant demands. The second, more systematic, wave of land reforms came in the 1950s, beginning in the liberated areas in 1953 and, by the time the campaign (and its rectification) was terminated in 1956, 810,000 hectares had been appropriated and distributed.

Ater the land reform, agricultural output increased rapidly in North Vietnam. But in the context of the overcrowded conditions of the northern deltas, the longer-term prospects for family farming presented a number of problems. Unlike the Mekong delta, where annual flooding renews the fertility of the soil, the dyke system of North Vietnam holds back the floodwaters and necessitates the addition of fertilizers by farmers. Substantial increases in land productivity would require capital investments in chemical fertilizers (or livestock to produce organic material), yet, even after the reform, farm sizes in the North were typically too small to produce the required surpluses. Such capital investments, moreover, were a necessity if North Vietnamese agriculture was to move away from the precarious balance whereby bad seasons could easily lead to widespread starvation. The aim of collectivization, which was introduced in 1959, was to give all farmers, both rich and poor, the chance to benefit from capital accumulation in agriculture and to prevent the possibility of peasants losing their land through the bankruptcies which would be the inevitable result of allowing private accumulation and a free market. Party leaders were afraid that a renewed development of capitalism in agriculture would undo the gains made by the poor peasantry during the land reform.

Collectivization can be considered as having been completed by 1968 when over 90 per cent of North Vietnamese peasants belonged to the higher-level cooperatives in which all land and means of production were collectively owned and remuneration was awarded in principle according to labour contributed. By this time North Vietnamese industry had also either been nationalized or collectivized and the social classes of the old regime had ceased to exist.[3] This does not, of course, imply that social inequality had ceased to exist, only that the material conditions for class formation on the basis of ownership and control over the means of production by one group in society to the exclusion of others had been eliminated.

The collectives also fulfilled a number of other important functions in

Vietnamese society. On the one hand, by enabling the consolidation of plots of land and re-organization of the labour force, they were able, by 1965, to achieve substantial gains in land and labour productivity—although it is doubtful whether per capita consumption rose by very much on account of the growth in population. The most important achievement of the cooperatives in the economic sphere was the construction of irrigation works by labour intensive methods so that the number of crops grown each year could be raised. In the social sphere the cooperatives also provided important benefits to many peasants, particularly women and the poor. Women benefited from the achievement of equal rights to income from the land, from the provision of child care, health care and education facilities, which both improved their welfare and status and relieved much of their workload, and from gaining equal rights to participate in village politics for the first time through the abolition of the male registration system. Cooperatives gave women economic and political independence and for this reason they were among the strongest supporters of the cooperativization movement. The establishment of schools, child care centres and clinics by the cooperatives also gave the vast majority of peasants access to education and basic health care which they had never had before. The collectivization movement saw major advances in public health and prevention of hitherto endemic diseases in the rural areas (McMichael, 1976). These factors, which were beneficial to peasants across the board, were important in helping to heal the rifts in village communities that had developed as a result of the land reform.

Changes in the economic structure of the DRV also brought about big changes in the occupational make-up of the population. At the time of independence, Vietnam had been a country in which the overwhelming majority were engaged in peasant agriculture. The industrial working class numbered no more than a few thousand and the indigenous bourgeoisie and petty bourgeoisie were tiny.[4] By 1975, however, the occupational structure of the DRV had been transformed. The northern industrial work-force (including mining) had grown to 11 per cent of the total labour force with a further 10 per cent in the construction and transport and communications sectors. Within industry there had been a dramatic shift away from artisan production to modern factory production.[5] There was also, by 1975, a sizeable work-force in commerce, services and administrative occupations— amounting to about 14 per cent of the total. The agricultural work-force had been reduced to 65 per cent (Vickerman, 1985, p. 230).

The revolution in Vietnam brought about big changes for women. Whereas in traditional Vietnamese society women enjoyed more economic and social independence than their counterparts in China, the various

attempts to Sinicize Vietnamese culture had left strong residues of Confucianism, particularly among the upper classes. A new family law introduced
by the Communists in 1960 abolished the practice of concubinage and gave
women equal rights within the family and the right to choose their own
husband. Earlier decrees had given them equal economic and political rights.
The Vietnam Women's Union, aside from its role of mobilizing women to
support the national liberation struggle, organized a campaign to promote
the 'New Culture Family', in which men and women would share in
household decision making and take equal responsibility for domestic labour.
A major objective of the policy was to break down the resistance of husbands
to women's participation in civil society, outside the home. In the context of
the national liberation struggle, this was an important requirement since,
with large numbers of men away at the war, women had to take on more and
more of the jobs traditionally done by men. During the war, women played a
major role in the militia, in operating and managing cooperatives and
factories, and in carrying out repair work on the Ho Chi Minh Trail.
Legislation was also passed to ensure that where women were the majority of
the work-force they must be represented at top management level.

The Trung Bo region needs to be mentioned separately in a historical
account of changes in the social structure because it combines elements
characteristic of both the Nam Bo and Bac Bo areas. The central region was
perhaps the least developed during the colonial period: it did not have the
mining exports and textile industry of Bac Bo and it did not have the
commercial development or export rice and rubber on a large scale as did
Nam Bo, although there was some exploitation of forestry products in the
central highlands. Having been governed officially as a Protectorate, the
central region retained many of the institutional forms of traditional
Vietnamese society, including widespread communal ownership of land.
Moreover, the small coastal plains, which contained most of the population
of the region, were very densely crowded; parcellization of landholdings was
intense and, as in Bac Bo, the inequality of land ownership was not as great as
further south. Two-thirds of the Trung Bo 'landlords' derived their main
source of income from their own farming activities, rather than from rent.

After 1954, northern Trung Bo underwent the same social transformation
as the Bac Bo region, but the provinces south of the 17th parallel changed in a
somewhat different way. During the anti-American war, the coastal plains of
southern Trung Bo were considered to be some of the strongholds of the
revolution. In order to maximize support there, the Party carried out its
united front policy by limiting expropriations of land to that owned by
foreigners and collaborators. 'Patriotic' landlords were subject to rent

reductions, but not expropriation and, in the areas under NLF control, they often sided with the Front. Commercialization of agriculture during the two decades after 1954 was not so great in Trung Bo as in Nam Bo, chiefly because of the much greater poverty of the region and the fact that strong support for the revolution provoked the greater use of American firepower to obliterate villages and defoliate crops. The exodus of people into the towns was highest in this region. Moreover, Thieu's Land-to-the-Tiller program, which in Nam Bo functioned largely to give *de jure* recognition to reforms already carried out by the NLF, was rather ineffective in Trung Bo. The large amount of communal land still in existence made its permanent alienation as private property a highly contentious issue and, given the lack of real political control in the villages by the Thieu regime, no action could be taken. Even where land could be distributed, the amount available for expropriation was small compared to Nam Bo where large holdings had been more common, so the reform made little real difference to the general situation of undersized plots and left the majority of peasants still poor.

Apart from a far greater level of urbanization, then, the social structure of southern Trung Bo had undergone a less radical transformation by 1975 than either North Vietnam or the Nam Bo region. After 1975 the conditions prevailing there—widespread poverty and lack of commercialized family farming, high incidence of communal land ownership and lesser degree of inequality than elsewhere, large tracts of wasteland often with unexploded ordnance to be cleared before it could become viable—were to make the achievement of collectivization of agriculture much easier than in Nam Bo, and the mistakes of the earlier Bac Bo land reform would appear to have been avoided.[6]

Social Change Since 1975

In the immediate aftermath of the 1975 victory, the regime followed the pattern established in the North after 1954 of allowing a period of economic recovery before beginning the process of creating socialist institutions throughout society. In the newly conquered areas of the South, only those enterprises owned by the former regime and open collaborators were nationalized, though in late 1975, following a campaign against compradors, a decree was also issued forbidding several American banks to resume business (this came, in any case, after US imposition in May 1975 of a total trade and financial embargo). By the middle of 1976, however, definite moves were underway to integrate the South into the socialist socio-economic system of the North. The historical development of the South was viewed officially in very negative terms in 1976:

the exploiting classes remain; the poisons of the enslaving culture and the social evils caused by U.S. neo-colonialism as well as the influence of bourgeois ideology in society remain potent; the reactionaries are still operating against the revolution; the negative aspects of capitalism and the spontaneous character of small-scale production are still to be overcome. [VCP, 1977, p. 42]

Social transformation was thus viewed very much in terms of a continuation of the struggle against US influence and the remnants of the old regime and there was litte analysis of the enormous structural changes which South Vietnamese society had undergone since the 1950s. In 1975 Truong Chinh declared that the differences between North and South were 'conditional and temporary' while the similarities were 'basic and decisive', though in April 1976, the Party theoretical journal did acknowledge that capitalism had 'struck relatively deep roots in the towns and cities' (but not in the rural areas, note) (cited in Porter, 1976b, p. 211). The early stages of the move towards socialism therefore tended to follow the pattern of the North. The main measures were the creation of joint state–private enterprises in modern industry, collectivization of agriculture and handicraft industries and the attempt to bring domestic circulation of goods under state control through the creation of a state trading network and administrative pricing system.

In Trung Bo these measures were rather successful. Collectivization of agriculture proceeded rather rapidly and, by the end of 1979, was substantially completed with 83 per cent of peasant households collectivized, chiefly in full cooperatives (*hop tac xa*). At the same time, output recovered and grew rapidly. In the Mekong delta, on the other hand, the collectivization campaign was an acknowledged failure. By mid-1980 only 50 per cent of peasants belonged, mostly to the lower level production collectives (*tap doan san xuat*), and only 36 per cent of the land had been incorporated. The reasons are not too difficult to see, given the great differences between the two regions in the past development of their social structures. The majority of peasants in Trung Bo accepted collectivization because it provided positive benefits in shared use of scarce means of production and draft animals, in collective labour to reconstruct damaged irrigation systems and reclaim the large tracts of land laid waste by the war, and it resolved the problem of how best to distribute communal lands and uncultivated lands without excessive parcellization. In other words, it succeeded because the great majority of Trung Bo peasants were either poor or very poor after the war. Large numbers of Mekong delta peasants, on the other hand, stood to gain little from collectivization—they owned their own means of production and had enough land; the low official purchase price of rice meant lower incomes than they could obtain on the free market and this was exacerbated by the fact that shortages of industrial inputs forced prices up causing much of the state supply to leak to the free market. To make ends meet in this situation, peasants had to devote much more attention to private plots than to collective fields, so output and state procurement were correspondingly low. Many collectives broke up after only one or two seasons. The government responded in 1978 by clamping down on the ethnic Chinese businesses that dominated private commerce in the rural areas but, while this succeeded in stabilizing the economic situation for a few months, it created severe political instability in the South and led to the sudden upsurge in the exodus of 'Boat People',[7] while ultimately failing to remove the real cause of the problem, which was that the economic system the government was trying to implement was not in the interests of the majority of the Mekong delta peasants. The free market merely went underground.

Since the introduction of economic reforms in 1979, the social structure in the whole country has become more fluid. On the one hand, there has been a resurgence of small-scale private enterprise and, on the other hand, there has been a slow, but steadier growth of collectivization in southern agriculture. In all parts of the country the household economy has come to the fore as a means of using individual incentives to stimulate the production and circulation of goods. In agriculture this has been combined with a system of contracting in the collectives, which allows peasants to keep for their own use anything they produce above the contracted amount. Price adjustments and the application of some unorthodox management techniques in the South[8] have also enabled the state to gain more control over the supply of staple food products and provided more positive incentives for peasants to join the collective system. It is difficult to judge the true effect of this because figures on the degree of collectivization contain an admitted margin of artificiality due to the poor operation of some collectives. Officially, collectivization of the Nam Bo region was completed at the end of 1985 with 90 per cent of peasant households joining production collectives. However, these are not full cooperatives—income is still awarded according to labour *and* means of production contributed (see Chapter 9)—and many of them are still not functioning properly. But the move towards collectivization in Nam Bo in the 1980s has not been accompanied by declining rates of government procurement and falling output levels as it was in the late 1970s. In his speech to the Sixth Party Congress in December 1986, the outgoing Party Secretary Truong Chinh, announced that the Party would set no more target dates for socialist transformation, but would proceed as economic conditions allowed (Duiker, 1987, p. 179).

Since the economic reforms, small-scale private enterprise has also been encouraged in industry and in areas of agriculture not considered suitable for collectivization under present circumstances. The latter includes production of most industrial crops, although in the past specialized cooperatives and state farms growing these have also been established in the New Economic Zones. But in the areas I visited in 1985, for example, collectivization of sugar and coconut farms in Ben Tre province was not being attempted and private enterprise was actively encouraged to open up *tram* oil production in the Plain of Reeds in Long An. These are family-based activities, not employing wage labour, but in industry private enterprises are allowed to employ ten or fifteen workers and there were in 1987 reportedly 3,000 such enterprises employing 25,000 workers in Ho Chi Minh City alone (*Far Eastern Economic Review*, 23 July 1987). Private enterprises in areas not approved by the government can, however, be subjected to heavy taxation even leading to bankruptcy, as happened with Ho Chi Minh City's restaurant industry in 1983, and the regime remains worried by a tendency for such enterprises to be concentrated in petty commerce, where returns are quicker, than in production itself.

The result of the reform policies is that in Vietnam today, there is a great mixture of social institutions and structures. There is no longer any large-scale private ownership of means of production in either the North or the South, in spite of continuing inequalities of wealth, especially in the South. State ownership exists alongside collective ownership, joint state–private ownership, small-scale private ownership, petty commodity production and trade (i.e., on an individual basis) and family farms. Wage labour in the state sector co-exists with wage labour in a small-scale private sector, where it may also be better paid, if individual reports can be generalized, although state employment remains attractive to many because of the greater security of employment and social benefits (annual leave, paid sick leave, maternity leave of six months, subsidized food prices). While the picture is less varied in the northern part of the country than in the South on account of the more firmly established socialist production relations, it is also changing. The new Party leadership is carrying out a determined attack on what it calls 'bureaucratism' and the 'administrative subsidy system' and on vested interests within the North Vietnamese bureaucracy, which have tended to obstruct changes. At the time of writing, then, it seems likely that the system of state and collective ownership that was established in the North in the 1960s may undergo substantial modification over the next decade.

Demographic Development

Population growth rate and variations in the density of population are two important determinants of growth and development. Rapid population growth has been a major concern of the socialist regime in Vietnam because it affects the size of the marketed agricultural surplus, which is a crucial factor determining the amount of domestic resources available for investment purposes and reduction of aid dependency. Increases in agricultural productivity that might have enhanced this surplus have in the past been largely absorbed by population growth. If per capita food output rises at a slower rate than population, living standards stagnate or decline and since 1975 Vietnam has been plagued by food shortages. The regime has therefore made strenuous efforts to reduce the rate of population growth. On top of this, high density of population, particularly in the key rice growing area of the Red River delta, combined with rather low densities in the more mountainous regions, has encouraged the government to try to relocate people and open up new areas for development. It is hoped that a reduction in the labour supply in these densely populated areas will encourage less underemployment, greater mechanization and higher productivity of labour in agriculture, thereby helping to raise the standard of living.

The effects of population growth and density are not the same, however, in all parts of the country. Whereas the society of the North Vietnamese deltas, for example, seems to have been caught in a 'low level equilibrium trap' as far as generating marketed agricultural surpluses goes, the relationship of population to productivity of agriculture in the Mekong River delta appears to be quite different. In the northern deltas, on the one hand, rapid population growth is discouraged not merely by government policy, but by economic considerations as the ability of the land to support more people at existing technological levels diminishes. In the Mekong delta, on the other hand, population density is not so high—even though rising fast in parts—and more extensive farming methods are still possible. The relatively high land to labour ratio in the Mekong delta has meant that population growth is encouraged and this is especially the case since the land reforms of the 1960s and 1970s have given the majority of peasants enough land to earn a living. Since withdrawal of the massive US aid subsidies of imported agricultural inputs, mechanization of southern agriculture has proceeded more slowly than before 1974 and, since the introduction of market-style incentives through the economic reforms of the early 1980s has encouraged output growth, the major response to the relative scarcity of labour has been to have more children. Population growth in the Mekong delta area has therefore tended to accelerate in the 1980s. Unlike the Red River and other northern deltas, however, this has not necessarily resulted in declining marketed surpluses. As an indication of the improved situation in the South since the introduction of the reforms, we can cite the official data on per capita output of paddy rice. This is only an indirect indicator, but we have no data available on the actual size of the marketed surpluses and we can assume that the higher per capita output above a minimum subsistence level, the more willing peasants will be to market a substantial portion of their crop. Table 5.1 illustrates the great differences between zones: the Mekong delta has achieved growth of per capita output in spite of its high population growth rate, while the Red River delta has barely sustained above subsistence output levels (officially put at 240 kg. of cereal per year).

Table 5.1 Population growth rates and per capita food output 1976–84

Regions†	Population growth 1976–84 %	Per capita food output*		
		1976 kg.	1984 kg.	Growth rate %
Red River delta	1.6	341	308	−1.3
Mekong River delta	3.1	457	511	1.4
Trung Bo	2.3	213	257	2.4
Total	2.6	241	296	2.6

* In paddy equivalent.

† See Table 5.2 for definition of regions.

Sources: Beresford, 1987, p. 266; General Statistical Office, 1980, p. 59; General Statistical Office, 1985, pp. 13–14, 90. Population figures have been revised to take account of data more recently released (see, for example, World Bank, 1986), but these are only available for the whole country.

In the short run, then, the problem may not be so much one of reducing population growth rates in the South, as one of redistributing the surpluses produced there to the rice deficient areas of the country. But the population density of the Mekong area is also increasing quite rapidly and, in the longer run, diminishing returns to increased labour inputs may lead to a similar situation to that prevailing in the North. Whether this happens will also depend very much on the rate of industrial growth and, correspondingly, the rate of mechanization and use of modern manufactured inputs in agriculture. In Part IV of this book it can be seen that for the time being, it is precisely the more rapid expansion in the availability of industrial inputs to agriculture which has enabled productivity in the Mekong delta to outstrip its high population growth rate (this has also been true of the southern Trung Bo provinces, particularly Quang Nam–Da Nang which accounts for much of the high per capita output growth of Trung Bo shown in Table 5.1), while more acute shortages of manufactured goods in the North have held this process back. Population cannot be looked at in isolation, then, but should be seen as one of a combination of factors influencing economic growth.

Table 5.2 shows some of the regional population densities and urbanization rates in Vietnam today. To some extent the densities shown in this table are misleading because a number of the provinces contain marked variations within them. The northern midland provinces, for example, have both densely populated deltaic plains and more sparsely populated upland regions. The same is true of all the Trung Bo provinces and, as well, some of these contain substantial cities (such as Da Nang, Hue, Nha Trang, etc.). The coastal plains of Trung Bo, which are the region's main rice growing areas, are in fact

Table 5.2 Population density and urbanization in Vietnam, by region, 1984

	Population density (persons per sq. km.)	Urbanization rates* (%)
Whole country	181	19.1
Municipalities		
Hanoi	1,346	34.9
Haiphong	930	30.2
Ho Chi Minh City	1,756	70.2
Vung Tau–Con Dao Special Zone	379	96.8
Red River delta		
Hai Hung	938	7.8
Thai Binh	1,106	6.2
Ha Nam Ninh	813	9.9
Northern Midlands		
Bac Thai	140	19.7
Vinh Phu	358	8.0
Ha Bac	410	6.8
Quang Ninh	137	41.3
Ha Son Binh	285	8.0

	Population density (persons per sq. km.)	Urbanization rates* (%)
Northern Highlands		
Ha Tuyen	65	7.3
Cao Bang	64	12.4
Lang Son	65	17.8
Lai Chau	22	15.9
Hoang Lien Son	58	12.8
Son La	39	15.8
Trung Bo		
Thanh Hoa	250	8.8
Nghe Tinh	151	6.5
Binh Tri Thien	110	24.7
Quang Nam–Da Nang	140	26.0
Nghia Binh	198	13.3
Phu Khanh	136	28.4
Thuan Hai	95	22.9
Southern Highlands		
Gia Lai–Kon Tum	27	19.5
Dac Lac	31	15.5
Lam Dong	49	30.6
Eastern Nam Bo		
Song Be	74	21.7
Tay Ninh	188	14.2
Dong Nai	198	25.6
Mekong River Delta		
Long An	248	9.9
Dong Thap	388	7.1
An Giang	505	15.7
Tien Giang	584	20.7
Ben Tre	523	7.6
Cuu Long	437	9.5
Hau Giang	407	17.4
Kien Giang	177	11.8
Minh Hai	201	17.9

* Percentage of the population living in urban centres. Municipal administrative divisions also include substantial rural areas.

Source: General Statistical Office, 1985, pp. 7–8, 18–19.

as densely populated as that of the Red River delta. However, the table does show quite clearly the contrasts between the very high densities of the main river deltas, on the one hand, and the highland regions, on the other. In recent years the government has made it a major policy priority to move people to the highlands, mainly by establishing New Economic Zones for growing industrial crops like rubber, coffee, tea and forestry products, as well as some livestock farms. Since 1975 about 2 million people have moved, either from overcrowded deltas of northern Vietnam, or from the cities where employment opportunities are scarcer, to the highland and foothill regions of both North and South.

The question of shifting large populations into these sparsely settled zones is, however, a sensitive one as it involves the majority ethnic group, the plains Vietnamese (Kinh), moving into areas often previously inhabited, or at least owned, by the country's minority tribal groups. The problems arise largely because, although the area is indeed sparsely populated, the indigenous people practise shifting cultivation which requires occupation of a very large area in order to avoid putting too much pressure on the fertility of the soil. The settlement of plains people inevitably encroaches upon the lands previously used by tribal groups and can create political tension. This was precisely the problem that the Thieu regime encountered when it tried to increase its political control over the southern highlands by allowing lowlanders to settle on traditional tribal lands. In fact the effect was the opposite of the one desired and many of the ethnic minority peoples were driven into the arms of the NLF. The socialist regime, on the other hand, recognizes that the success of its effort to develop the highland regions and to redistribute population depends very much upon its success in persuading the hill tribes to settle down and engage in more productive forms of cultivation and livestock management than they have practised up to now. This project in turn depends upon the ability of newly settled farmers to obtain improved inputs and modern techniques to maintain the soil fertility in a given area. Otherwise, there is a positive incentive for the ethnic minority groups to resume their pattern of shifting cultivation and clashes with the new settlers from the plains become likely. Given the acute shortages of modern farm inputs in the Vietnamese economy and repeated references by leaders to the need to persuade the hill people to settle down, it would seem that the program has not so far met with a great deal of success. The issue has acquired even greater sensitivity in recent years because of the conflict with China. Many of the ethnic groups inhabiting the northern border area are closely related to people living on the other side and this has led to fears, on the part of the regime in Hanoi, of a possible fifth column or of Chinese infiltration of Vietnam by using minority people from its own side of the border. There has therefore been a need in Hanoi to tread with even greater care where the ethnic minorities are concerned, so as not to antagonize them and break the bonds of support for the regime which were forged by the Viet Minh in the early 1940s at the beginning of its struggle with the French.

Large-scale population movements are less problematical where newly settled areas had been previously uninhabited or had already been developed for commercial use before the war. This has been true for many of the New Economic Zones established in South Vietnam. The latter have opened up new areas for cultivation in the Mekong delta and have begun the process of rehabilitating tracts of land that were heavily affected by war damage (as, for example, the former 'Free Fire Zone' around Ho Chi Minh City) or had fallen into disuse (like many of the rubber, coffee and tea plantations of the highlands). But in these areas the often primitive conditions of living in the first few years have created difficulties for sustaining the new populations. A major role of the armed forces and of special youth brigades has been to open up these areas and build the initial infrastructure to make them more habitable for the civilian settlers who follow. Since this policy was adopted in the late 1970s, the numbers of people preferring a return to urban slum life to the hardships of the NEZ has fallen dramatically.

A further problem for the policy of redistributing population arises, however, in trying to encourage people to leave the crowded deltas at the government's desired rate. The tradition of ancestor worship in Vietnamese culture means that most people are naturally reluctant to leave the village of their patrimony. Villages have also been bound together by the system of 'insiders' and 'outsiders' which made it difficult for individuals to acquire land or exercise political rights in villages not their own. The only emigration system that made sense, both to the *ancien régime* and to the Marxist regime, in opening up new lands for settlement, was to move people in groups from the same original village. Such a system would work quite well provided there was a surplus labour force in the villages of origin. But in many North Vietnamese villages, although the land farmed by each family was often insufficient to provide a living for all its members, the demand for labour at certain times of the year was sufficient to absorb the available supply. During periods of high labour demand there was in fact a shortage in many parts of the Red River delta and farmers could often supplement the meagre income from their own plots by taking casual work in other villages where the seasonal labour demand was slightly different. Extra income could also be earned by handicraft labour in the off-season: in fact, under the socialist regime the development of small-scale artisan industries has become a major means of absorbing extra labour in the cooperatives. Thus, while the overcrowding and low land per capita would appear to suggest a surplus of labour in the Red River delta, the actual situation is quite different. Given the prevalence of labour-intensive farming methods, the existence of labour shortages in the peak season and the ability to supplement income by seasonal migration patterns or handicrafts, there is a reluctance on the part of villagers to move away permanently. This economic motivation to stay put is reinforced by cultural attachment to place of origin. However, it has also meant that the full potential of the existing labour force is underutilized and that large numbers of North Vietnamese peasants can still only find seasonal employment.

Characteristics of the Labour Force

In 1984 the total social labour force of Vietnam consisted, according to the official statistics, of 23.1 million people, a rise of 5 million people over 1976. Agriculture continued to be the main source of employment, accounting for 71 per cent of the work-force (16.5 million people) in 1984. Manufacturing industry employed 11 per cent and the so-called 'unproductive' sectors, like health, education and administration, accounted for another 6.8 per cent. The armed forces should be included in this last category, but no separate figures for them are published. Most Western commentators, however, estimate the size of the armed forces at about 1 million which would make them over 4 per cent of the work-force and so it would seem that either the estimates are too high or they are excluded from official figures (cf. Table 5.3). No comprehensive data are published either on the amount of unemployment, although this has been the subject of frequent comment and policy measures designed to overcome it in recent years. One recent estimate of urban unemployment put it at about 1 million.[9] The same source went on to suggest rural underemployment involving much larger numbers of people.

According to the official data, the main structural changes in the pattern of employment since 1975 have been a rise in the share of agriculture and a decline in the share of unproductive sectors. The decline in the share of unproductive employment has been continuous since 1975, but the rise in the share of agriculture has occurred primarily after the introduction of economic reforms in 1979 and this period has also seen a marked fall in the share of the construction industry. These changes reflect the changed economic priorities of the government, in response to an economic crisis

Table 5.3 The structure of employment, 1975–84*

	1975	1980	1984
Productive sectors			
Industry	10.2	11.2	11.0
Construction	5.3	5.0	3.3
Agriculture	67.0	67.9	71.3
Forestry	0.5	0.5	0.5
Transport	2.1	1.9	1.7
Communications	0.3	0.2	0.2
Trade	5.6	5.2	5.0
Other	0.7	0.5	0.2
Unproductive sectors			
Education	3.1	3.3	2.6
Health	1.0	1.1	1.2
Administration	1.2	1.3	1.0
Other	3.0	1.9	2.0

* Persons of working age, between 15 and 65.
Source: General Statistical Office, 1985, p. 22.

during 1978–80, which have involved strenuous efforts to increase food production, raise the productivity of labour, shift the structure of investment away from new, large projects towards small projects generating quick returns and completion of existing projects.[10]

In 1984, 16 per cent of the total labour force worked in the state sector (the proportion rises to 30 per cent in industry). The rather low overall share of state employment is accounted for by the predominance of agricultural employment which is either collective (over two-thirds in 1983) or family-based. Within the state sector 45.8 per cent of the work-force were women. Women were most concentrated in foresty, trade, education, health, services and tourism, finance and banking, where they constituted over half of the work-force. They were under-represented in construction, transport, science, cultural occupations and administration. Women were nearly 70 per cent of health workers, but only 24 per cent in transport[11] and 27 per cent in science and administration. However, the trend since 1976 has been to even up the representation of women in virtually all branches of the state sector. It is not possible, on the basis of the available data to say with very much precision how much segmentation on the basis of gender exists within these branches, though the existing evidence suggests that it remains fairly extensive. Women made up 65 per cent of the total work-force in the light industry (predominantly consumer goods) sector in 1979 (Vietnam Women's Union, 1981, p. 18), for example, as against 44 per cent in industry as a whole. But the existence of women in the more skilled occupations and in heavy industry is greater than for most developing countries in the region. According to data published by the Vietnam Women's Union (1981, p. 22) women were 35 per cent of skilled workers, 42 per cent of technicians and 26 per cent of graduate cadres in the state sector in 1979. In recent years the Women's Union has organized campaigns to achieve better opportunities for women to receive on the job training and technical education to improve their skill levels, and they have also fought to have women's work re-evaluated so that pay scales take proper account of commensurate levels of skill or heaviness of labour compared to jobs predominantly done by men.

Outside the state sector, women form the highest proportion of the work-force in agriculture—over 60 per cent—and in the small industry and handicrafts sector where they are 65 per cent (Vietnam Women's Union, 1982, p. 22). The predominance of women in agriculture was a historical development partly caused by the exodus of men to the army during the war,[12] but Vietnamese women have also traditionally done heavy labour in the fields. During the war women rose to senior management positions in many of the cooperatives and undertook jobs traditionally done by men. But the necessity to demobilize large numbers of troops after the war and the policy of providing them with jobs commensurate with their rank in the army, meant that there was a return to a more traditional division of labour. The division of labour in farming is thus still very much carried out along gender lines with women predominating in those areas which have been least mechanized, e.g., transplanting (White, 1982b; White, n.d.) Moreover, Houtart and Lemercinier have shown in their detailed study of a cooperative in the Red River delta, that the women there still did most of the housework and took prime responsibility for cultivation of the family land (the 5 per cent of cooperative land that is set aside for the personal use of individual households). Their average working day is considerably longer than that of the men who thereby have more time available to become involved in political activities and in the management committees (Houtart & Lemercinier, 1981). The effect of the economic reforms has been to increase the amount of predominantly female employment in petty commodity production and trade and even those women with factory jobs have had to take on such work in order to overcome the erosion of their state salaries by inflation. The reforms have thus tended to increase the workload of women and increase their segmentation into the less technologically advanced areas of the economy.[13]

The Vietnamese work-force is an educated and skilled one as the regime has always placed emphasis on achieving a high degree of literacy and technical skill. Indications of the educational level and its historical development are given in Table 5.4. Virtually all Vietnamese receive some primary level education and, according to the World Bank, 48 per cent of children of secondary school age in Vietnam are enrolled in schools, as against an average for low income countries of 31 per cent (World Bank, 1986). Official Vietnamese statistics suggest that 3 per cent of the work-force have also received some form of post-secondary education, either in vocational schools or in colleges and universities (General Statistical Office, 1985, p. 30). Nearly half of these, however, work in the education sector itself where they form over half the work-force and in industry the ratio is only 3 per cent. Women are fairly equally represented in the general education system and, as can be seen from Table 5.4, have made great progress to date in gaining technical education, but increased workloads as a result of economic reforms may be eroding this to some extent and account for the Women's Union's anxiety to promote on the job training and vocational education for women. Women still apparently experience difficulty in getting a university education, and this may be partly due to the fact that it is seen as an avenue of entry into the bureaucracy, which, so far, has been a more exclusively male area of employment.

Table 5.4 Education in Vietnam 1955–80

	1955*		1980	
	No. enrolled	% female	No. enrolled	% female
General education:				
Grades 1–5	654,722	24	7,890,000	52
Grades 6–9	55,608	25	3,159,000	47
Grades 10–12	5,755	—	688,000	48
Teacher-training colleges	1,808	—	91,866	n.a.
Universities and colleges†	1,191	10	158,800	25
Vocational schools†	2,752	10	169,500	41

* North Vietnam only   † Data are for 1955 and 1979.
Source: *Education in Vietnam*, 1982.

The health of the work-force has been a cause of concern in recent years. Compared with the situation prevailing in the 1950s, considerable advances in public health had been made by 1975, particularly in the DRV, which had a strong emphasis on prophylactic medicine. Vietnam also has more doctors per head than other countries of comparable income levels (World Bank, 1986) and an impressive array of paramedical facilities that enable the delivery of elementary health care to all. The Vietnamese system of treating drug addiction, which was a major problem in the South during the war, by combining acupuncture, physical exercise and meditation with job retraining has been widely praised. The special centres set up to deal with rehabilitation of an estimated 100,000 drug addicts and 500,000 prostitutes, many of whom also had to be cured of venereal diseases, were a major and rather successful feature of the regime's efforts to deal with the enormous social problems created by the war in the southern cities. Other side-effects of the war have been more intractable: mosquitoes breeding in bomb craters, for example, have caused the spread of malaria which the DRV had earlier made progress towards its complete eradication. Malnutrition has also been a source of declining health in the population, especially among urban dwellers in recent years. It has been suggested, though I have not found any quantitative evidence on this, that food shortages have reduced the level of resistance to diseases and contributed to falling labour productivity and shorter life expectancy. Vietnam's hospitals continue to suffer from acute shortages of modern medicines and the system as a whole has been forced to rely heavily on traditional remedies, even where these may not be the most efficacious.

Conclusion

The social structure of Vietnam has undergone dramatic changes in the three decades since the establishment of the DRV, most notably in the elimination of class based inequalities, improvements in the educational and skill levels of the work-force, establishment of a basic health infrastructure and creation of a much more diversified occupational structure. But a number of intractable problems remain. Efforts to achieve economic development are retarded by extremely high population densities in some of the prime agricultural areas and the effects of food shortages may already be discerned in re-emergence of basic health problems. Efforts to redistribute population and to achieve a lower growth rate have met with limited success. Moreover, the effect of economic reforms designed to increase farm output would appear to have stimulated population growth in the Mekong delta and this may eventually threaten the economic growth process as a whole.

Part III
The Political System

The political system of the SRV is dominated by the Communist Party. Not only is it the sole political party with the capacity to form a government, but its influence is felt directly and indirectly at every level of political life. In this part of the book we will begin by looking at the political system with the Party, before going on to study the constitution and formal government structure. In the last chapter of this Part we will look at the possibilities for participation in the political process by individuals and other social organizations. It should be borne in mind, however, that it is difficult to maintain a clear separation in practice between these three spheres of activity because of the pervasive influence of the Party and the deliberate blurring in socialist countries of the distinction between state and civil society.

The Vietnamese have evolved a distinctive set of political institutions which, while in some respects borrowed from foreign 'models', have been essentially designed to meet specifically Vietnamese conditions and have served successfully to sustain the legitimacy of Party rule over four decades since the establishment of the DRV in 1945.

These institutions have undergone numerous changes as the Vietnamese have sought to adapt to new circumstances, often brought on by forces beyond their control. The most recent such change has been the re-unification of the country in the 1970s and, while this initially brought few alterations to the way the Communist Party leaders viewed the long-term development of the political system, the debates which opened up, over economic policy in particular, towards the end of the 1970s have produced a number of new developments which may affect the shape of the political system in the future. Notable among these are the attempts to get a clearer distinction between Party and bureaucratic functions, to break the grip of the bureaucratic administrative system and encourage local initiative.

While it is widely acknowledged that the Vietnamese leadership does respond to pressure from below in formulating these changes, little is known about the actual relations between state and population or the mechanisms by which political interests can be expressed and translated into policy outcomes. Much more research into this area is required, but some tentative conclusions are drawn here.

The Party Structure

The structure of the Vietnamese Party has remained basically the same since its inception. Local party cells (*chi bo*) usually contain from three up to ten members. If there are more than ten Party members at a particular location they are divided up into fractions of not more than five, but these fractions are still administered by the executive committee of the *chi bo*. The next level is the district committee (or ward in urban areas) and above these are the provincial and municipal organizations. In the Indochinese Communist Party there were, in addition, three regional committees for the northern, central and southern regions and two special bureaux for Vietnamese residents in Laos and Siam.[1] At the top of the structure is the Central Committee (Trung Uong Dang Bo) consisting, in 1987, of 124 members and forty-nine alternate members.[2] At each level, the Party committees, including the Central Committee, are elected by Party Congresses comprising delegates elected by the level below (Figure 6.1). Day to day functions are carried out by administrative committees elected by the Party committees or *chi bo* at each level.

Party membership expanded very rapidly between 1945 and 1951 under the united front policy of the Viet Minh (Table 6.1), but was reduced again over the next decade as the political criteria for membership were tightened up and a drive to bring more people of poor peasant and worker origins and reduce the weight of intellectuals and even landlords was launched by the Second Congress in 1951. From 1960 to 1976 the Party grew at a slower pace, roughly in line with the rate of population growth, with emphasis on recruiting younger members and women. But growth has slowed to less than 2 per cent per annum since 1976 as the economic crises of the 1980s have led to a renewed drive to eliminate bureaucratism, arrogance and corruption in an attempt to revitalize public confidence in the Party's leadership. Thousands of Party members have been expelled in the 1980s and renewed calls have been made to expand the working class and youthful component. There are no reliable estimates of the social composition of the Vietnamese Communist Party at present. However, women do seem to have a rather low rate of participation. A recruitment drive launched in 1967 attempted to increase female membership from the very low 5.4 per cent in 1965 and by

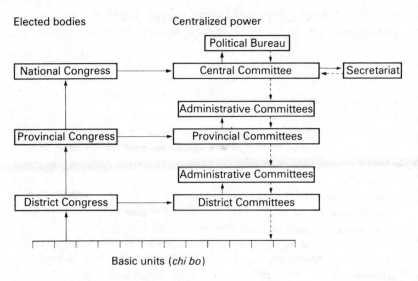

Figure 6.1 Organization of the Vietnamese Communist Party

Note: Solid lines indicate election: broken lines indicate control

Table 6.1 Party membership, 1930–86

1930 February	211
1945 August	5,000
1946 end year	20,000
1947 end year	50,000
1948 end year*	180,000
1949 end year	700,000
1951 February	760,000
1960	500,000
1968	800,000
1970	1,100,000
1976 December	1,500,000
1982 March	1,727,784
1986 December	1,800,000

* Including 66,000 in the south.

Sources: Kolko, 1986, p. 46; VCP, 1980, pp. 30, 148, 260; Elliott, 1975, p. 46; *Yearbook on International Communist Affairs*, 1984; Truong Chinh, 1986.

1973 the number had reportedly risen to 25 per cent. But at the 1976 Party Congress, women were only 14 per cent of delegates (Eisen, 1984, p. 252).

Between 1941 and 1945 and again during the Resistance War against the French, the Central Committee was often not able to meet, despite its small size, and Party affairs were run by a Standing Committee of the Central Committee based in the Bac Bo region. However, the difficulties of communication during this period of clandestine activity and guerrilla warfare meant that the regional Party Committees also had a great deal of autonomy. The Nam Bo Committee, in particular, showed a tendency to act on its own: in 1940 it organized an uprising which the Central Standing Committee regarded as premature. The Central Standing Committee sent senior cadres to the south in an attempt to head it off, without success—an event which had serious consequences for the Party's ability to organize in the South during the August Revolution and its aftermath (see Chapter 3). There is also evidence that the Nghe-Tinh uprising of 1930 was organized by local committees acting independently of the Central Committee (Huynh Kim Khanh, 1982).

Since the regularization of the DRV state a Political Bureau is formally elected by the Central Committee as its executive body fulfilling the same functions as the earlier Standing Committee (Table 6.2 for membership in 1987). The Political Bureau comprises the Party Secretary-General and a number of other senior Party leaders (there has been no chairman since Ho Chi Minh's death in 1969). Its present membership is thirteen with one alternate member. At least five of the present Political Bureau, including the Secretary, are southerners or have strong political links with the South. Two are from the military. There are no women, nor have there been since 1945. Also elected by the Central Committee is a Secretariat, headed by the Secretary-General and currently comprising thirteen members, to carry out administrative functions and help frame policy for the Central Committee and Political Bureau. Table 6.3 lists the Secretaries-General since 1930.

In effect, the Political Bureau is the most powerful institution within the Party since the Central Committee meets only once or twice a year at plenums which normally concentrate on a particular theme. These plenums are, however, often very important meetings and major changes in policy direction are usually decided by the Central Committee. For example, it was a Central Committee Plenum, meeting in May 1941 which formed the Viet Minh, and that of January 1959 which took the decision to step up the level of armed struggle in the South. In recent years, the most important meetings of the Central Committee have been the Sixth Plenum (Fourth Central Committee) in August 1979, which initiated major reforms in the economic

Table 6.2 Membership of the Political Bureau, 1987

Party post		Government post
Party Chairman	Vacant	
Secretary-General	Nguyen Van Linh*	
Members	Pham Hung*	Prime Minister
	Vo Chi Cong*	President of State Council
	Do Muoi*	
	Vo Van Kiet*	Deputy Premier, State Planning Minister
	Le Duc Anh*	Defence Minister, Army C-in-C
	Nguyen Duc Tam*	
	Nguyen Co Thach*	Deputy Premier, Foreign Minister
	Dong Si Nguyen*	Deputy Premier
	Tran Xuan Bach	
	Nguyen Thanh Binh	
	Doan Khue	General, People's Army
	Mai Chi Tho	Interior Minister
	Dao Duy Tung (alternate)	

* Indicates member or alternate member of outgoing Political Bureau. Nguyen Van Linh was dropped in 1982 and reinstated in 1985.

Table 6.3 Secretaries-General of the Vietnamese Communist Party

Date	Name	Observations
1930 October–1931	Tran Phu	Died or killed in prison
1935 March–1940	Le Hong Phong	Guillotined
1940–1956 November	Truong Chinh	Resigned after land reform errors
1956–60	Ho Chi Minh	Le Duan took over duties before 1960
1960–1986	Le Duan	Died in office, July 1986
1986 July–December	Truong Chinh	Retired, December 1986
1986 December	Nguyen Van Linh	Elected 6th Party Congress

sphere, and the Eighth Plenum (Fifth Central Committee) in 1985, which reaffirmed and deepened the reform process.

Like other communist parties, the Vietnamese Party adheres to the principles of democratic centralism, therefore it is incumbent upon Party members to carry out orders from higher echelons and to observe strict Party discipline at all times. Day to day functioning of the Party is highly centralized and higher committees also have the power to remove elected individuals from their posts and make new appointments between congresses. This means that the Political Bureau is undoubtedly the most powerful institution in the country since, as the leading body of the Party, it also has the power to issue directives to the government. The Party's role as the 'only force leading the State and society' is enshrined in the Constitution (Article 4).

The democratic process, on the other hand, is carried out via periodic Congresses, culminating at the National Congress of the Party which, since peace was re-established in 1975, is held every five years. The first official Congress of the ICP was held in Macao in 1935, however its decisions cannot be considered very important as it reaffirmed the Comintern line of emphasizing class struggle in the colonial countries only a few months before the Comintern itself underwent a change, bringing in the anti-fascist Popular Fronts of 1936–39 (Huynh Kim Khanh, 1982). The Second Congress was held in 1951 and was important in that it re-established the Party's existence after its *de jure* dissolution in 1945, changing the name to Vietnamese Workers' Party and providing for the setting up of separate parties in Laos and Cambodia, and heralded a renewed turn towards class-based politics. The Third Congress was held in 1960 after it had become clear that there would be no re-unification election. Its role was largely to affirm the basic direction of building a socialist industrial system in the North, based on a 'priority to heavy industry' strategy, while undertaking armed struggle in the South. The Fourth Congress was held in 1976 in a re-unified country and it was here that the decision to proceed with the transition to socialism in the South was confirmed. The country's Second Five Year Plan was ratified at this congress—previous efforts to continue the economic planning system established in 1960 having been disrupted by US escalation of the war. The Fifth Congress, scheduled for late-1981, was in fact delayed for several months by intense disagreements within the Party over economic policy and was held in March 1982. This Congress was notable for the trenchant self-criticism by Party leaders over the economic crisis of 1978–80 and a number of important decisions emerged about restructuring investment and utilizing market-type individual incentives during the Third Five Year Plan. The Sixth Congress was held in December 1986, again apparently delayed slightly by the intensity of debate mainly focusing on problems in the economic field. It also focused on the need to rejuvenate the Party leadership as well as tackle serious problems of corruption and bureaucratism.

The fact that the Party Congresses usually meet for only a week or two to ratify a series of decisions, which have, in fact, already been taken by the Political Bureau and Central Committee, gives a rather misleading impression of the extent to which inner Party democracy does function. Congresses should be seen as the culmination of the political process rather than its beginning. The more important arena of activity is the prior discussion and consultation around the main agenda items of the Congress—the drafting of the Political Report, delivered by the Party Secretary, the Economic Report and the selection of candidates both for the Congress delegates and for the Party Committees. Important documents like the Political Report are initially drafted at the Central Committee level, probably by the Secretariat, and are then circulated down to the lower levels for discussion and comment. The different views expressed by lower level organizations are then aggregated and sifted by the higher levels. While little information is available on the details of these discussions, it seems likely that a process of bargaining takes place in order to achieve compromises between, for example, different regional interests or ideological positions. Indirect evidence for this is provided by the sometimes contradictory statements which can appear at different parts of the final draft, suggesting that changes have been made to accommodate interests of groups within the Party who are concerned with particular sections of the report. Documents may be drafted and re-drafted several times before a sufficent degree of unanimity is reached to allow the Congress to go ahead, but even then, a perusal of speeches delivered at the Congresses can reveal substantial divergences of opinion among the delegates. That the pre-Congress discussion is not just a formality can be seen from the unusual reference by Truong Chinh in the opening of his speech to the Sixth National Party Congress to the 'outspoken suggestions to the draft' and 'many heartfelt proposals' which had been received (Truong Chinh, 1986, p. C1/1).

Congresses have also been an important means by which the Party has responded to problems caused by ossification of its structures, corruption, arrogant behaviour by cadres and bureaucratism. The Sixth Party Congress in 1986, for example, was preceded by a six-month long 'criticism and self-criticism' drive in which the record of cadres was examined at every level, large numbers were expelled or demoted and, in the elections of delegates to the various Congresses and executive committees, many new people were brought into leadership positions. This was by no means a unique occurrence in the history of the VCP: a similar shake-out had been instigated around the 1951 Congress, for example, after the leadership became worried by the lack of poor peasant participation in the Party. Although the lists of candidates are drawn up by higher level committees, the Party leaders are constrained by the need to maintain a high level of Party unity and sustained levels of commitment among rank-and-file members if the Party as a whole is to thrive and retain public confidence. Though little detail is known about internal Party election procedures, it is likely that a similar process of consultation and bargaining between higher and lower levels takes place over candidate selection as over policy statements. Party congresses and their preparatory debates and personnel selection procedures are therefore the main means by which the Party as a whole responds to political pressures both from within its ranks and from the society.

Collective Leadership and Factionalism

One of the major distinguishing features of Vietnamese communism ever since the foundation of the Party has been its collective leadership. While Ho Chi Minh was undoubtedly pre-eminent within the Party during his lifetime, the style of leadership which he established was one of consultation, persuasion and moral example rather than any overt attempt to impose his will. Moreover, Ho's essentially pragmatic approach meant that success in achieving the overall goals of the Party became a more important criterion for judging the correctness of a political line than adherence to a particular ideology. This enabled the Party to avoid forming ideological factions and maximized the flexibility of its leaders. Ho created a tremendous reserve of loyalty, both to himself and to the Party, by bringing all the leaders into the decision-making process and especially by encouraging local leaders to use their initiative within the basic parameters of Party policy. The latter was necessary, in view of poor communications during the early years of insurrection and resistance, but was also turned into a virtue because it enabled local Party leaders to react creatively to changes in the fortunes of the revolution in their area. Conversely, the Party centre also showed loyalty to its local committees—in 1930, for example, when the regional committees in northern Trung Bo organized an ill-timed insurrection, the central organization supported the movement to the best of its ability, at great cost to itself. These features of Party activity during its early history helped to forge the unity which was essential to survival over the long decades of struggle.

The collective decision-making style established by Ho Chi Minh was formally incorporated into the Party structure at the 1960 Congress. It enabled the VCP to avoid many of the problems of succession after Ho's death (in 1969) which have plagued other parties with more individualistic leaders. In the first place, for any one leader to try to concentrate power in his own hands would have constituted an act of disloyalty to Ho. Secondly, it would have encouraged the formation of organized factions which might have been a dangerous development at a time when peace negotiations were commencing with the United States. The United States certainly looked for signs of disunity in the Hanoi leadership which it could exploit during this period immediately following Ho's death.

Collective leadership was therefore deliberately maintained by the VCP after 1969. Ho Chi Minh's position as Chairman of the Party was left vacant to ensure that no individual could claim his mantle. And the most important positions in Party and state were kept separate. (Ho had been both Party Chairman, and interim Secretary during 1956–60, and President of the State Council.) Le Duan, who became Party Secretary in 1960, had no post in the government. The State Presidency was given to the ageing Ton Duc Thang and thenceforth became much more of a ceremonial post than under Ho. Within the state apparatus, the Prime Ministership (held by Pham Van Dong) and the chairmanship of the National Assembly Secretariat (held by Truong Chinh) were the most powerful posts. In this way, the problem of succession was solved in a manner which emphasized the continuity of the Vietnamese collective leadership tradition.

This tradition has been maintained in the 1980s as a second major transition from an earlier generation of leaders has taken place. The death of Le Duan in mid-1986 and the advancing age, and sometimes ill-health, of several of the other senior Party personnel created the necessity to bring about major changes in the composition of the leadership. The matter was given added urgency by the severity of economic problems caused by ill-planned reforms carried out in September 1985 which had shaken public confidence; and there was also widespread public perception of corruption even at high levels (though not concerning the former close associates of Ho Chi Minh). The Sixth National Congress in December 1986 therefore presented the opportunity for a shake-out of ossified Party structures and to bring new, younger cadres into positions of responsibility. Here again, however, the collective nature of the Vietnamese leadership made the transition easier—even though the change was carried out in the midst of a sharp debate over the course of economic policy. Because no single individual can concentrate power in his or her own hands, it is possible to reach compromises in appointing the new leaders so that no group is forced into an oppositional position. While this may make change a much slower process in the Vietnamese Party than in others, it also means that there are no wild swings of policy—as for example were seen in China in the 1960s and 1970s—and periodic renewal of the leadership also allows for continuity and maintenance of Party unity at the same time.

In December 1986, three of Ho Chi Minh's closest associates retired from their positions in the Political Bureau. These were Pham Van Dong (whose health was reported to be poor), Truong Chinh and Le Duc Tho (who had negotiated with Kissinger in Paris). Truong Chinh had served as Party Secretary briefly after Le Duan's death and his post was taken by Nguyen Van Linh. The latter is also a veteran Party leader at 72 years of age in 1987, having joined the Thanh Nien in Haiphong in 1929 and spent most of his Party career in the South. Linh does not hold a government position. The three retired leaders have been appointed as special advisers to the Central Committee and it is not clear exactly what their role will be or how much effective power they retain. But of the Political Bureau elected by the 1982 Party Congress, nearly half were replaced in 1986. Thus the new leadership, although there has been a significant change in personnel, also contains a large element of continuity with the past and with the traditions of the VCP. This continuity is also reflected in the re-election of veteran Party leader Pham Hung (aged 75) to the number two position in the Political Bureau and his subsequent elevation to the Prime Ministership in place of Pham Van Dong.

The pattern of continuity and change was repeated at other levels by provincial and district elections as younger people were brought in to the Party hierarchy. But while most of the top leadership gained revolutionary experience before 1954, this does not mean that it is ideologically rigid or unable to respond to the needs of a population, two-thirds of whom were born after that date. The collective nature of the leadership and the tendency to compromise inherent in its decision-making procedures make it flexible in this regard.

More than any other socialist state, then, Vietnam has an institutionalized system for transferring power from one generation to the next. Political power resides in the collectivity of the Political Bureau, that is, in the institution, and not with any individual or faction leader of that body. The death or retirement of a key leader does not, therefore, lead to instability— even at times of fierce policy disagreements (as was the case in 1986). Indeed the major sources of political instability in Vietnam are the uncertain development of the economy and in the relationship of the Party as a whole with the population, *not* in faction fighting or internal power struggles.

Collective leadership and essential Party unity have been maintained in spite of often intense internal disagreements. The main areas around which such disagreements have focused have been (a) the strategy for combining economic development of the DRV with effective support to the struggle for national re-unification in the South in the 1960s, which involved debates over the type of military strategy to be pursued as well as over the economic strategy for the North; and (b) the pace of socialist transformation of the South and economic strategy for the reunified country since 1975. Nevertheless, unity has been maintained because the different positions taken by Party leaders on these issues have not gelled into organized factions and because of the tendency to compromise which has arisen through the collective leadership structure. These factors notwithstanding, there have been frequent attempts by Western scholars to identify factions within the Party which might point to a breakdown of unity or a growing monopoly of power by one individual or faction.[3] Unfortunately, such attempts have mostly ended in disaster: Le Duan, for example, has been variously described as pro-Soviet, influenced by Maoism, a neutral arbiter and ambitious seeker of personal power. Le Duan and Le Duc Tho had, according to one author, developed a bitter enmity, while according to another author they had formed an unbeatable power bloc. The labels change with the issues at stake and depend very much on the time of writing. The problem with these efforts to identify factions which are either committed to one or another external 'model' or pit 'ideologues' against 'pragmatists' is that they neither take account of nor explain the real political processes by which the Vietnamese Communist Party operates.

In the first place, they ignore the independent origins and traditions of the

Vietnamese Party. This independence was stamped on the Party by Ho Chi Minh, who constantly emphasized the need to apply the insights of Marxism to the specific conditions of Vietnam. Party strategists have in consequence always been aware of the constraints imposed upon policy by the historical and material conditions prevailing. It was precisely this awareness that gave them the ability to exploit political, military and diplomatic developments to achieve their goals. Consciousness of material constraints imposed by external developments, for example, or the small size of the Vietnamese working class, made them adopt a flexible and non-doctrinaire approach without which, it hardly seems plausible that they could have succeeded against such enormous odds. Debates within the VCP tend, therefore, to take the form of debates over the most practical way to achieve a given, agreed upon, set of goals. These goals in turn stem from the independent origins of Vietnamese communism as a national liberation movement basing itself upon mass demands for social justice. At their most general level, these goals are summed up by the phrases 'large-scale socialist production' and 'collective mastery', by which it is understood that Vietnam is to become an advanced industrial country (instead of poor and backward) in which the Vietnamese people (as opposed to foreign occupying powers or parasitical exploiting classes) are the political and economic power. The very definition of 'socialism', then, is a response to the way the Vietnamese communists saw their own society in the colonial period. It is not something artificially derived from Marxist ideology (indeed some Vietnamese Communist ideology seems to be more closely derived from indigenous cultural traditions) or from the Soviet Union or China.

In the second place, it needs to be pointed out that the VCP has understood from early days that aid from its socialist allies was always conditional upon the satisfaction of their own national interests—a lesson that was most starkly revealed at Geneva in 1954. But Ho Chi Minh in the 1920s had already criticized the Europo-centric views of fraternal parties and differed with Comintern policy on colonial countries (Huynh Kim Khanh, 1982). The experiences of the ICP in the 1930s were a further lesson in the futility of simply following external prescriptions. Since the 1940s the Vietnamese leadership has responded in what it collectively sees as a realistic way to external pressures and opportunities, but to label particular leaders as pro-Soviet or pro-Chinese is to suggest that some leaders, unlike those of the Chinese and Soviet parties themselves, do not see the interests of the Vietnamese revolution as paramount. Such a description may be valid for parties in other countries which have little or no domestic power base, but it hardly accords with the historical record of Vietnam.

What this means is that while factions and alliances may form from time to time within the VCP, they are based not on personal disposition (ideologue or pragmatist) or external attachment, but on responses to specific issues facing the Vietnamese revolution. The extraordinary variety and rapidity of social, economic and political change taking place in Vietnam over the four decades since 1945 has meant that the leadership is subjected to a multitude of pressures from different regional, class, occupational, religious, ethnic and cultural sources. The various political institutions and organizations—the Party, mass organizations, People's Councils and National Assembly—act as transmission belts passing information up to the Political Bureau from these interest groups and as arenas for consultation and debate. The responses of the leaders at the top will not depend primarily on their personal pre-conceptions, but on which groups in the society at large have access to the transmission belts of the institutions and organizations to which they are connected and how individual leaders see the information they receive as affecting the overall legitimacy and effectiveness of Party rule. Factional alignments can, therefore, and often do, shift quite dramatically.[4] For this reason it is better to view all the Vietnamese leaders as revolutionary pragmatists, non-doctrinaire in outlook, but committed to a set of fundamental revolutionary goals. The collective style of leadership, by encouraging compromise and avoidance of factionalism, ensures both continuity of these goals and flexibility in the Party's approach to achieving them.

Chinese Communist Party Influence on Vietnamese Communism

A good way to illustrate the relationship between ideology and practice in the Vietnamese Party is by analysing its relationship to the Chinese Communist Party. This relationship between the VCP and its powerful northern neighbour has ranged from close (as 'lips and teeth') to highly antagonistic at different points in history. On the one hand, the Vietnamese have borrowed much from China at certain periods and have often commented on the similarities of the two societies as factors which make Chinese experience more relevant to Vietnam than Soviet ideas. Mao Zedong was also by far the most prolific writer on theoretical issues concerning the transition to socialism in the former colonial world of Asia—earlier Soviet writers tending to adopt a more Europo-centric view. Individual Vietnamese leaders (e.g., Truong Chinh) have often been described as belonging to a pro-China or

Maoist-influenced group within the VCP (Chen, 1969; Fall, 1960; Thai Quang Trung, 1985). However, the actual degree of influence of the Chinese Party on elements of the Vietnamese leadership is more difficult to disentangle, especially given that pronouncements of the latter tend to reflect compromises reached through the collective process of decision making. It will be argued here that the reality supports the view that a revolutionary pragmatism, rather than ideological commitment to particular 'models', has been a major characteristic of Vietnamese communism. By extension, the study of the relationship between these two parties can throw light on the nature of the VCP's relationship with the CPSU which may presently be regarded as a more important influence than the CCP.

The Vietnamese Party did not begin to borrow extensively from Chinese theoretical writings until the 1940s when Chinese and Maoist works on guerrilla warfare in particular were an important influence. But the history of the two parties was intertwined in a practical way from earliest days with the foundation of Thanh Nien in Canton. Vietnamese cadres studied at the Whampoa Military Academy in the 1920s and several revolutionaries from Vietnam had also been members of the CCP. At the same time, it could not be said that Chinese influence was dominant in the 1920s or 1930s.

Ho Chi Minh's views were developed quite independently of the Chinese leaders.[5] Ho was well ahead of Mao in asserting that revolution in colonial areas must be carried out largely by the peasant masses, but like Mao, his views were at variance with the policies emanating from the Moscow-based Comintern in the late 1920s.[6] After the foundation of the ICP, however, it was the Comintern view that prevailed through the 1930s in Vietnam. As Comintern influence diminished in Southeast Asia in the 1940s, the broad similarity of views between Mao Zedong and Ho Chi Minh on the nature of the struggle in the colonial countries re-emerged—particularly on the need to rely on the peasantry as the main force (though not the guiding force) of the revolution and the idea of building broad cross-class alliances to defeat imperialism. Chinese and Vietnamese social systems also had many characteristics in common. It is not surprising, therefore, that Ho, who was a strategist and tactician rather than a theoretician, encouraged Vietnamese cadres to study the theory being developed in China.

When he returned to Vietnam in 1941 and established his base at Pac Bo, Ho translated a number of Chinese military works and wrote about Chinese guerrilla experiences in Yenan.[7] Later on, Party Secretary Truong Chinh took on the role of interpreter and popularizer of theory. Chinese influence is evident in the latter's first major work, *The Resistance Will Win*, written in 1947 and based upon Maoist theory of guerrilla warfare. Vietnamese military theorists borrowed ideas on people's war, protracted war, the interlocking relationship of guerrilla and regular forces and the notion of fighting a war without a frontline. They also adapted Mao's idea of the guerrilla war developing in three stages—defensive, equilibrium and counter-offensive—in which the revolution would first regroup and conserve its forces, then begin to attack the enemy, always choosing the place and timing of the attack in order to maintain the strategic initiative and, finally, as the enemy became demoralized and over extended, to launch a counter-offensive which would rely not necessarily on military superiority, but on political advantage as well.

Vietnamese leaders made adaptations to these theories; for example, taking into account the small size of their country compared with China, they argued that a close relationship with the masses and a highly disciplined army could offset the disadvantages of having to fight in a small area (Duiker, 1981, pp. 129–30) Another more significant area in which they differed from the Chinese was in their emphasis on the role of the cities in the revolution. As Maoist theory developed the concept of the encirclement of the foreign/comprador-dominated cities by a revolutionary countryside, the Vietnamese moved in a different direction, stressing the importance of an uprising by urban workers and intellectuals, destroying the colonial power from within its own bastions as well as from without. The success with which the August Revolution combined the two elements of urban and rural uprising led Vietnamese leaders to stick to this formulation, even after 1968 when it became clear that their ability to mobilize the cities of the South was greatly diminished. They continued to try to find a way of activating the urban population, particularly the workers, right up to the final victory in 1975. But this only partly stemmed from the classical Marxist view of socialist revolution led by the proletariat. Its fundamental root was the more pragmatic notion that to succeed, the revolution must develop a broad united front, isolating its enemies so that they cannot combine against it—the policy of 'winning more friends, making fewer enemies', which had been a guiding principle of Ho Chi Minh from the start.

In the 1940s, however, these differences with China—and others which were to develop in the 1960s—were less apparent. From 1947 the Vietnamese began receiving armaments from China (Chen, 1969, p. 189), though at this stage Ho was still attempting to work with the Guomindang as well as the CCP. In addition, CCP armed units were able to find sanctuary on Vietnamese territory (Chen, 1969, pp. 192–193) up until the time when the Guomindang was finally driven out of southern China in early 1950. In January 1950 the newly established PRC accorded diplomatic recognition to the DRV and this act was soon followed by the Soviet Union and other socialist regimes. (The United States responded by recognizing the French-sponsored 'Associated State of Vietnam' of Bao Dai.) The establishment of a common border between the two states enabled a rapid increase in the quantity of arms supplied to the DRV by China and Chinese advisers were also attached to the PAVN.[8]

The greatly increased level of contacts between the DRV and PRC in the late-1940s was accompanied by new productions of theoretical works from China. The Vietnamese adopted much Maoist thinking on 'New Democracy', although here again the practical aims of Vietnamese policy dictated such borrowings. Moreover, it should be remembered that there was a long tradition within international communist theory—going back to the Second Comintern Congress in 1920 and the Baku Congress of Toilers of the East—which stressed the potential importance of the indigenous bourgeoisie in the colonial countries in supporting a national democratic revolution, analogous to the bourgeois revolution in Europe in freeing up political structures, but led by the proletariat in the colonies because the bourgeoisie was too weak to seize power on its own behalf.[9] Mao's revival of these ideas accorded with the Vietnamese leaders' own perceptions of the need for a broad united front to drive out the imperialists.

Similarly, at a time when the VCP felt that it needed to strengthen poor peasant support for the struggle against France, the Chinese experience of land reform seemed a suitable example to follow, albeit with variations to suit Vietnamese conditions. By 1956, however, after the Party had effectively lost control over the land reform process, Truong Chinh as Party Secretary accepted responsibility for the mistakes committed and resigned his position.[10]

In other areas of agricultural policy the VCP borrowed from Chinese theory and practice, but selectively. Collectivization was carried out by stages, beginning, as in China, with 'mutual aid teams' (or 'production solidarity teams' in Vietnamese parlance) and going on to lower-level and higher-level producer cooperatives (see Chapter 9). But in Vietnam there was no Great Leap Forward—cooperativization was both more gradual and less radical in concept. At no stage did the Vietnamese contemplate establishment of communes incorporating several villages as the basic unit of account (see Elliott (1976) for a detailed comparison).

The leaders of the Communist Party in Vietnam have thus responded to perceived demands from the population affecting the legitimacy and effectiveness of Party dominance in an essentially pragmatic way, by adapting theoretical insights within the broad framework of Marxism-Leninism to Vietnamese conditions. As conditions have changed over time, through the impact of war or international events, or through internal social change, the pragmatism of earlier times became the conservatism and 'ideological dogma' of the new situation. This has led to intense intra-Party debates which have, in turn, slowly generated a new consensus and collective Party commitment to a new policy direction. Such an analysis does not preclude the idea that individuals have adopted views which persistently favoured a particular type of solution, for example a preference for centralization over decentralization, but implies that factions have not been built around adherence to any ready-made system of ideas. And there have never been any *organized* factions. Vietnamese leaders have always viewed the material conditions of their society and the global economy as the fundamental parameters constraining their decisions and they have rarely put 'politics in command'. Hence the distinction between 'ideologues' and 'pragmatists' is misleading—except in the fluid sense mentioned above.

This doctrinal flexibility of the Vietnamese Party has generated serious conflicts with the Chinese Communist Party since the latter, under Mao Zedong, decided that it had hit upon a model of universal applicability to the situation of colonial and semi-colonial countries (Chen, 1969, p. 215). Vietnamese leaders went along with this for a while,[11] as long as the Maoist theoretical formulations appeared to suit the requirements of the Vietnamese revolution and particularly where it was deemed necessary to maintain Chinese material support. But the VCP began to develop criticism of the Maoist model after 1964 and the launching in China of the Great Proletarian Cultural Revolution. By 1970 this had become fairly open: in a speech made early that year, Le Duan made an explicit criticism of the idea that the Chinese experience had universal applicability: 'there has never been, nor will there ever be, a single formula for carrying out the revolution that is appropriate for all circumstances and at all times' (Elliott, 1975, p. 43).

A particular point of contention during the Cultural Revolution was the Chinese recommendation that Vietnam should escalate the guerrilla war in the South in response to US bombing of the North and rely on 'human wave' tactics to launch an invasion across the Demilitarized Zone. DRV leaders, on the other hand, wanted to buy Soviet missiles and develop a more technology-intensive and effective anti-aircraft system—which is what they eventually did. Chinese interests here were clearly related to strategic factors as well as an ideological preference for 'red' over 'expert' (or fear of technocratic dominance which might arise with a high-tech army). The Chinese wished to keep the Vietnam War as much as possible in the South to reduce risk to their own territory. They were afraid that a concentrated effort by the DRV to defend the North would lead to further escalation of US ground-force involvement and that its own vociferous statements in support of the DRV might lead even to an attack on China itself. To avert such a possibility, China made it known to Washington during 1964–5 that, militant public threats to the contrary, it would not use its own troops to support Vietnam unless directly attacked (CIA, 1983). The Sino-Soviet dispute, which escalated during the Cultural Revolution, also meant that China tried to minimize Soviet influence in the Southeast Asian region. One way that it did this was to disrupt the passage of Soviet supplies to Vietnam (Funnell, 1978, pp. 149–50).

Disagreements between the Chinese and Vietnamese Parties over these issues were aggravated by Vietnamese criticism of the personality cult of Mao which reached extreme heights during the Cultural Revolution. While the Vietnamese themselves have never been wholly free of this sin—there are quasi-religious overtones to the way 'Uncle' Ho Chi Minh has been treated, especially after his death[12]—it is out of keeping with the emphasis on collective leadership. There has never been any promotion in Vietnam of 'Marxism–Leninism–Ho Chi Minh Thought' as a universally valid theoretical apparatus. An apocryphal story of Ho indicates his own attitude to it: asked by a foreign reporter if he intended to produce his own 'Little Red Book', Ho is alleged to have replied with a wink, 'Tell me if there is any subject Mao hasn't covered and I shall try to fill the gap.' Indeed Vietnamese criticism of this aspect of Chinese Party practice was as explicit as it could be without openly attacking Mao. In his major February 1970 speech, made five months after the death of Ho, Le Duan said:

A man, however, exceptional the qualities he may have, can never know all things and all facts in all aspects and in all their varieties. Therefore it is necessary to have collective intelligence. Only with a collective decision based on collective intelligence will we be able to avoid subjectivism that leads to errors and sometimes to dangerous consequences . . . [cited in Elliott, 1975, p. 42]

The Vietnamese also revealed their opinion of the factional struggles taking place in China, under the guise of attacking 'capitalist roaders within the Party', in Le Duan's statement in the same speech that 'if we overestimate the influence of the exploiting classes and the counter-revolutionary forces, and if we only concern ourselves with quelling them, while losing sight of the essential task of organizing, promoting and carrying out the three revolutions,[13] we would commit a serious error' (Elliott, 1975, p. 41). In other words, Vietnamese leaders stressed the overriding importance of Party unity and the need to keep a united front against the United States in the South while strengthening the economy of the North to sustain this war. Class struggle for its own sake would see the defeat of the goal of national re-unification.

These tensions were aggravated in the 1970s when the Chinese leadership cordially received Henry Kissinger and Richard Nixon in Beijing at a time when Nixon had already resumed bombing North Vietnam. China both encouraged the DRV to concentrate on military matters at a time when the DRV leaders thought negotiations were opportune and, in 1971, told Pham Van Dong on one of his visits to Beijing that since China could not retrieve Taiwan from the imperialists, the Vietnamese could hardly hope to liberate South Vietnam. The apparent inconsistencies in the Chinese position reflect a consistent Chinese Communist appreciation of their own stategic interests. The Chinese leadership showed that it was prepared to put pressure on the Vietnamese to make concessions, which would accommodate Nixon's strategy of buying time for the Thieu regime, in order to win an improve-ment of its own relations with the United States. At the same time, it sought to keep Vietnam divided and dependent upon it, by pushing for continuation of the war in the South and supporting the anti-Vietnamese xenophobia of Pol Pot in Cambodia in order to reduce Vietnamese and also Soviet influence in the Indochinese peninsula. It also sought to exploit differences within the Vietnamese leadership by cultivating the NLF leadership (which established its own legation in Beijing) and supporting its more aggressive military leaders against those in Hanoi who favoured negotiating while fighting (Funnell, 1978, p. 160). Under Mao and the so-called 'Gang of Four', the CCP continued to give succour to the more chauvinist elements within the Khmer communist movement playing on Cambodian fears of Vietnamese domina-tion and it also used the key positions of ethnic Chinese in the Thai and Malaysian Communist Parties to promote the Maoist 'model' in other countries of the region. After the death of Mao and China's vastly improved relations with the United States, the emphasis in this policy of isolating Vietnamese communism within the region shifted to developing good relations with the ruling elites and ethnic Chinese business communities of Southeast Asia.

Relations between the two Communist Parties in the period since the establishment of the PRC have thus been intimately bound up with relations between the two states and the divergent trends of revolution within their national boundaries. This has been most particularly true in the period since China began to emerge from its diplomatic isolation and adopt more of a 'great power' attitude in international relations during the 1970s, but as early as the Geneva Conference in 1954 the tension caused by the clash of state interests was clear. These tensions in state interests have, from time to time, been hidden from view by the VCP's pragmatic adaptation of Chinese theoretical insights to the problems of their own socialist revolution.

Socialist Constitutional Practice

In the socialist countries, constitutions have a rather different status and function from those of the capitalist states. Western constitutions define the boundaries between state and civil society, setting out areas of state function and, more particularly, areas in which the state may not encroach upon private activity. The legal framework established in such constitutions is essential to the functioning of the capitalist system based, as it is, on contracts between buyers and sellers in the market place. Rights and freedoms set out in constitutional law serve to limit the arbitrary use of state power over the 'enjoyment of property' as well as to foster the legitimacy of a system in which great disparities in wealth and income are sustained by an economic mechanism, rather than by force or religious canon (as in feudalism, for example). Constitutions in many Western capitalist states have also enjoyed a remarkable degree of stability, reflecting the stability of the socio-economic order and the central role of the legal framework in reproducing it. However, it is worth remembering that the stability of these constitutions is contingent upon the continued viability of the underlying economic system—when this is severely threatened, as in Weimar Germany for instance, the constitution can prove as fragile and irrelevant as those of the socialist countries are often purported to be. This conditionality in practice of Western constitutional law contrasts sharply with liberal democratic theories which assign to the constitution a determinant role in economic and political life and it means that the differences between capitalist and socialist constitutions in reality are often exaggerated.

In Marxist theory, on the other hand, systems of law are designed explicitly to ensure the continuation of class rule. Constitutions of capitalist countries are deemed to be instruments for reproducing the dictatorship of the bourgeoisie while those of socialist countries are for preserving the dictatorship of the proletariat. As such, constitutions do not acquire the independent and determining role which they are seen to have in liberal democratic theory: hence in the view of Marxists it is perfectly legitimate for the ruling class to change the constitutional framework in accordance with changing economic and social conditions. Stability in the constitution and unconditional adherence to its provisions are therefore not considered necessary, or even desirable, goals. Moreover, at least until very recently, socialist countries have not tried to base their economic systems upon commodity relations, but have used extensive political control over economic and social life. Since the Party, in its role as vanguard of the proletarian dictatorship, rather than the market place has been the ultimate source of economic power, the idea at the core of Western constitutional practice of legally enforceable contracts, has little relevance. The socialist system is one *par excellence* of *political* determination.

Socialist constitutions in this respect play a very different role from those of normally functioning capitalist societies. Rather than seeking to regulate relations between the state and civil society, the socialist constitution has no real legal function. It serves more as a statement of Party intentions or socio-economic goals, often bearing little relation to the actual functioning of the system. A written constitution, for example, can signify the need of a Party newly installed in power to create a modern nation state along Western lines. This would be true of early constitutions of Vietnam, a country in which the notion of nation state had no precedents. Prior to the establishment of boundaries by the French in the early twentieth century, the idea of the Vietnamese nation has traditionally been based on common linguistic and cultural heritage and lacked a clearly defined *territorial* base. But the French had divided this new territory into three sub-regions which competed for resources and also ruled the whole of Indochina as a single federated unit (including Laos and Cambodia), blurring national distinctions. The Vietnamese constitution of 1946, then, provided the revolutionary regime with an identity equivalent to those of other nation states in the modern world—with national boundaries, clearly defined citizenship, modern parliamentary system and elections and relations of state and civil society defined by a system of rights and obligations. However, much of the constitution conflicted with the actual functioning of the system by Party rule, hence its main role must be seen not as regulating state–society relations (as in the West), but primarily as an instrument legitimating the establishment of the Vietnamese nation state. Later variations in the constitution can be seen as legitimating new developments in Party rule, for example, the measures taken towards socialist transition.[1] This legitimation function of constitutions is, of course, also present in Western systems, but as an adjunct to their regulatory functions. The latter are almost completely absent from socialist constitutional practice for reasons outlined above.

The 1946 Constitution of the DRV

Vietnam (excluding the American client regime in the South) has had three constitutions since independence. The first was promulgated in 1946 by the first National Assembly. This early constitution was drawn up by a committee headed by Ho Chi Minh and thus bore the hallmarks of his influence; in particular, an appreciation of the delicate situation of the DRV was apparent in its composition. The 1946 constitution was designed to appeal to as broad a section of Vietnamese society as possible and also to head off possible criticism abroad—from Nationalist China, for example, which was then promoting the claims of the VNQDD, or from the United States. The document was also drawn up with an eye on French politics. It bore little resemblance to the Soviet 1936 constitution (which was to form the basic model for Chinese constitution building), but contained quotations from the US Declaration of Independence while much of its framework derived from French law. The right to private property was guaranteed. It was a constitution designed for a period of prolonged anti-colonial struggle in which the tactics of the united front would be the Party's guiding principle.

The 1959 Constitution

The DRV's second constitution was framed by a commission established in late 1956 and was adopted at the end of 1959. As with the first constitution, the historical background is important. Whereas the 1946 constitution can be seen as seeking to legitimize the newly established Vietnamese nation state as part of a strategy of maximizing domestic and international support for a regime which still faced enormous obstacles to its continued existence, by the late 1950s some fundamental changes in the situation of the DRV had taken place.

The decision to draft a new constitution was taken after it had become apparent that the re-unification elections, scheduled for 1956 under the Geneva Agreement, would not be held. On the one hand, the DRV was now firmly established in the North and the majority of those most likely to oppose a transition to socialism had emigrated to France or the South. Land reform had been completed and those former landlords who remained in the North no longer posed a threat to the regime through their economic or political power at the village level. The northern half of the country would therefore have the opportunity to begin creating a socialist society. On the other hand, it seemed likely that the South could not be regained except after a prolonged period of struggle. The focus of Party strategy there would remain on the struggle for re-unification and this would necessitate continued united front tactics.

The new constitution took three years to draft amid an intense intra-Party debate. The main issues of this debate revolved around the question of armed struggle to regain the South and the ways in which this attempt would affect or be affected by economic development in the North. As it became apparent by 1959 that the Party apparatus in the South faced imminent extinction unless a more concerted armed struggle was undertaken, the grounds of the debate shifted towards a discussion of how best to ensure that a commitment to warfare in the South would not result in a fundamental weakening of the northern economy. Many Party leaders were concerned that new class divisions would appear in the North if private farming and market forces were permitted to dominate in rural areas in the wake of the Land Reform and came increasingly to favour commencement of collectivization. This was also seen as a means of rapid capital accumulation, by concentrating otherwise fragmented surpluses produced by small farmers and providing an important boost to industrialization. Industrialization would, in turn, enable the North to support a higher level of combat in the South. By 1959, then, the majority view in the Party favoured a fairly rapid transition to socialism as the basis for industrialization and the major conclusions stemming from this view were incorporated into the new constitution.

The 1959 constitution drew upon constitutional models of other socialist countries for the first time, although it retained some of the distinctive French-inspired touches as well (Fall, 1960, p. 284). The aim of creating a communist society in Vietnam was made explicit in this constitution: central planning and collective and state forms of property were given pride of place, although private property was permitted provided it did not undermine the socialist economic system. Until 1958 local government functions had been carried out by Committees for Resistance and Administration, containing combined civilian, military and Party elements, but a reorganization in 1958 after the restoration of peace (Fall, 1965, p. 20) saw the separation of civilian and military roles with the establishment of locally elected People's Councils. These were incorporated into the 1959 constitution. Another new specifically socialist feature of the 1959 constitution was the establishment of People's Control Organs, with both civilian and military sections, to oversee and ensure the legality of the work of government bodies. Finally, while the French provincial boundaries were retained, two 'autonomous zones' created in 1955 and 1956 in areas where most of the ethnic minorities lived (i.e., the mountainous regions of northern and north-western North Vietnam), were given their own zonal assemblies, administrative committees and militia forces. The inclusion of these in the 1959 constitution was in line with PRC practice.

The 1980 Constitution

National re-unification in 1976 provided the occasion for preparation of Vietnam's third constitution. Yet again a drafting committee was set up, by decision of the National Assembly, following the first nationwide elections since 1946. The committee reported in 1979 and the new constitution, which remains in force today, was formally promulgated in 1980. Again the lengthy drafting period was a reflection of intense debate over the direction Vietnamese society should take in the aftermath of re-unification, at a time when the economy was wracked by crisis caused by poor harvests, misallocation of resources, renewed military mobilization against Democratic Kampuchea and China and political instability in the South. The problem of absorbing the South, with its vastly different social structure and chaotic economy was a major source of divided opinion with the majority of Party leaders in the late 1970s favouring fairly rapid transformation along similar lines to the North two decades earlier. The conclusions reached in this debate around 1978–9 can be seen reflected in the constitutional framework.

In many respects, the 1980 constitution of Vietnam borrows from the 1977 constitution of the Soviet Union. An important inclusion, for example, is the constitutional role assigned to the Communist Party. Article 4 states that the Party is 'the only force leading the State and society, and the main factor determining all successes of the Vietnamese revolution.' A similar clause appears in the Soviet constitution,[2] but not in that of China or the earlier DRV constitutions. The new clause in fact regularizes something which has been applied in practice by the Party since the inception of the DRV, but its inclusion may also be a reflection of the desire of those drafting the constitution to emphasize the *socialist* nature of Vietnam under the leadership of the working class (Articles 1–3).[3] The basic structure of government is also similar to that of the Soviet Union, except that where the latter is a federal system, Vietnam is unitary. The highest legislative authority is the National Assembly (equivalent to the Soviet Union's Supreme Soviet) which elects a Council of State or 'collective presidency' equivalent in function to the Soviet Union's Presidium.[4] The highest executive body is the Council of Ministers as in the Soviet Union (in China the Council of State fulfils this role). Other government structures which are basically the same as those set out in the Soviet constitution include the system of law courts and People's Control Commissions. Both the Soviet Union and Vietnam (but not China) include in their constitutions provision for the use of People's Assessors to sit alongside judges and with the same powers in the court system. These are elected, though in Vietnam the method of election is not specified.[5]

There are, however, important areas in which the Vietnamese constitution diverges from the 'models' established by other socialist states. First among these perhaps is the emphasis which the Vietnamese have placed on the role of the working class in their revolution. This partly reflects Vietnamese recognition of its lower stage of socialist development—after all, according to the preamble of the Soviet constitution, 'socio-political and ideological unity of Soviet society . . . has been achieved. The aims of the proletariat having been fulfilled, the Soviet state has become a state of the whole people' (cited in Lane, 1985, pp. 346–7). The Vietnamese, in contrast, have not even completed their industrialization program, hence still perceive the need for a vanguard Party, the 'general staff' of the working class (*Constitution of the Socialist Republic of Viet Nam*, p. 12), to construct socialism. But, Vietnamese orthodoxy in stressing the proletarian dictatorship also differentiates them sharply from their erstwhile allies and benefactors in China for whom the idea of 'people's democracy' remains the appropriate category for this less developed state of socialism. One suspects that anti-Chinese sentiment is an important motive here, since in other respects the characteristics of the united front are retained in the Vietnamese constitution (e.g., Article 9 on the mass organizations and the tradition of 'national unity').

Secondly, the Vietnamese constitution differs from earlier socialist models concerning the position of national minorities. The Soviet constitution goes as far as permitting Union Republics, in principle, to secede—a reflection of Lenin's views on the nationality question and his efforts to combat Russian chauvinism associated with tsarist imperialism. The Chinese constitution, on the other hand, explicitly forbids secession and this in turn is a reflection of historical tendencies within China—regional warlordism and the fact that national minorities often straddle sensitive border areas. The Chinese have attempted to accommodate national aspirations within a unitary state by the creation of 'autonomous regions' with limited governmental functions, though this has usually been offset by constitutionally sanctioned promotion of the Chinese language and substantial in-migration of the majority Han Chinese to these autonomous regions. In its 1959 constitution Vietnam had also established autonomous regions (Viet Bac and Tay Bac), but the abandonment of this in the 1980 document probably reflects concern in Hanoi to limit the political (as opposed to cultural and linguistic) independence of national minorities. Most ethnic minorities live in border areas, a significant proportion along the troubled borders of Cambodia and China. Concern was expressed in Hanoi at the possibility of a fifth column being created among the tribal groups in these zones.[6] Moreover, at the time of unification, to be consistent with the earlier constitution, a third autonomous region in the mountain provinces of the South would need to be created. Here, the Party's relationship with local minorities was even more uncertain. The French and then the Americans had financed and assisted an organization known as FULRO (Front Unifié de Lutte des Races Opprimés) to fight the Viet Minh, mobilizing tribal chieftains and others who felt threatened by the Communist policy of encouraging sedentary farming and mass literacy to drive out superstition and clan-based exploitation systems. The ethnic minorities of the South were thus more divided over their support for the communists than those of the North. While wishing to preserve minority languages and cultural differences, the Vietnamese constitution skirts around these problems by stressing the unitary nature of the state and, by abolishing the autonomous regions, avoids the need to say anything about secession.

Thirdly, neither Soviet nor Chinese constitutions contain any equivalent to the Vietnam Fatherland Front, which comprises the various political parties (Communist, Democratic and Socialist) and mass organizations within the framework of the united front. Again emphasizing the role of the working class, however, the Vietnamese constitution gives pre-eminence to the Vietnam Confederation of Trade Unions (VCTU), allowing it to 'take part in State affairs and supervise the work of State bodies and participate in the management of factories' (Article 10), a role which is open also to other mass organizations in the Soviet Union (Lane, 1985, pp. 348–9). In Vietnam the President of the VCTU also has the right to attend meetings of the Council of Ministers and representatives of the Fatherland Front and its other affiliates may also be invited to attend (Article 106). This right does not exist in the Soviet Union or China, although in both Vietnam and the Soviet Union trade unions have the right to table draft laws which they seek to implement.

There are many other differences of wording and emphasis between the Vietnamese constitution and its Soviet 'model', reflecting differences in outlook and varying conditions facing the two countries. The Vietnamese constitution, for example, contains no mention of the international division of labour which forms an important part of the equivalent Soviet clause on international cooperation and fraternal solidarity (Article 14 for Vietnam,

Article 30 for the Soviet Union), an indication of greater Vietnamese concern for economic self-reliance at the time of drafting. Whereas the Soviet Union 'permits' the existence of the individual economy, Vietnam 'encourages, guides and assists' it.[7] The Vietnamese constitution, in its chapter on the rights and obligations of individuals, lays greater stress on obligations of citizens to state and society compared with the Soviet Union which stresses citizens' rights (though in a qualified way). This may reflect the difference between the Asian and European traditions of the two countries. The Vietnamese constitution also makes what may be a unique contribution to socialist constitutional law in its assertion that 'The family is the cell of society' (Article 64), apparently relegating those *ex loco familiae* to an inferior legal status. In detailing membership and functions of government bodies, the Vietnamese document is sometimes deliberately vague on procedures for appointment or election where both the Soviet and Chinese constitutions are more explicit. This gives greater leeway, without overtly breaching constitutional strictures, for Party intervention to override or pre-empt decisions normally taken, for example, by the legislature.

The list given here is by no means exhaustive, there are many other points of difference, but it serves to counteract the argument often voiced in Western analyses, that the Vietnamese socialist system is but an echo of the Soviet one, a consequence of alleged Soviet domination over the Vietnamese Party.[8] A study of the Vietnamese constitution shows that although it has pragmatically borrowed from different sources (American, French, Chinese and Soviet for the most part), it retains a distinctive Vietnamese flavour rooted in the history and traditions of Vietnamese communism.

The Structure of Government

As in other socialist countries, it is very difficult to discuss the government of Vietnam in isolation from the actual everyday operations of the Party. The Vietnamese polity is characterized by extensive Party intervention in affairs of state in spite of an awareness that the role of the Party ought to be chiefly in providing policy guidelines and in mobilizing people towards its political goals, rather than concerning itself with day-to-day management of the government. Party cadres play an important role at all levels of the government apparatus and indeed promotion is often predicated upon political criteria rather than technical competence, so that the higher echelons of government are almost entirely dominated by Party members. At ministerial level senior Party members hold nearly all the posts (Table 7.1) but this is also

Table 7.1 Membership of the Council of Ministers, 1987

Name	Government position	Party position
Pham Hung	Chairman (Prime Minister)	Political Bureau
Vo Van Kiet	Deputy Premier, Chmn. State Planning Commission	Political Bureau
Nguyen Co Thach	Deputy Premier, Foreign Minister	Political Bureau
Dong Si Nguyen	Deputy Premier	Political Bureau
Vo Nguyen Giap	Deputy Premier	Central Committee
Nguyen Khanh	Deputy Premier, Secretary to Council of Ministers	C. C. Secretariat
Nguyen Ngoc Triu	Deputy Premier	Central Committee
Nguyen Van Chinh	Deputy Premier, Dir. Govt. Inspectorate	Central Committee
Doan Duy Thanh	Deputy Premier, Foreign Trade Minister	Central Committee
Tran Duc Luong	Deputy Premier	Central Committee
Le Duc Anh	Defence Minister	Political Bureau
Mai Chi Tho	Interior Minister	Political Bureau
Dau Ngoc Xuan	1st vice-chmn. State Planning Commission	Central Committee
Vo Dong Giang	Chmn. State Commission for External Economic Relations	–
Dang Thi	Chmn. State Commission for Economic & Cultural Cooperation with Laos and Cambodia	Central Committee
Do Quoc Sam	Chmn. State Commission for Capital Construction	Central Committee (alternate)
Dang Huu	Chmn. State Commission for Science & Technology	Central Committee
Phan Van Tiem	Chmn. State Prices Commission	Central Committee (alternate)
Hoang Quy	Finance Minister	Central Committee
Lu Minh Chau	Dir. State Bank	Central Committee
Hoang Duc Nghi	Min. for Supply	Central Committee (alternate)

Name	Government position	Party position
Nguyen Ky Cam	Min. for Labour, Disabled Soldiers & Social Affairs	Central Committee
Phan Ngoc Tuong	Construction Minister	Central Committee
Bui Danh Luu	Transport Minister	Central Committee
Phan Thanh Liem	Engineering & Metals Minister	Central Committee
Vu Ngoc Hai	Energy Minister	Central Committee
Vu Tuan	Light Industry Minister	–
Nguyen Cong Tan	Agriculture & Food Industry Minister	Central Committee
Phan Xuan Dot	Forestry Minister	Central Committee (alternate)
Nguyen Canh Dinh	Water Conservancy Minister	Central Committee
Nguyen Tien Trinh	Marine Products Minister	–
Hoang Minh Thang	Home Trade Minister	Central Committee
Tran Van Phac	Culture Minister	Central Committee
Tran Hoan	Information Minister	Central Committee
Tran Hong Quan	Secondary Vocational & Higher Education Minister	Central Committee (alternate)
Pham Minh Hac	Education Minister	Central Committee (alternate)
Phan Hien	Justice Minister	–

true of Western parliamentary systems. Ministerial positions are by their nature highly politicized. Not enough information is available to be able to say to what extent politicization of top administrative positions prevails or a Soviet-style 'nomenclature' operates for these jobs. In recent years there have been efforts to increase the level of technical competence in such posts, but this does not of necessity conflict with continued politicization—depending on the extent to which technically skilled persons are also attracted into the Party.[9] Unlike the Chinese, the Vietnamese have never accepted any fundamental distinction between 'red' and 'expert'.

In discussing the formal structure of Vietnamese government, then, it is necessary to bear in mind that the main decision-making bodies are not the organs of government itself, but those of the Party, principally the Political

Bureau. The Political Bureau plays a central role in initiating legislation and in directing the work of the legislature and ministries. It also has the power to issue decrees independently of the formal government apparatus and these have the force of law. While this gives Vietnamese and other socialist governments a markedly different character on the surface from their Western counterparts, we shall see in Chapter 8 that the actual inputs to the decision-making process may not be so different.

The National Assembly

The highest legislative authority in Vietnam is the National Assembly (Quoc Hoi) which, in 1987, consisted of 496 deputies elected for five-year terms. Under the constitution, the Assembly is the 'highest State authority' (Article 82). Theoretically, then, it is the most powerful government institution, but this is far from the reality. As is the case with most Western parliaments, the National Assembly acts primarily as a rubber stamp for decisions taken at a higher level, usually in Vietnam by the Political Bureau. Legislation presented to the Assembly is drafted by Party bodies (e.g. the Political Bureau or Secretariat), by the Council of Ministers or, occasionally, by one of the mass organizations and voted on, usually unanimously, during biannual sessions lasting about a week. An important difference from Western legislatures, however, is that the National Assembly is not a forum for public presentation of criticism of government policy. In Vietnam the votes taken within the legislature are seen as expressing the unity of the people and, as with Party congresses, they are seen as the end of the political process rather than its main arena. However, the legislative procedure does provide a means whereby deputies can represent the interests of their constituencies through making suggestions and criticisms of draft bills, within a policy framework laid down by the Party. Determination of the framework itself is largely an extra-parliamentary process and in this there is again little difference from other socialist and non-socialist systems.

For electoral purposes constituencies are based on provinces and municipalities (except that Hanoi and Ho Chi Minh City each have four). Within each constituency a deputy is elected for every 100,000 voters with an extra deputy if more than 50,000 are left over. This gets rid of the urban bias in the electoral system of the DRV prior to 1975 (Duiker, 1983, p. 83). Voters in each constituency are presented with a list of candidates selected by the Fatherland Front and its affiliated organizations, which implies that if not Party members, they are at least approved by the Party. But for the April 1987 elections the list of candidates was for the first time drawn up at public selection meetings where contenders had to face questions and criticism. Traditionally some choice has been available to the electorate: Table 7.2 suggests that for a constituency of one million voters and ten seats, there would normally be a choice from at least twelve or thirteen candidates. Since a candidate must receive 50 per cent of the vote to be elected, voters could theoretically force a new election by failing to vote for the selected candidates. I know of no case, however, where this has happened.

Table 7.2 Electoral choice

Election date	No. seats	No. candidates	Ratio candidates to seats
1946	n.a.	n.a.	n.a.
1960	362	458	1.35*
1964	366	448	1.30*
1971	n.a.	n.a.	n.a.
1976	492	605	1.23
1981	496	614	1.24
1987	496	829	1.67

* Until 1971, ninety-one deputies elected from the South in 1946 retained their seats without re-election. Their seats were abolished with the formation of the PRG in 1971. The ratios given here are for those seats subject to election only.

Candidates for the National Assembly are selected so as to represent the different sections of Vietnamese society comprising the united front. Composition of the Assemblies elected in 1976, 1981 and 1987 is given in Table 7.3. It shows a preponderance of non-manual workers, while peasants, in particular, are under-represented compared with their weight in the population. Women are also greatly under-represented and, if anything, have suffered a setback since the end of the war. On the whole, however, representation of manual workers, women and ethnic minorities is considerably higher than in Western parliaments. The number of Party cadres (i.e., full-time Party workers) has shown a marked tendency to decline.

Apart from legislation, the functions of the National Assembly include the election (or removal) of the Council of State, National Defence Council, Nationalities Commission, Council of Ministers and appointment of such officers as Procurator-General of the Supreme People's Control Commission and Chief Justice of the Supreme Court.[10] In practice these decisions are also

Table 7.3 Social composition of National Assembly, 1976 to 1987

	1976		1981		1987	
	No.	%	No.	%	No.	%
By occupation						
Workers	80	16	100	20	91	18
Collective peasants	100	20	92	18	105	21
Soldiers	54	11	49	10	49	10
Cadres	141	29	121	24	100	20
Intellectuals	98	20	110	22	123	25
Democratic 'notables' and religious groups	13	3	15	3	9	2
Handicraft and cooperative workers	n.a.	n.a.	9	2	19	4
Others	5	1	—	—	—	—
By other categories						
Women	132	27	108	22	88	18
Ethnic minorities	67	14	73	15	70	14
'Third Force'	5	1	—	—	—	—

taken outside the formal structures, by the Party leadership, but as with the discussion of the political process within the Party we cannot assume that the leadership is entirely unresponsive to pressures emanating from different sections of the community. Unfortunately little solid information is available on the nature and content of inputs to the legislative process and any conclusions are necessarily tentative. But it seems likely that the actual functioning of the system, as distinct from the formal role assigned to the legislature, may not be very greatly different from those of the West.

The Council of State

The Council of State is defined in the constitution as 'the highest continuously functioning body of the National Assembly and ... the collective Presidency of the Socialist Republic of Vietnam.' It is elected by the National Assembly from among its deputies and consists of a chairperson, a secretary-general, several vice-chairpersons (currently six) and members. The total membership in 1987 was fifteen. Political Bureau member Vo Chi Cong was the Chairman. Eleven of the fifteen were senior Party members and the army, national minorities and mass organizations are all represented. Interestingly, five members of the State Council had been senior figures in the NLF or the PRG before unification. The Council acts in lieu of the National Assembly when the latter is not in session and, in addition, it convenes and presides over the Assembly, supervises the activities of People's Councils and rescinds or abrogates the decisions of these if they are deemed to be 'seriously detrimental to the interests of the people' (Article 100, Clause 10), and ratifies or abrogates international treaties.

As in the Soviet Union, members of the Council of State may not be concurrently members of the Council of Ministers since the latter are responsible to the former when the National Assembly is not in session.

The Council of State replaces the Presidency in the 1959 constitution. Under Ho Chi Minh the Presidency was a rather powerful position, but it declined in importance after his death with the appointment of Ton Duc Thang, who was then even older than Ho. After Thang's death in March 1980, his deputy, the former chairman of the NLF, Nguyen Huu Tho, was appointed, but by then the process of changing the constitution was already under way. With the new constitution the chairmanship of the State Council has gained in importance in the hands of Truong Chinh, who was elected in 1981. The current chairman (elected in June 1987) is Vo Chi Cong, a prominent Party leader with strong connections with the South—he is third-ranking member of the Political Bureau, was a former vice-president of the NLF and for several years headed the Party Commission for Transformation of Southern Agriculture as well as being a former Agriculture Minister. The importance of these two recent chairmen in the Communist Party hierarchy has vested their position in the state apparatus with greater significance than the former Presidency. The chairman of the Council of State also holds the important position of chairman of the National Defence Council which is charged with mobilizing human and material resources for defence purposes. Through their links with the mass organizations, which select candidates for National Assembly elections and also have the right to submit draft legislation, members of the State Council have a potentially important power base.

The Council of Ministers

The Council of Ministers is the 'highest executive and administrative' body of the state. It is elected by the National Assembly and responsible to it (though unlike the Council of State, its members can be non-deputies—as is currently the case with General Vo Nguyen Giap). As presently constituted the Council consists of a Chairman (the Prime Minister), nine deputy premiers, a secretary-general, twenty-two ministers (a reduction from twenty-six in 1982) and seven heads or deputy-heads of State Commissions (State Planning, External Economic Relations, Price, Science and Technology, Capital Construction, Economic and Cultural Cooperation with Laos and Cambodia). The directors of the State Bank and the Government Inspectorate also have ministerial rank. The President of the VCTU has the right to attend meetings (this post was vacant in 1987) and heads of other mass organizations may attend by invitation.

The Council of Ministers is the government of Vietnam, the equivalent of a Western Cabinet and with much the same powers, but in addition some of its powers overlap with those of the State Council (e.g. in supervising and if necessary rescinding resolutions of the People's Councils and People's Committees). This arrangement of overlapping functions might not work very well were it not for the fact that decisions are usually not made by these bodies, but by the Party and transmitted to the organs of government by the senior Party members who fill the top posts.

In 1987, following recognition by the 1986 Party Congress of the need for serious economic reform, an attempt was made to streamline and rationalize the ministry. The former practice of dividing ministries by function has been modified in favour of achieving better vertical integration—several ministries concerned with agriculture and food production were amalgamated, as were the ministries of Coal Mines and Power (to form a new Energy ministry) and those for Labour, War Invalids and Social Welfare. There have also been numerous cabinet reshuffles in the wake of economic crisis and reforms in the 1970s and 1980s. The extent of the search for new, successful economic measures is reflected in the fact that by April 1982 only twelve of the ministers appointed following unification in 1976 retained their jobs and by mid-1987 only three of these remained. Of the forty-one individuals appointed to ministerial posts in the 1982 reshuffle, only fourteen were still in the ministry in June 1987. All the original PRG members who were added to the DRV cabinet in 1976 have gone, including the sole woman in the ministry for ten years, Mme Nguyen Thi Binh, who has now been replaced by a man (though remaining head of the National Assembly's foreign affairs standing committee).

These dramatic changes are partly a reflection of the Party's desire to fill key government posts with more expert leaders: several jobs have been taken by people promoted from within the department concerned. But more importantly, they reflect a shift in the political composition of the ministry as the Party has grappled with economic problems created by unification. The present ministry contains a high proportion of reform supporters and several of these—notably Pham Hung (Prime Minister), Vo Van Kiet (Planning), Mai Chi Tho (Interior), State Bank director Lu Minh Chau and Minister for Internal Trade, Hoang Minh Thang, have strong associations with the successful economic policies pursued in the South since 1982. The head of the newly formed State Commission on External Economic Relations, Vo Dong Giang, is also a southerner and former NLF central committee member.

People's Councils

Vietnam is divided below the central level into three levels of administrative responsibility. Immediately below the central government are the provinces and municipalities. (There is also one Special Zone, Vung Tau-Con Dau, under central authority.) These in turn are divided into districts and townships or, in the cities, precincts. Below these are rural communes and urban wards. At each level there are corresponding People's Councils, each Council in turn electing its executive People's Committee. All People's Councils are directly elected.[11] They are responsible both to the electors *and* to higher authorities which have the power to rescind their decisions (see above).

Local administrations have the power to draw up budgets and plans and during the past decade the Party has heavily promoted the idea that the district should become a more important unit of planning. The idea has been to build integrated agro-industrial complexes at the district level, with small towns providing services, repairs and simple manufactured goods to the agricultural sector, both as a way of increasing decentralization of economic management and of decreasing village autarky. However, little has been achieved in this direction—in some areas of the South, for example, efforts to make the district more important disrupted existing patterns of trade and division of labour, which cut across district and even provincial boundaries, creating economic difficulties and increasing local autarky instead of diminishing it, so that a reversal of the measures was needed. Moreover, district leaders complained that although they had the power, in principle, to raise revenues and plan economic developments, they lacked the means in actuality. There was too little left over after central and provincial appropriations for any meaningful increase in district economic activity to take place.

As far as local government is concerned, then, the commune (basically a village-level unit) remains a more important unit of administration than the district.

Provincial governments are also an important source of power and the central authorities have frequently found it necessary to warn against regionalism and a propensity for provinces to promote autarky. A problem arose in the early 1980s, for instance, when provinces were permitted to establish their own import-export companies, that they tended to hoard foreign exchange earnings and preferred to import goods rather than buy them from elsewhere in Vietnam. Since then, regulations have been introduced to ensure that provincial foreign trade companies are only able to keep a portion of their foreign exchange earnings.

People's Courts and Control Commissions

The judicial system in Vietnam consists of People's Courts, at each administrative level, and Military Tribunals. Special Tribunals may be established by the National Assembly or Council of State for special purposes. All judges of the People's Courts are elected for a term corresponding to that of the electing body—in the case of the Supreme Court, which is elected by the National Assembly, five years; in the case of provincial courts, four years, and lower courts, two years. In addition to the judges, trials are also presided over by People's Assessors elected, by unspecified means, for periods of two and a half years for the Supreme Court or two years in the lower courts. People's Assessors have the same power as judges, but it is not clear how many of each category sit at a given trial. Judgments and sentencing are by majority decision.

Minor disputes and petty crime are usually dealt with by organizations established at grass-roots level such as residents' committees in urban wards.

The People's Control Commissions were originally established under the 1959 constitution to provide a means of centralized control over government bodies. They fulfil a sort of ombudsman function. Procurators and members of the Control Commissions are appointed by the Procurator-General of the Supreme Control Commission who is elected by and responsible to the National Assembly. Procurators at the lower levels, who have the power to prosecute, are responsible only to the procurators at higher levels and are independent of local government control.

Interest Groups and the Political Process

In many other socialist systems, including the Soviet Union and post-Mao China, the notion of conflict of interest in a socialist society is explicitly rejected by the official Party line. In Vietnam, however, one of the major themes of critics of collectivization as practised up to the late 1970s has been that it generated conflicts of interest between three different social groupings: individuals, cooperatives and the state. Individuals lacked adequate material incentives to contribute to collective production, cooperative managers were squeezed between the demands of the state for enlarged surpluses and the low prices paid for these, the state failed to achieve the increases in supplies of food and raw materials necessary for its industrialization and export programs. The results were that peasants turned increasingly to sideline production, disrupting cooperative and state plans; cooperative managers became demoralized and resorted to such practices as handing out blank contracts to workers or misusing cooperative resources for their own ends; the state resorted to coercive measures to try to break down the autarky of the villages, but encountered resistance from cooperative managers and members alike. (Many forms of resistance were available, ranging from under-reporting of production to attacks on government procurement officials.) The explicit aim of those seeking to reform the system of agricultural cooperation was to reconcile these three interests by providing incentives to peasants that more closely related income to labour input and allowing both individuals and collectives to retain a higher percentage of output. The central authorities thus hoped to expand their own surplus extraction from a greatly increased total output. Earlier efforts to deflect growing political pressure from peasants for reform had been resisted by Party leaders on the grounds that low agricultural prices were offset by the availability at below-market prices of industrial products (Le Duan & Pham Van Dong, 1975). But in fact the existence of severe shortages of industrial goods (in part as a result of the pricing system itself) meant that cooperatives were, for the most part, unable to raise their incomes or meet government quotas without resorting to corruption, black market activity or (at that time) illegal contracting of land. There can be little doubt that pressure from the peasants, expressed politically through Party channels and also via mass organizations and National Assembly deputies (as well as at conferences like that organized at Thai Binh in 1974 ostensibly to gain compliance for the then Party policy of tightening administrative management in the cooperatives), contributed to the decision in 1981 to allow the Haiphong authorities to pilot widespread implementation of the product contract system (see Chapter 11) as a prelude to its introduction nationwide.

Another area in which Vietnamese analysts have identified conflict of interest between groups in society has been in the singling out of bureaucratic resistance to the program of economic reform. This critique has also extended into the Party itself, even to its highest levels (VCP, 1982; Ton That Thien, 1983, p. 697). The attack levelled at the bureaucracy and some elements of the Party has been most trenchant, referring to the power and privilege which some individuals gained due to their position in the 'bureaucratic administrative subsidy' system and which they have proved reluctant to relinquish. At the 6th Party Congress, outgoing Party Secretary, Truong Chinh, said

The struggle for renovation is not only held back by force of habit, but also runs up against the privileges and prerogatives of some people who stick to the old mechanism. This is a struggle inside the Party and the state organs, among comrades and right with ourselves. [Truong Chinh, 1986]

In a related critique the reformers have also attacked regional particu-larism which stems from the ability of local leaders to resist central interference by virtue of the relative self-sufficiency of the local economy. The solution, according to the reformers is to create a genuinely national market based on a nationwide social division of labour; i.e., to break down the autarky of regions by economic means, and to decentralize economic decision making to the level of the enterprise, breaking down the ability of the bureaucrats to allocate resources on the basis of political criteria independently of real costs and benefits to society. But it is not yet clear how this will be achieved. The tendency of bureaucrats to obstruct such reforms can be a major limiting factor and much will also depend on how other interest groups in society react—urban workers, for example. This is difficult to see owing to the lack of outlets for workers' pressures—the trade unions remain weak *vis-à-vis* the government and these clashes of interest must be sorted out largely within the Party.

The working class is not overtly mentioned as a group having interests diverging from state policy—it may be seen as too subversive of the received orthodoxy that the state is led by the working class. But urban workers are clearly one of the worst-off sections of Vietnamese society today, and this much is admitted. As employees of the state (as factory workers or civil servants), workers[1] have been hit by shortages of food and other consumer goods (including housing), high rates of inflation and low salaries. They are victims of the fiscal crisis of the state whose revenues have not matched the cost of subsidies to unprofitable industries and the provision of food and welfare at low prices to the workers themselves. The existence of the food subsidy has been used to justify payment of low wages and, indeed, these can hardly be increased to an adequate level without adding further inflationary pressure to the economy in the short run. On top of this, economic stagnation and high rates of population growth have led to rising unemployment levels, particularly affecting new entrants to the work-force.

In the long run, then, workers stand to gain considerably from economic reform, whether this is through an increase in the number of small-scale individual and private enterprises providing jobs and alleviating shortages or by elimination of the 'bureaucratic subsidy' system which props up uneconomic firms at great cost to the rest of the economy. But in the short run, the serious uncertainty engendered by the reform process is likely to generate worker resistance to change in some areas at least. In a situation of already high unemployment, the threatened closure of uneconomic factories and loss of job security, paid leave and social welfare benefits that go with state employment would lead workers to join with management and the bureaucracy in resisting closure. Greater hardship for workers has also been caused by poorly designed policies, such as the price and currency reforms introduced in 1985 (Chapter 11) which led to chaos in the market place and precipitated the country into a round of hyperinflation.

All these problems have been discussed openly in the Vietnamese press, however, and this propensity for frankness, which the Vietnamese leadership has shown periodically throughout its history, is a major factor underlying continued public confidence in its ability eventually to find a solution. Conflicts of interest have not broken into widespread lack of trust and passive or open resistance that has been a feature of some East European societies. An important reason for this is that the Party has been genuinely responsive to persistent pressure from below, even if this often takes a long time to work its way through the system. Such open discussions in periods of crisis also provide Western analysts with an opportunity to view the actual Vietnamese political process, at least in some of its aspects, instead of the formal or ideal process which is put forward for foreign and domestic consumption when the system is functioning normally.

An irony of the current interest group conflict in Vietnamese society is that at a time when the role of the Party as the 'only force leading state and society' has been enshrined in the constitution, the Party itself has come increasingly to recognize the existence of independent sources of political power. While the present attempt to implement reforms is officially presented largely in terms of a struggle between the Party and the bureaucracy (or sections of it), the reality is that the bureaucracy also constitutes a power base for a number of important Party leaders. The interests of the bureaucracy (and possibly other groups as we have seen above) are articulated by political leaders associated with the more conservative positions in the economic debate. Taking this line of argument a step further, I would suggest that different ideological positions within the Party should be seen as articulating the interests of particular groups or combinations of groups in the community. Therefore the conflict portrayed in the media as one between Party and bureaucracy should be seen in reality as a struggle between the bureaucracy and these other groups, expressed as a struggle for dominance within the Communist Party. In this view, the existence of the Party as the main arena for interest articulation leads to the formation of coalitions of interest which, through a process of bargaining and compromise, generate Party policy. In Western democracies, functional interests find political expression in the formation of different political parties as well as coalitions of interest within the same party: usually a fundamental class division forms the main cleavage between parties. But the process of bargaining and coalition formation which determines actual policy outcomes is essentially similar to what I am suggesting here for the single-party system in Vietnam.

Since 1979 in Vietnam, the advocates of economic reform have gained, with some temporary setbacks, increasing ascendancy within the VCP. The rise to dominance of the reform policy can be attributed to two major factors: firstly, the popularity among the peasant majority of the improved system of individual and collective material incentives and, in particular, its proven ability to overcome the crisis of agricultural production in southern Vietnam; secondly, and relatedly, the greatly enhanced economic performance of the South based on creative use by the southern Party leadership of the possibilities contained in the reform package to bring out the dynamic agricultural and industrial potential of the region (often by ignoring and in other ways circumventing instructions from Hanoi). It seems to me no accident that in the 1987 government changes in Hanoi several key positions were awarded to individuals with strong associations with the southern political and economic system. These changes reflect a coalition of interests between peasants and southerners gaining ascendancy over more traditional

Vietnamese socialism represented by bureaucrats, war veterans and workers (mainly northern urban dwellers).

A caveat should be entered here: it is difficult and dangerous to try to attribute a direct correspondence between a set of ideas emerging at a given point in time and the needs of a particular interest group, especially such broadly defined ones. The situation may become more confused if, for example, leaders try to draw a wide range of groups into the coalition by making concessions to interests articulated by opposition leaders or if differential impact of a policy on a single group, like the peasantry, leads one section to attack it. Such attributions are therefore useful only as broad guidelines. They nevertheless serve to illustrate the point being made here about the nature of relations between Party and society in Vietnam; i.e., that the Party serves as the main institutional means for pulling together diverse sectional, regional and functional ranges of interests in society, provides a forum for the articulation of those interests and for the formation of alliances and compromises which determine policy outcomes at the central level.

I do not wish to suggest that all these coalitions of interest have an equal chance of success—I am not arguing the case for socialist pluralism. The likelihood of influencing the policy outcome depends, as in all societies, on the ability to dispose of resources within the economic system. The centralized power of the Vietnamese Communist Party, then, is not something which results from the charisma of individual leaders or force of arms, but out of a collective ability to articulate the interests of important sections of Vietnamese society. However, the VCP could never have succeeded in defeating the French and Americans if it had not had the capacity to act in the interests of the vast majority of Vietnamese people. It can only continue to exercise a leading role so long as it retains this ability to respond to pressure from below and to implement policies which appeal to a wide range of interests beyond the bureaucratic elite. Failure to do this in the longer run would result in loss of legitimacy.

Political Participation

Ordinary citizens have the opportunity to participate in political life through four main channels: firstly, through the mass organizations—the trade unions, peasants' associations, women's union, youth union or various religious bodies—which were established to bring most of the population under the umbrella of the national united front; secondly, through electing National Assembly and People's Council deputies (discussed in Chapter 7); thirdly, through joining the Communist Party (Chapter 6); fourthly, by writing letters to newspapers.

Since Party members are strategically located in all of the non-Party bodies, especially at the higher levels, this provides the Party both with access to information about the needs of people participating in these bodies and a means of disseminating and implementing the Party line within them. Letters to newspapers can also be used as a means of promoting debate and delimiting its scope within bounds set by Party policy. Party domination of the mass organizations (which also select candidates for election as deputies) thus puts it in a key position to tap popular opinion, including potential opposition to its policies (but excluding system-rejecting opposition, which remains outside the official political framework and which we will discuss below), to pass the information collected upwards, supplying inputs to the centralized decision-making processes of the Party. This means that participation in the political process is not only open to citizens who wish to become involved, but is not, contrary to the suggestion of many Western writers, an entirely meaningless activity.

The mass organizations thus have a dual function; on the one hand to implement Party and state policies in their area of responsibility—the function usually stressed in Western literature—and, on the other hand, to act as a transmission belt channelling information to the Party without which it could not formulate policies to meet changing conditions. Mass organizations do not normally function to express the interests of their members in an organized fashion as would be the case, for example, with Western trade unions. They are not seen as organized pressure groups: this would not be in keeping with the principle of democratic centralism, according to which there is a need for centralizing authority to override particular interests in the name of universal ones, and might also lead to the formation of organized political opposition, breaking down the carefully balanced unity that has enabled Party rule to sustain its broad legitimacy for so long. The mass organizations are expected to help contain opposition both by educating their members about the Party line and by keeping the Party adequately informed on any potentially explosive issues affecting their members. Failure to carry this out properly or failure of the Party to respond can result in serious problems for a socialist regime, as happened with the demand for independent trade unions in Poland and an outbreak of strikes in Yugoslavia in 1987. Thus while the possibility for members of these organizations to air critical views publicly is circumscribed, and while the channels through which problems can be raised are informal and the response uncertain, there are also definite limits upon the ability of Party and government to ignore such problems.

The Fatherland Front (Mat Tran To Quoc) is the most broadly based of the mass organizations. It was founded in North Vietnam in 1955 as the successor to the Lien Viet (League for National Union of Vietnam, an umbrella body established in 1946 incorporating the Viet Minh as well as other mass organizations such as the Women's and Youth Unions). In 1976 the Fatherland Front absorbed the National Liberation Front for South Vietnam and the Alliance of National Democratic and Peace Forces. Huynh Tan Phat, the former secretary of the NLF, became president of the Fatherland Front.

The Fatherland Front attempts to enrol the widest possible segment of Vietnamese society, including all 'patriotic' Vietnamese. Organizations which are affiliated include, apart from the above mentioned, the VCTU, Peasants' Association, Democratic and Socialist Parties, the Committee for Solidarity of Patriotic Vietnamese Catholics and the Vietnamese Buddhist Church. No figures are available on total membership of the Fatherland Front.

Of the other mass organizations, the Vietnamese Confederation of Trade Unions is accorded the highest prestige by the Party and government apparatus. Founded in 1946 to organize the tiny Vietnamese working class within the framework of the united front, the VCTU now has over 3 million members. In 1976 the South Vietnamese Trade Union Federation for Liberation was absorbed. This had been an illegal organization under the Thieu regime. Legally operating trade unions of the former regime were abolished, but as these had never acted independently of the southern government, the effective organizational capacity of southern workers was not fundamentally altered by this change. The VCTU functions essentially as an arm of the Vietnamese state concerned with welfare and working conditions of workers. The trade unions also participate in factory management, acting more like the industrial relations department of a capitalist firm than a Western trade union. An important proviso here, though, is that in Vietnam the state has awarded a large number of benefits to industrial workers which are not available in countries of comparable development levels and would probably not have been won by independently organized unions acting on their own. These benefits include two weeks annual leave, paid sick leave and maternity leave (six months), on the job training and in-service courses, some limited child-care facilities. This is not to say that trade unions do not act as an important conduit for expression of worker dissatisfactions, but they do not normally act to represent workers' interests to the Party.

While the trade unions have been mobilized to help implement the reforms in industrial management since 1985, they are currently in an awkward position because of the conflicting and often hostile response of workers to the new measures.

The Vietnam Women's Union was founded in 1930 which makes it the oldest of the mass organizations. It currently has 11.4 million members (*The Far East and Australasia*, 1986) which is more than a third of the female population, but around 80 per cent of the adult women, and is open to all women. Its president is Nguyen Thi Dinh, a former deputy commander of the NLF armed forces and one of the handful of women on the Party Central Committee. She is also a Vice-Chairman of the Council of State.

Like the trade unions, the Women's Union functions mainly to disseminate and implement Party policy among women, i.e. as an arm of the state. Historically, then, it has placed far more emphasis on mobilizing women to support the goals of national liberation and state socialism than organizing around specifically women's issues. During the war the VWU concentrated on the 'Three Responsibilities' movement to build 'socialist rear areas', urge husbands and sons to go and fight and to donate supplies to the armed forces. In addition to their more traditional roles, women all over Vietnam took responsibility for organizing local militia forces as well as production. Since 1975 the VWU has again mobilized women to support the war effort against Democratic Kampuchea and China and to contribute to boosting production. But in peacetime it has also tended to concentrate on numerous areas of social policy affecting women *in their traditional roles*. Because petty commerce has been traditionally an area of women's work, the VWU has organized campaigns to bring traders into cooperatives and because women are housewives they are mobilized into price-watch committees to report on and combat speculation and hoarding. The Union has also taken part in activities concerned with education and social welfare— for example, the holding of a Conference of Exemplary Mothers to help educate women in child care and the setting up of institutions for rehabilitating prostitutes or caring for war orphans.

As in the case of the trade unions, it has been the Party and government, rather than organization by the Women's Union *per se* which has been responsible for the main advances which women have made in achieving equality with men in Vietnamese society and in breaking down the traditional role structures. For several years after the war, however, the VWU had to sit by and watch the newly achieved status of women eroded in many areas as men took over responsible positions formerly held by women and 'normalcy' was restored to gender relations as well as to economic life (Eisen, 1984, p. 253). Though the Union did maintain its campaign to create a 'New Culture Family' based on greater equality within the household between men and women, it could do little about the changes taking place in society at large which obstructed further progress in this regard. By its own admission, the VWU had not found a way of overcoming the tenacity of 'feudal attitudes' among men (Eisen, 1984, p. 253).

In its report to the 5th Congress of Vietnamese Women held in May 1982 (shortly after the highly self-critical 5th Party Congress), the Central Committee of the VWU launched a strongly worded critique both of the shortcomings in achieving emancipation of women and of its own activities (Vietnam Women's Union, 1982). The report especially pointed to the difficulties created for women by the persistence of technologically backward production and the extra burden of combining housework and outside work under conditions of indequate transport, services and welfare establishments. The lack of full equality with men was emphasized as was the failure to make progress in spite of numerous laws and policies favouring them in principle. While men often did not take the policies seriously, the VWU also looked at its own role and called for a study of the concrete realities of women's lives as the basis for finding solutions, rather than the 'tedious and arid' political education it had previously concentrated on (Vietnam Women's Union, 1982, p. 39). The Union also saw a need to bring women's problems to the attention of other organizations such as the VCTU and Ho Chi Minh Youth Union, rather than limiting itself within the 'framework of its own hierarchy'.

Some concrete steps have been taken. A Centre for Women's Research has been established and several campaigns around issues affecting women in the work-force were undertaken—particularly in the areas of in-service training and promotion opportunities and maternity leave. The latter campaign, around extension of maternity leave from $2\frac{1}{2}$ to 6 months, was, according to Women's Union cadres, fought hard all the way up to the Political Bureau.[2]

Admittedly, these activities of the VWU have concentrated on issues affecting women who work for the state, as yet a rather small minority of the female labour force, though 35 per cent of state employees. Not yet tackled seriously have been the possibly deleterious effects on women's social position of the economic reforms in the countryside and, in spite of the wide-ranging debate in Hanoi in recent years, this may be too large a question at this stage. Economic benefits to the peasantry as a whole may still be more important to rural women than the less tangible losses of economic and social independence resulting from the product contract system. Much more information is needed about the effects on women before it becomes clear that they actually perceive their interests to be threatened. Thus the lack of response by the VWU so far may simply stem from the lack of a perceived need to respond.

I have dealt with the Women's Union at more length than the other mass organizations, largely because it is a body with which I am more familiar. Moreover, the activities of the VWU may be illustrative of the activities of the mass organizations in general, if for the most part they act as organs of the state in areas affecting their membership, but are also capable of articulating the interests of these members or even representing these interests to the Party leadership at times. In the case of the VWU, however, it may be the very lack of influentially placed cadres which has forced it to act more as an organized pressure group, where other mass organizations may be able to exert influence through less formal channels because they have more cadres who are also highly placed in government and Party. These are questions which require further investigation.

To my knowledge the other mass organizations have not been much studied and I know little about their operations beyond what has already been said in general terms. The youth organizations are, however, slightly different from the others in that they are seen as training grounds for future Party cadres. There are two organizations: the Pioneers, to which most primary school children belong, and the more overtly politicized Ho Chi Minh Youth Union, which, in 1986, had 4 million members (*The Far East and Australasia* 1987, 1986). These two bodies are charged with imbuing patriotic ideals, a collective spirit and commitment to Party rule among young people.

'System-Rejective' Opposition

Vietnam has no significant intellectual dissident movement like those of the European socialist states. This may be partly due to Vietnamese cultural heritage in which intellectuals were incorporated into the state via the mandarin system and partly due to the opportunities for dissident intellectuals to leave the country.[3] There was, however, a brief 'hundred flowers' interlude in the 1950s when a literary journal, *Nhan Van* (Humanities), appeared for a few issues before being closed by the government for going too far in criticizing Party policy (Duiker, 1983, p. 131). In the late 1970s a newspaper (*Tin Sang*), which published rather critical articles, was also permitted to exist in the South, but it was closed in August 1981 during a campaign against 'decadence', corruption and black marketeering, 'bad books and noxious music'. It may be going too far to describe *Tin Sang* as 'system-rejective'.[4]

There has also been large scale emigration by other groups who found themselves in fundamental opposition to Party policy (Chinese businessmen and supporters of the former South Vietnamese regime, for example). By far the majority of emigrants, however, have been people fleeing from difficult material circumstances caused by the extreme dislocation of the southern economy following US withdrawal and advent of the new system. The extent to which these can be described as political refugees is debatable. Their departure can be viewed as a form of protest at government policies in attempting to deal with a crisis which was only partly of its own making. In large measure, the flood of 'boat people' during the economic crisis of 1978–80 can be attributed to the lack of well-functioning mechanisms in the South for channelling information upwards to the central Party level, which would enable a potentially destabilizing situation to be defused through readjustment of policies. In the early years after re-unification, Party leaders fell victim to euphoria and over-optimism, on the one hand, and wariness of the southern urban population, on the other hand, which blinded them to the signals of an impending political crisis.

Among the remaining sources of opposition to Party rule, there are some which, though potentially disruptive, lack any real capacity to challenge the system. Such opposition is strongly suppressed by the regime, but this is only one reason for its inability to constitute a fundamental threat. The major reason is that it is highly fragmented, based on narrow sectional interests and lacking in appeal to the broader society.

This group includes FULRO (Front Unifié de Lutte des Races Opprimés), an organization of ethnic minorities along the border with Cambodia and Laos. Initially set up with French backing to combat the Viet Minh, it lapsed into obscurity in the 1970s, but has recently been revived with assistance from Thailand and China and carries out minor guerrilla activity in the mountain areas.

Another group which has been a source of opposition is the Chinese community. This group has always had a rather suspect loyalty—in the North because many retained Chinese citizenship and Party membership, in the South because of its class position and links with Taiwan. In 1971, at a time when relations with China were becoming strained, the DRV held a Congress of Overseas Chinese attended by 200 delegates, which urged them to contribute to 'the defence of the security of China' by joining the Vietnamese struggle against the United States (Woodside, 1971, p. 496).

Apparently an appeal to defend what was for most their country of birth was considered insufficient motivation. Tensions came to a head during 1978-9 as the two countries went to war and Chinese business in the South suffered from socialization measures. But the advent of economic reforms and a reduction of international tension has, at least for the time being, lowered the temperature.[5]

The third source of opposition is from religious groups. There are four major groupings: Catholics, Buddhists, Hoa Hao and Cao Dai, which have all at some stage expressed opposition to Communist authority. Of these, the Hoa Hao and Cao Dai are now probably the most acquiescent. The Hoa Hao are a fundamentalist Buddhist sect with an estimated following of $1\frac{1}{2}$ million (*The Far East and Australasia*, 1986), chiefly in the western Mekong delta. It strongly opposed the Communists after 1945 and had its own armed forces, but its hierarchy has been dismantled (Duiker, 1983, p. 11). The Cao Dai continues to have a significant following in the South (of around 2 million) and has been allowed to retain its hierarchy in spite of earlier antagonism towards the Communists.

Active religious opposition seems to have come mainly from Buddhists and Catholics. There have been several reports of arrests of Buddhist monks (mostly from the highly politicized An Quang pagoda in Saigon, which was also the source of opposition to the RVN regime) and the same is true of some Catholic priests and their followers, who have been accused of plotting with officials of the former regime to overthrow the government. Many of the latter group came to the South from North Vietnam in 1954 and were strongly committed to the Diem regime. Relations of the Party with the Catholic hierarchy in Vietnam were reasonably good, however, and links with the Vatican retained, though the rise of Solidarity in Poland since about 1980 has brought a deterioration in this situation.

Finally, there are the officials of the former regime itself. A number of these have organized a National United Front for the Liberation of Vietnam under a former vice-admiral of the RVN Navy. It is mainly California-based and in 1983 claimed to have 500 guerrillas operating inside Vietnam. It also has a radio station based on Thai territory. Most officials of the old southern regime underwent re-education in special camps after 1975. The vast majority were released before 1979, when the official figure of those still in detention was 20,000.[6] Many of these have since been released also. Large numbers have joined the lists of those leaving the country, while others have been re-arrested for plotting against the government or trying to leave illegally.

Part IV
The Economy

One of the most pressing problems facing the regime since 1975 has been that of incorporating the southern half of the country. This region, which had continued along a capitalist path of development during the first two decades of socialism in the North, proved to hold quite different political, social and economic problems from those which had faced the DRV in 1954. Nevertheless, this was not well understood at the time, and most DRV leaders appear to have felt that a fairly simple transference of the northern development strategy and social structures would suffice. In fact some important sectors of southern society resisted the implementation of the northern socio-economic system and this has led, in the 1980s, to a process of gradual re-evaluation and re-vamping of policy towards the South.

The picture in 1975 was clouded by the fact that the country had only just emerged from a long and costly war. Chronic shortages and low productivity of both industry and agriculture in the DRV were thought to be largely war-related and, subsequently, much of the continued poor economic performance during 1975–80 was attributed to wars with Pol Pot's Cambodia and with China. The ability of many of the older generation of revolutionary leaders to cling to these explanations delayed the rise to power of a reform-minded leadership which had already begun to express its critique of the 'heavy industry first' industrialization strategy as well as many of the bureaucratic aspects of collective agriculture in the mid-1970s. The latter group argued that the DRV's economic problems were not simply the result of war, but were generated by the operation of the socialist system itself.

Without the addition of the South and the decision, taken by 1976, to embark upon a rather quick socialist transformation program in that region, the much needed economic reforms in the North might have been further procrastinated. But, as we shall see below, it was precisely the attempt to transform the South along northern lines which precipitated an economic crisis in the whole country and gave the reformers their opportunity to seize the initiative.

Vietnam is unique among the socialist countries in having made the attempt to incorporate a large capitalist region into its socialist system two decades after the establishment of that system. The lessons of this attempt have proved vital to the future development of socialism in Vietnam and it is therefore impossible to understand the present structure and development of the Vietnamese economy without taking the unification process into account. In this part of the book, then, we will begin by looking at the economy of the DRV between 1954 and 1975. While the achievements of the DRV were not inconsiderable, especially given the enormous impact of the war, Chapter 9 will focus particularly on the weaknesses in the structure which rendered it unable to progress under the impact of the unification process. The following chapter will look at the southern economy as it stood at the end of the war and the factors which led to failure of the 'northern model'. The final chapter in Part IV will assess the process of integration since 1980 and the influence of economic reform on the overall structure and development of the Vietnamese economy today.

9 The Economy of the North, 1954–1979

In 1954, that part of Vietnam ceded to the DRV under the Geneva Agreement was an overwhelmingly agrarian society. Modern industry reportedly accounted for only 1.5 per cent of material output in 1954 (Le Chau, 1966, p. 225). From a population of about 13 million, only a few thousand were employed in modern industrial enterprises, chiefly the Nam Dinh yarn and textile mills, Haiphong cement plant, Hon Gai coalfields, some breweries and cigarette factories. A rather larger number were employed in small manufacturing workshops and, because of the system of contract labour, an even larger group—numbering many hundreds of thousands—had had some experience of wage employment in factories, mines and on the rubber plantations of southern Indochina. Nevertheless, the vast majority of the labour force was engaged in farming.

The reasons for this state of affairs were that in a little over ninety years of their *mission civilisatrice* in Indochina, the French had developed only those areas of the economy which could serve the metropolitan economy. French private investment in the colony was not especially large and was concentrated in developing the export of rice, rubber, maize, coal and rare minerals for French industry and agriculture. While textile, beer, cigarette and cement industries were developed to serve the Indochinese market, the majority of manufactured goods available in the colony were imported. The domestic market for manufactures was itself very restricted, owing to the heavy taxation and corvée burden imposed upon the peasants in a largely abortive attempt to render the state budget financially independent of France. On their departure in 1955 the French in any case dismantled most of the industries they had established.

The end result of the colonial period was the creation of an impoverished and embittered peasantry, who saw the solution to their problems in the VCP's political program of abolishing all the (highly regressive) French taxes, combined with the redistribution of land and elimination of rent and usury. The tax burden imposed on peasants had resulted in high levels of indebtedness and concentration of land ownership (Truong Chinh & Vo Nguyen Giap, 1974; Ngo Vinh Long, 1973). Reforms in this area were therefore begun by the DRV as early as 1953 in its liberated areas and then extended to the whole area north of the 17th parallel between 1954 and 1956 (Chapter 3).

In spite of political difficulties with the land reform, the period 1954–60 was one of rapid growth for North Vietnamese agriculture and saw a mushrooming of industry as well. By 1960 industry accounted for 18 per cent of national income (Nguyen Tien Hung, 1977, p. 104) and 7 per cent of employment (Vickerman, 1985, p. 230).

In 1959 the DRV embarked upon the collectivization of agriculture. In this it would appear to have followed the Chinese model up to a point. 'Mutual Aid' teams or 'Production Solidarity' groups were established first. These institutionalized already existing collective practices of traditional Vietnamese wet rice agriculture (such as joint transplanting and harvesting, lending of tools and draft animals). The next stage was the setting up of 'production collectives' (*tap doan san xuat*) or 'lower-level cooperatives'. Land and means of production were contributed to the production collectives in exchange for a small rent (in proportion to the amount contributed). A system of work-points was also established according to which workers were remunerated, in kind, after the harvest according to the number of workpoints accumulated by each individual. Norms were established for agricultural tasks (so many hectares ploughed per day, so much fertilizer distributed, etc.) and workpoints allocated on the basis of completion of these norms. Income was then distributed to workers from the harvest, *after* payment of the collective's taxes and compulsory deliveries to the state, as well as that portion set aside for collective accumulation and social funds. Facilities such as health clinics, child care and assistance for poor and disabled members of the collective were met from the latter fund.

Income distribution in the collectives was thus carried out according to a dual system of distribution according to means of production contributed, on the one hand, and labour, on the other. In the third and final stage of the collectivization process, in which the advanced production cooperatives (*hop tac xa*) were established, all remuneration was based on labour contribution and the rents to former owners of land and means of production were eliminated. By 1968, virtually all of North Vietnam's peasants were incorporated, at least on paper, into these advanced cooperatives. After this time, a process of gradually increasing the size of the cooperatives was set in motion by amalgamating smaller cooperatives, usually at village level, but nothing on the scale of China's communes was ever attempted (Elliott, 1976). Nor did the Vietnamese try any of the more radical aspects of Chinese communal life—communal eating, for example, which was experimented with during China's Great Leap Forward.

The impact of the collectives and cooperatives on the economy was mixed.

In 1960, the first full year, output suffered and a number of other features common to collectivization in other countries—reduction of livestock numbers, for example—were apparent. Subsequently, however, output rose consistently above 1950s levels and this seems largely to have been due to the labour accumulation projects carried out by the collectives. Over half of state investment in agriculture during the years 1960–4 went into the construction of irrigation and drainage schemes. But investment expenditure alone does not reflect the full extent of the effort, which was highly labour-intensive, making use of surplus labour resources in the collectives during slack periods of the agricultural calendar. The great advantage of carrying out these projects under collective auspices is that individual blocks of land can be consolidated in a way which rationalizes land use, water supply can be equitably controlled and adequate maintenance of channels can be ensured. When irrigated farming is carried out on a purely individual basis, disputes tend to break out over the location of channels and earthworks and over allocation of water (e.g. with farmers close to the source of supply leaving insufficient water for those further away). Difficulties also break out where individual farmers fail to carry out adequate maintenance of irrigation channels which others depend upon.

The irrigation works carried out by the collectives and cooperatives were responsible for increased cropping intensity[1] and rising labour productivity prior to 1965. The advent of collective farming also gave most Vietnamese women an independent source of income for the first time and enabled them to gain a voice in village councils.[2] Another economic advantage to women was the establishment of collectively-run child care and educational facilities, which gave them more time for remunerative labour. The establishment of health care centres and advances in the prevention of disease were beneficial to all levels of rural society and may have helped to improve the productivity of labour. Poor families were able to gain access to more advanced means of production, though these were not yet widespread, while the sight of human beings harnessed to the plough because they could not afford a buffalo or ox disappeared from the Vietnamese landscape.

The collective system did not perform as well as expected, however. Grain output levels tended to stagnate, after their 1961 recovery, at around the 6.5 million tonnes per annum mark (while population grew at more than 2 per cent per annum). This compared with a growth rate of nearly 10 per cent per annum during 1955–9, the period immediately after the land reform. Yields per sown hectare did not increase markedly during the 1960s either, though there were some improvements in labour productivity (measured by the somewhat crude yardstick of gross output per worker)

(Vickerman, 1985, p. 230), allowing the siphoning off of workers into industrial and other off-farm occupations.

The residual nature of peasants' remuneration in the cooperatives had important implications: in very poor areas or as a result of bad harvests, income distribution after the state and collective funds had taken their share could mean rather little was left over for the peasants. As a result, collectives frequently experienced difficulties in mobilizing labour and in maintaining labour productivity on collective land, as opposed to family plots which came to provide an increasing portion of peasant subsistence requirements (Gordon, n.d.; Beresford, 1985a). Cash incomes could be earned by sale of produce from these 'individual' or 'family' plots which were allocated to each member household from 5 per cent of the collective's land set aside for this purpose.

Rapid industrialization was also a feature of the period from 1959 to 1964. The modern industrial sector had been nationalized from the departing French, and the only sector left to non-state enterprises from then on was handicrafts. These were usually organized on a cooperative basis after the official phase of 'socialist transformation' began in 1957. The real value of industrial output grew by 15 per cent per annum (Nguyen Tien Hung, 1977, p. 140), with the output of the capital goods sector growing at almost 20 per cent per annum, during the early 1960s. Electricity, coal, cement and phosphate ore production rose by 300–1,000 per cent during 1957–65 while output of some key consumer goods like cloth, soap, paper, cigarettes and sugar rose at similarly spectacular rates (Nguyen Tien Hung, 1977, p. 144; Vo Nhan Tri, 1967, p. 231; Vien Kinh Te Hoc, 1980, p. 97). But, as in the collective agriculture system, problems were already beginning to appear in the industrial system by 1965. Shortage of all kinds of goods, but especially raw materials for industry, was to become a chronic and endemic feature of the DRV economy from this time onwards.

Unfortunately, the US bombing campaign, known as 'Rolling Thunder', which began in early 1965, obscured a major cause of these difficulties (which was the development strategy adopted by the regime) and led to a postponement of economic reform until the late 1970s. The effects of the bombing on the northern industrial economy were indeed drastic, so that many North Vietnamese leaders attributed sluggish growth afterwards to this cause, ignoring the pre-existing problem which the bombing had only served to exacerbate.

US bombing of the North, which was continuous from 1965 to 1968, was halted following the Communists' New Year (*Tet*) Offensive of 1968 and resumed with even greater intensity during 1972—culminating in the massive 'Christmas' bombing of Hanoi and Haiphong of that year. It does not appear to have affected agricultural output, in spite of the fact that the dykes protecting the countryside of the Red River delta from floods were a target and frequently breached. The data available do suggest, however, that industry was very seriously damaged. The index of real output value fell to only 92 per cent of its 1964 level in 1967 (*Vietnamese Studies*, 1976, p. 209) and Table 9.1 shows that physical output declined drastically as a result of the bombing.

Table 9.1 Output index of major industrial products

	1965	1968	1970	1972	1974
Electricity (kwh)	100	59	94	87	162
Coal (tonnes)	100	57	64	40	88
Phosphate ore (tonnes)	100	n.a.	32	29	25
Cement (tonnes)	100	12	91	27	61
Machine tools (no.)	100	n.a.	100	n.a.	110
Diesel motors (no.)	100	n.a.	105	n.a.	119
Electric rotary engines (no.)	100	n.a.	179	n.a.	165
Pig iron (tonnes)	100	n.a.	23	n.a.	76
Timber (cu. m.)	100	66	80	69	63
Car tyres & tubes (sets)	100	n.a.	90	n.a.	138
Chemical fertilizer (tonnes)	100	83	126	124	238
Ploughs & harrows (no.)	100	n.a.	171	n.a.	142
Livestock fodder processing machines (no.)	100	n.a.	25	n.a.	150
Insecticide (tonnes)	100	n.a.	93	n.a.	109
Paper (tonnes)	100	37	62	46	82
Rush mats (pairs)	100	n.a.	158	n.a.	128
Cloth (m.)	100	83	89	73	96
Chinaware (pces)	100	n.a.	113	n.a.	123
Fish sauce (litres)	100	n.a.	527	n.a.	532
Sugar (tonnes)	100	45	45	42	45
Cigarettes (packs)	100	100	131	122	164
Soap (tonnes)	100	50	50	62	75
Bicycles (units)	100	101	73	72	72
Salt (tonnes)	100	113	129	98	107

Source: Nguyen Tien Hung, 1977, p. 144; Vo Nhan Tri, 1967, p. 231; Vien Kinh Te Hoc, 1980, p. 97; *Vietnamese Studies*, 1976, p. 210.

Industrial disruption caused by the air war was only partially due to physical damage to plant—which was, however, of especial importance in the case of certain capital intensive and technologically complex industries like steel-making and coal-mining. Another problem was the massive destruction of communications and transport networks which hampered the ability of industry to obtain raw material supplies. The loss of expensive railways, bridges, etc., necessitated the allocation of even more investment funds for their restoration, further delaying increases in output of essential raw materials and consumer goods. The DRV response to the bombing campaign is justifiably well known: bridges were repaired innumerable times while industrial installations were dismantled and, along with most of the urban populations, evacuated to rural areas. Rapid decentralization of the economy under the pressure of bombing was one of the key elements enabling industrial production to continue throughout the war. Nevertheless, many of the external economies associated with urban concentration of industry would have been lost.

Chronic Economic Imbalance

Although agriculture was left largely to its own devices during the war and a *de facto* reversion to family farming was tolerated in many areas, the restoration of peace brought renewed pressure to advance the cooperativization process and, at the same time, revealed a number of important weaknesses in the cooperative system. These were to have ramifications for the functioning of the entire economy.

In the mid-1970s, a number of critics of the collective agriculture system were already pointing to the failure of output to expand rapidly (Table 9.2), the stagnation of land yields and, most importantly, the decline of labour productivity since 1972. The proximate causes of this poor performance were seen to be the inability of collective (as opposed to individual) farming to mobilize labour: peasants were both avoiding participation in collective work where possible and working at low intensity when they did turn up (Beresford, 1985a). The chief consequences, from the point of view of the socialist state, were that in spite of increasingly favourable (to farmers) terms of trade between industry and agriculture, marketed agricultural surpluses were insufficient to support the state's accumulation requirements. Moreover, the ever higher prices the state had to pay to acquire grain from the peasantry, in order to resell to urban workers at heavily subsidized prices, was, by the mid-1970s, a major drain on the state budget.

Table 9.2 Output and productivity of North Vietnamese agriculture

Year	Output m.t	Yield t/ha.	Labour productivity 1960 = 100	Year	Output m.t	Yield t/ha.	Labour productivity 1960 = 100
1955	4.4	1.72		1965–8	6.7	2.28	118
1957	4.9	1.92		1969–71	6.2	2.30	136
1958	5.4	2.06		1972	7.1	2.57	145
1959	6.4	2.43		1973	6.4	2.43	135
1960	5.4	1.98	100	1975	5.3	1.89	130
1961	6.7	2.24		1976	6.4	2.18	
1962	6.6	2.19		1979	6.2	1.91	
1963	6.7	2.22		1980	6.0	1.93	
1964	6.6	2.18					

Source: Nguyen Tien Hung, 1977, pp. 118, 127; General Statistical Office, 1980, pp. 56–7; 1983, pp. 56–7; 1985, pp. 89–90; Vickerman, 1985, p. 230.

Attention was turned to urgent measures to increase agricultural output and marketed surpluses that could be acquired by the state. Earlier efforts to improve output under collective management had concentrated on irrigation projects. These provided a once-off boost to production, by increasing the ability of land to sustain more than one crop. But as irrigation schemes grew in size and were extended to more difficult terrain they became more expensive to build and maintain with correspondingly lower returns to labour expended.

Initial increases in agricultural surpluses had been rapidly absorbed by the rising population and so a new way of renewing growth had to be found. The orthodox response was to increase the size of cooperatives and reform the management system to provide greater centralization of decision making, more technical expertise in agricultural management and to achieve economies of scale through increased division of labour. Reforms along these lines were accordingly introduced during 1972 (*Vietnamese Studies*, n.d.; Fforde, 1982), but without producing the desired result. Grain output in North Vietnam, after peaking at just over 7 million tonnes in 1972, fell to 6.4 million tonnes in 1973, 5.3 million tonnes in 1975, recovered to 6.4 million tonnes in 1976, but fell again to 6.2 million tonnes and 6.0 million tonnes in 1979 and 1980. This fall occurred in spite of a few individual success stories with the new management system (*Vietnamese Studies*, n.d.).

One problem was that the new management system represented an attempt to achieve greater national integration of the largely self-sufficient and autarchic villages by administrative methods in a society which lacked the resources and organizational skills to carry this out in a widespread and coherent manner. But this was not the only reason for the failure. In some areas where the prerequisites for success of the new system were not lacking, there was, nevertheless, a failure to sustain productivity growth following the reform. There were also occasional reports of peasant resistance to attempts by cadres to collect taxes and quotas (Nguyen Duc Nhuan, 1982).

A number of problems can be identified in the collective system of agriculture. These were not tackled by the 1972 reforms and have been the object of a new series of reforms introduced since 1979. These later reforms will be discussed in Chapter 11: here we will focus on the nature of the problems and their impact on output of agriculture and on the economy as a whole (for a more detailed treatment, see Beresford, 1985a).

(1) The division of labour

A major economic goal of the collectivization movement was to industrialize agricultural production, to transform it from small-scale, petty commodity production into a system in which economies of scale could be derived from production in much the same way that they are achieved in modern industry, i.e., by capitalization of the production process and reorganizing the labour force along proletarian lines. This goal has featured constantly in Vietnamese writing on collective agriculture (encapsulated in the slogan 'towards large-scale socialist production in agriculture') alongside the goal of 'collective mastery' meaning the socialization of the relations of production (i.e., the organization of production and appropriation of economic surplus on a collective or societal basis). Not only does technical change and the increased division of labour greatly enhance the productivity of labour and its surplus-producing capability, but, in Marxist theory, it is the collective nature of production by the factory proletariat in modern industrial economies which forms the material basis for the eventual overthrow of the system of private surplus appropriation based on private property. Collective agriculture in socialist theory therefore plays a dual role: on the one hand, its aim is to bring about a technical revolution in agriculture, leading to industrialization and productivity gains; on the other hand, by creating a new agricultural proletariat engaged in social, as opposed to individual production, it creates a firm basis for consolidating social appropriation and socialist property forms.

Much debate has occurred, however, over the way in which this should come about. There has been a divergence of views within the Vietnamese Communist Party over the possibility of consolidating socialist production relations in the absence of prior industrialization of the economy which could sustain rapid technical progress in agriculture. For those who take an affirmative view in this debate, the establishment of collective property relations and collectively organized labour is a sufficient condition. For example, Le Duan, then Secretary of the Party, speaking at an agricultural conference in 1974 claimed that the 'national democratic revolution' had created the necessary preconditions for collectivization, rather than it being the outcome of developing the forces of production (Le Duan & Pham Van Dong, 1975, p. 32). But as we have already seen, the reorganization of labour that occurred as a result of collectivization produced a one-off effect. The surplus expansion which resulted was soon absorbed by a fast growing population. On top of this the new organization of labour contained a number of characteristics which mitigated against further gains in output via increased labour productivity. Further increases would therefore have to come from capital inputs, which were not forthcoming because low agricultural surpluses hindered industrial growth, while imports were largely devoted to maintaining consumption levels of urban areas and to the development of a heavy industrial sector with few linkages to the rest of the economy.

The basic problem with the new division of labour in the cooperatives was that it gave a veneer of industrialization where in fact there was none. Peasants were divided into specialized production teams according to the type of work to be carried out (ploughing, spraying pesticide, fertilizing, cultivation, etc.). No one was given actual responsibility for or control over the final product, only for delivering so much fertilizer per hectare, or ploughing so many hectares per day. Quality control was difficult because of the time lapse and intervention of others in the production process between completion of the task and harvest time. Close supervision of these tasks was also difficult owing to the spatial dispersion of workers. Income received was directly related to the number of workpoints earned in a day, but the harvest from which it was distributed depended as much on the efforts of others as on one's own. There was thus an in-built tendency, in carrying out many jobs, for people to 'rely on others'. This problem was related to the technical aspects of agricultural production, which enabled individual workers to retain a large degree of control over their pace and quality of work (the only real constraints being seasonal and climatic). This can be contrasted with modern factory production in which the labour process is governed by machines[3] and problems of labour supervision and quality control are correspondingly reduced. Thus the new division of labour in Vietnamese cooperatives was artificial: it created problems of supervising labour because the cooperatives did not have the resources or skilled cadres to carry that out properly. Where supervision was inadequate, labour productivity declined. In many cooperatives the problem was resolved by *de facto* abandonment of collective production.

(2) The Incentive System

One reason for early success of collectivization had been that everyone benefited from the construction of irrigation schemes and the establishment of health, education and welfare facilities. But, in many cooperatives, the residual nature of workers' remuneration meant that peasant incomes did not rise and, in fact, many may have fallen below subsistence levels. This was particularly true of areas in which little or no real surplus was being produced above subsistence requirements. On most cooperatives there was in fact little internal accumulation, while state investment in agriculture was both small as a proportion of its total investment effort and concentrated upon state farms which contributed only a tiny proportion of the total output. The investible surpluses extracted from the cooperatives did not, therefore, contribute to growth of cooperative incomes (except in certain favoured areas) and thus a very real conflict of interest appeared between the cooperatives and the state.

In many cases, the purpose of the workpoint system—to distribute income according to labour—was defeated because once minimum food requirements had been met for all members, there was little left over. Compression of the share of total income going to workers therefore led to a very flat distribution of income between cooperative members and reduced incentives to work hard in the collective sphere. Moreover, much of the investment carried out by the collectives, which should have raised the productive power of the farms, was in fact wasted: peasants had little incentive to use machinery and chemicals effectively since increased collective output would result in increased siphoning off of surplus at low prices rather than rising peasant income.

Even though prices of key agricultural products (grain, pork meat) tended to rise relative to those of manufactured goods over the period up to the late 1970s (White, 1985, pp. 105-6) and taxes were periodically reduced, thereby raising the purchasing power of peasants, the real problem lay in the inability of many collectives to operate at a profit. Costs of production remained high compared to returns from collective farming and this problem was exacerbated by chronic shortages of manufactured goods, which forced many peasants and collective managers alike to resort to black market operations to meet their needs. Thus the lack of return on investment (of labour and capital) in collective agriculture provided a strong impetus for individuals to resort to the private sector. Low mobilization and low productivity of labour in the collective fields was matched by increasing attention devoted by peasants to their household plots. In some cases, collective land was itself illegally distributed to individual families (Gordon, n.d.).

Part of the poor performance of North Vietnamese agriculture, especially that of the second half of the 1970s, can be attributed to the uncertainties of climate (see Chapter 1). But the new management system, introduced in the early 1970s, did not help to overcome the effects of poor weather and indeed may have worsened them for the reasons outlined above. It did not tackle the lack of individual or collective incentive embodied in the system and in order to mobilize labour effectively it relied on supervision and administrative methods. These not only increased greatly the number of cadres needing to be supported by the already poor cooperatives, but were of dubious value for the consolidation of 'collective mastery'. The flow of agricultural produce to urban areas and industries dried up, resulting in the need for a massive food import program and shortages of raw material for industry. As an agricultural crisis bit in 1977–8, the ramifications began to be felt throughout the economy. But this was really only the intensification of a pattern that had persisted throughout the period since 1960.

North Vietnamese agricultural output had been sustained in spite of, rather than because of, the type of collective structures which had been established. The benign neglect which the countryside had experienced at the height of the war had helped to paper over the cracks, so it was not until peace was restored and the government made efforts to strengthen the 'socialist' character of the cooperatives that the real weaknesses of the system were fully exposed. What these weaknesses meant was that in the late 1970s when the attempt to incorporate the South coincided with a series of poor agricultural seasons and renewed hostilities, this time with Pol Pot's Cambodia and with China, the economy was unable to cope with the shocks. Instead of experiencing a downturn of a rising trend line of growth, the agricultural crisis of the late 1970s precipitated a reversal of economic growth, which, in the context of an economy as poor as Vietnam's, implied a renewal of the threat of famine for much of the northern population and called into question, for the first time, popular confidence in the leadership of the Communist Party.

Maurice Dobb (1967) has argued that the fundamental constraint on growth in underdeveloped societies is the size of the marketed agricultural surplus because it is this which determines the rate at which new workers can be absorbed into the industrial labour force. We can go further than this and point to the importance of an adequate subsistence wage for workers in maintaining the productivity of an existing labour force. If wages fail to rise in line with the cost of living or (as in the case of North Vietnam where part of wages for urban workers were paid in the form of a subsidized food ration) food supplies are reduced, labour productivity will decline correspondingly. Under wartime conditions, labour productivity may be maintained temporarily by use of moral incentives (exhortation to work for the war effort, for example), but even this device is likely to fail if wages (including the social wage) fall below minimum subsistence levels and the physical health of workers is affected. The failure of the collective agricultural system, at the micro-level, to produce sustained increases in marketed surpluses was thus a fundamental source of the problems of Vietnamese industry in the period under consideration. This failure was exacerbated at the macro-economic level by the development strategy pursued by the DRV government and by the government of the SRV up until the 1980s.

From the commencement of the First Five Year Plan (1st FYP) in 1961, the DRV had pursued a strategy of priority to 'heavy industry'[4] development. In this, it had followed the practice of most other socialist countries since Stalin had adopted the same policy for the Soviet Union in 1929. The theoretical basis of the strategy had been developed in the 1920s by Soviet economists, particularly Fel'dman, who had argued that the rate of growth was a function of the share of investment in national income. By raising the rate of investment and compressing the share of consumption (i.e., subsistence incomes of workers and peasants), more factories, railways and power plants could be built and the national income would grow much faster than if a higher share was consumed. In this view, the shortages of goods being experienced all over the socialist economies were attributed to lack of industrial development and the solution was seen as pushing industrialization at a faster pace. Like others before it, then, the Vietnamese government began to invest heavily in steel making, coal mining, electric power generation, rolling stock, machine tools, cement and other basic industries. The development of consumer goods industries received only a minor portion of the state's investment effort in industry (Table 9.3) and, although lip service was often paid in the DRV to the principle that a balance should be maintained between the growth of industry and agriculture, insufficient effort was devoted to the production of an increased supply of modern inputs for the agricultural sector.

The result was the development of an industrial structure with few linkages to the rest of the economy, which remained overwhelmingly agrarian and backward. During the war, most of the consumer goods reaching the population in the rural areas were imported from China. The Vietnamese steel industry obtained most of its raw materials from China and exported most of its output to China (White, 1982a, p. 10). Moreover, the establishment of technically complex industries (like steel making) in a country with poor infrastructural development and lacking a pool of industrially experienced and skilled workers, created abnormally large teething problems (see Rawski, 1980, pp. 22–4, for comparison with China). The tying up of resources in large-scale construction projects created demands (for wage goods and raw materials) that could not be met by existing industrial capacity nor through imports because of the scarcity of foreign exchange. The consequences were that such construction projects tended to drag on well beyond their scheduled completion time, while failure of new productive capacity to come on stream at the designated time, led to further

Table 9.3 Structure of state investment outlays, 1955–84 (percentages)

Year	Industry	Agriculture	Industry by group		Industry by management	
			Group A†	Group B‡	Central	Regional
Democratic Republic of Vietnam						
1955–57	31	15	66	34	100	—
1958–60	46	12	67	33	98	2
1961–64	53	21	78	22	94	6
1965–68	33	14	82	18	75	25
1969–71	40	21	76	24	75	25
Socialist Republic of Vietnam						
1975	—	14	—	—	65	35
1976	32	20	67	33	63	37
1977	32	26	76	24	63	37
1978	32	24	69	31	59	41
1979	36	24	72	28	67	33
1980	41	19	72*	28*	74	26
1981	42	27	84	16	74	26
1982	53	16	85	15	75	25
1983	40	17	—	—	71	29
1984	36	24	—	—	71	29

* Estimate.   † Producer goods.   ‡ Consumer goods.
Sources: General Statistical Office, 1980, pp. 39, 41, 44; 1983, pp. 39, 41, 44; 1985, pp. 75–6.

imbalances downstream. Because of supply uncertainties, enterprise managers had a strong incentive to hoard scarce materials, thus exacerbating the shortages, or resort to parallel markets causing the government to lose control over economic activity.

Even before the US bombing affected output in the mid-1960s, there were reports that industrial capacity utilization rates were only around 50 per cent, the main cause of the problem being a chronic shortage of raw material supplies and spare parts. Moreover, both workers and management cadres were affected by the shortages of food and other basic wage goods. Unable to obtain sufficient means of subsistence through the official state distribution system, urban employees were forced increasingly to resort to the free market. But state wages were too low to afford the higher prices on the free market and so many employees had to take second jobs in the private sector, often resorting to moonlighting and illegal use of state property for private purposes. The disappearance of building materials, for example, from state construction companies was a common occurrence. Workers could earn much higher salaries working on their own account at weekends, than for a 40-hour week in their state firm or government office. Enterprise managers would often condone the practice, in exchange for a cut, or engage in their own black market purchases and sales, sometimes for personal profit, sometimes simply to enable the firm to meet its plan. These factors made the shortages and low labour productivity of the state sector worse and also helped to undermine the socialist goals of the regime in so far as the private sector, in spite of government efforts to suppress it, became one of the chief means of keeping the economy viable.

The other major means of relieving the problem was foreign aid. During the war, North Vietnam received substantial amounts of foreign aid from China, the Soviet Union and Eastern Europe (Table 9.4). After 1960 a very high proportion of this aid was devoted to imports of capital goods and raw materials, but after 1965 it would seem that the emerging shortages of consumer goods forced a switch towards imports of these goods. At the end of the war, however, a number of factors combined to ensure that the beneficial effects of this aid would decline. On the one hand, the terms on which aid was given began to shift: Soviet aid, which tended to come in the form of long-term, low-interest or interest-free loans, grew in importance, while Chinese aid, which tended to be in the form of grants, showed a relative decline. The need to repay loans required that the aid could show (directly or indirectly) a rate of return if Vietnam was not to acquire a Mexican-style debt problem.[5] This contributed to the rise of Soviet pressure in the late 1970s and early 1980s for Vietnam to make more effective use of its aid and to pay more

Table 9.4 Estimates of foreign aid to socialist Vietnam (US$ millions per annum)*

Year	China	Soviet Union	Eastern Europe	Other	Total
Democratic Republic of Vietnam (average)					
1955–65	42	33	8	—	88
1965–75	149	178	80	n.a.	n.a.
Socialist Republic of Vietnam					
1976	n.a.	500	142	192	n.a.
1977	n.a.	500	142	305	n.a.
1978	—	500	142	459	n.a.
1979	—	n.a.	n.a.	419	n.a.

* These are Western estimates and highly conjectural.
Sources: Honey, 1962, p. 115; Thrift & Forbes, 1986, pp. 58, 72; Fforde, 1985, p.195.

attention to the problem of investment effectiveness in general. On the other hand, Chinese commodity aid, which had contributed so much to stabilizing Vietnamese society during the war (by supplying grain for the urban population at the rate of about half a million tonnes a year (Siamwalla & Haykin, 1983, p. 66; Fforde, 1982, pp. 49–50) as well as other consumer goods and raw materials), was stopped in 1975, amid deteriorating relations between the two countries. Vietnam was now faced with achieving self-sufficiency in grain—in the longer term the South could be expected to fill this role—or using its scarce foreign exchange reserves to import grain. Even without the agricultural crisis which beset the South in the late 1970s (see next chapter), lack of transport facilities would prevent extensive shipments of grain to the North in the short run, so the second option, of food imports, was the only real choice (Table 9.5). Reduced foreign aid levels after 1975 therefore placed further pressure on resources, given the essential continuation of the 'heavy industry' priority of the Second FYP (1976–80) and increased imbalances in the economy.

Conclusion

At the time of unification of the country the North Vietnamese economy had achieved a high level of socialization: most peasants were members of

Table 9.5 Grain imports to Vietnam 1975–84, ('000 tonnes)

Year	Rice	Wheat and wheat flour	Maize
1975	350	463	141
1976	148	497	89
1977	197	971	96
1978	35	1278	105
1979	287	1281	20
1980	193	731	48
1981	12	443	–
1982	197	127	–
1983	42	43	–
1984	*	359	n.a.

* Figure for wheat and wheat flour includes rice imports.
Source: General Statistical Office, 1979, p. 66; 1980, p. 87; 1983, p. 74; 1985, p. 167.

cooperative units and nearly all staple food production was carried out by these units; industry had also been incorporated into the socialist sector—modern industrial plants were owned by the state at the central or provincial level and handicrafts were run by cooperatives set up by districts or within agricultural cooperatives. But this socialization of ownership had not been accompanied by very effective forms of socialized production: powerful incentives existed in the way both industry and agriculture were organized for workers and peasants to transfer much of their productive effort to non-collective and non-state activities—either the legitimate activities of family plots, or the illegitimate black market variety. While some recognition of these problems had begun to emerge in the DRV by the end of the war, it was not yet widespread—the difficulties of managing a war-time economy and the availability of foreign aid diverted attention from them. The program for transformation of the South thus took the establishment of the same institutions for granted. However, the reactions of southerners to the imposition of the 'northern model' were a key element in bringing about a fundamental process of reform, as we shall see in the following chapters.

The economic problems facing Vietnam at the end of the Second Indochina War were immense. Not only were there serious difficulties to be overcome in the North (VCP, 1977, pp. 30–4), but there was also the question of how to deal with the extensive war damage, social dislocation (war refugees, prostitution, drug addiction, orphans, hostile political elements, unemployment) and economic chaos of the South.

A great deal of attention has been focused on US bombing campaigns against North Vietnam, but it is often forgotten that the South suffered far more extensive and sustained bombing during the war. Ecological damage was also largely confined to the South where some 72 million litres of herbicides were sprayed over about 12 per cent of the forest area and 5 per cent of agricultural land, mainly during Operation Ranch Hand in the late 1960s (Vietnam Courier, 1983). Apart from long-term effects on the health of the population, which are still only partly understood, the most lasting effect of this defoliation appears to have been extensive erosion of top soil, making subsequent recovery of the economy of affected areas difficult. In the first few years after the war a highly dangerous campaign to remove unexploded ordnance from agricultural land was also carried out, resulting in numerous accidental deaths. Even today, peasants are occasionally killed or maimed in this way. So many bombs were dropped and mines laid that not all have yet been discovered.

In addition, the war and the existence of large armies (over 1 million South Vietnamese armed forces, half a million Americans at peak strength in 1969, plus tens of thousands of Australians, Filipinos, New Zealanders, South Koreans and Thais) created enormous social problems in South Vietnam's cities. Approximately 10 million people, or half the population of the South, were uprooted during the war (Thayer, 1982). Many of these were herded into concentration camps called Strategic Hamlets where they were supposed to be safe from attack by the National Liberation Front. In fact, this method of rural 'pacification' proved disruptive to agricultural production and normal village life and the Hamlets did not succeed in achieving their aim of isolating the poplation from NLF influence. They were eventually torn down by their residents.

Many people also moved into South Vietnam's urban areas. The Saigon urban agglomeration grew from an estimated 500,000 people in 1945 to 3.5–

4 million thirty years later (Nguyen Khac Vien, 1985, p. 140; Thrift & Forbes, 1986, p. 153); Da Nang, on the central coast, grew even faster, from 50,000 in 1955 to over half a million by 1975 and other cities like Nha Trang, Quy Nhon and Can Tho also underwent population explosions. Many of the new urban dwellers found employment in the service of the military establishment, while others survived as best they could. By the end of the war, there were approximately 3 million unemployed in the southern cities (about half of these in Saigon alone). There were an estimated half million women engaging in prostitution, 100,000 drug addicts, 400,000 amputees, 800,000 orphans and millions of persons suffering from disease (see Nyland, 1981, p. 438). Because of the rapid urbanization, housing and infrastructure were inadequate in the cities: nearly half the population of Saigon was said to inhabit slums; water and sewage drained unprocessed into the river; parts of the city were periodically flooded; electricity supply was inadequate and food had to be brought from as far away as Dalat in the highlands (Thrift & Forbes, 1986, p. 153).

By the end of the war, a third of the southern population lived in cities. But these were not industrial cities, they were parasitical cities sustained by American aid and by US military and related expenditure. US economic assistance was provided under the Commercial Import Program (CIP) and was tied to goods purchased in the United States or in one of a small number of approved countries. Under this program, South Vietnam imported a range of goods—from the food required to feed its urban populations (over half a million tonnes of grain a year) to luxury items, as well as raw materials for the few industries which had been established and agricultural inputs. In the late 1960s, the US aid which financed these imports amounted to as much as one-third of South Vietnam's GNP (Asian Development Bank, 1971, p. 617). Over the period 1960–74 it enabled the southern population to spend, on average, the equivalent of 115 per cent of its Gross Domestic Product annually without incurring external debt (Le Khoa *et al*., 1979, p. 114).

In the face of the consumer bonanza brought on by US aid, the uncertainty engendered by war and the ready availability of essentially unproductive employment (both legal and illegal) in the service and commercial sectors, the productive capacity of the South Vietnamese economy stagnated. Exports declined drastically. South Vietnam became a net importer of rice from 1965 and rubber exports fell from an average of 75 million tonnes p.a. in 1958–62 to 26 million tonnes average in 1969–73 (Le Khoa *et al*., 1979, pp. 43–4, 136, 138). While these traditional exports were to a small extent replaced by new ones in the final two years of the southern regime (especially by marine and timber products), the regime's export income was only able to cover 3 per cent of imports in 1969–70 (Asian Development Bank, 1971, pp. 596–7).[1]

Industrial production suffered a similar fate. The share of manufacturing output in GDP fell from 11 per cent in 1960 to 6.5 per cent in 1972 (while services increased their share from 48 per cent to 52 per cent) (Le Khoa *et al.*, 1979, pp. 117–18). GDP itself grew only very slowly, at 2.8 per cent per annum (in constant 1960 prices) from 1960 to 1974—a per capita decline (Le Khoa *et al.*, 1979, p. 114). Most of the industries in existence in 1975 had already been established prior to 1954 and production was concentrated in a few areas—chiefly beverages (in fact two French-owned breweries from which 30 per cent of total industrial output was derived in 1970), tobacco (a further 13 per cent), food processing (10 per cent), textiles (9 per cent), and chemicals (8 per cent) (Moody, 1975, pp. 89–90). There was also a diversity of other small industries, but all except the more traditional ones (e.g. fish sauce making, rice milling) were almost completely dependent upon imported raw materials and spare parts and suffered very severe shortages when US aid was cut in 1975. Some of these had the capacity to recover quickly by using locally produced raw material (e.g., sugar refineries, cigarette manufacturers) and some were able to make ingenious use of left-over war material, etc., but others which were engaged in assembly of imported machinery or required imported parts or inputs continued to experience difficulties for a number of years as a result of both the US trade embargo (imposed in May 1975) and continued foreign exchange scarcity.

The problem of transforming the urban areas of South Vietnam was, then, vastly different from that facing the regime in the North in 1954, simply because of the scale of these cities, but with the additional factor that unlike the North, where, in the period immediately after Geneva, people hostile to the socialist regime were able to emigrate to the South or to France, no equivalent evacuation from the South had been organized in 1975. This meant both that the regime had to compete economically with entrenched private capital in the South and that it was suspicious of large segments of the South Vietnamese population and failed to make good use of intellectuals and skilled administrators and workers—even those who sympathized with the regime.

In the rural areas of South Vietnam there had been fundamental social transformation in the two decades since 1954, largely as a result of the revolutionary movement. The pattern of land ownership established under the French colonial regime had been one of acute inequality, with the majority of peasants farming as tenants on the estates of a relatively small number of landlords, many of them absentee landlords residing in the cities.

The wealth of these landlords derived from their extraction of agricultural surplus as rent. This surplus formed the basis of the export trade before 1965. But productivity of agriculture did not rise because landlords lacked interest and tenants the means of investing in new techniques. As pressure to increase surplus extraction for export increased and population also rose, the consumption of peasants fell accordingly (Norlund, 1986).

Land reforms and rent reductions were begun by the Viet Minh during the First Indochina War and were a major contributing factor to the popularity of the Communists in the rural areas. In some areas these reforms were reversed by the Ngo Dinh Diem regime which carried out its own reform in 1956. This reform was rather generous to landowners who, at that time, provided one of the political mainstays of the Diem regime (Sansom, 1970). After the founding of the NLF in 1960 and the rapid gains made by the Communists between 1961 and 1965, the Communist reform process was resumed and, in a belated attempt to defuse the land issue and restore its own position, the Thieu government also carried out a reform in 1970–2 (the Land To The Tiller Program). In Nam Bo, where this last reform had its greatest impact, the effect was largely to ratify occupation of land by peasants to whom the NLF had previously allocated it.

By the mid-1970s, then, the distribution of landownership in the leading rice-producing area, the Mekong delta, was fairly egalitarian. Only a quarter of peasants were classified as poor: the rest were 'middle' or 'rich', which meant that they had access to at least enough land and means of production to sustain their families by farming (Table 10.1). It was these peasants who now produced the marketed grain surplus in the South—estimated at about

Table 10.1 Land distribution in eight villages of the Mekong River delta in 1978

Category	% households	% land	Average land per capita (ha.)
1. Non-agricultural households	2	*	0.04
2. Agricultural labourers	23	8	0.12
3. Lower middle	57	56	0.35
4. Upper middle	15	25	0.57
5. Rich	3	11	1.19

* Less than 0.5 per cent.
Source: Tran Huu Quang, 1982, p. 32.

half of total output of the delta region (Ngo Vinh Long, 1984, p. 287). With the abolition of landlordism and retention of agricultural surpluses by peasants themselves, the opportunity arose, not only for peasants to increase their living standards, but to invest in modern farm inputs to increase productivity of the land. Thus a substantial market developed in the rural areas of South Vietnam for the goods imported under CIP. Consumption of imported fertilizer, agricultural machinery and manufactured consumer goods rose dramatically in the period 1969–74 and with it came a boost to agricultural output and productivity (Table 10.2).

Table 10.2 Rice production in South Vietnam, 1956–84

Year	South Vietnam* m.t.	Mekong Delta m.t.	Growth rate (whole South)* % p.a.
1956–59 av.	3.3	—	6.9
1960–64 av.	5.0	—	9.5
1965–69 av.	4.7	—	−0.4
1970–74 av.	6.5	—	6.8
1975	5.4	4.2	−23.9
1976	6.6	4.7	22.2
1977†	6.0	4.4	−9.1
1978†	5.5	4.0	−8.3
1979	6.3	4.4	14.5
1980	7.3	5.3	15.9
1983	8.6	6.3	5.6‡
1984	9.4	6.9	9.3

* South Vietnam includes Quang Nam Da Nang southwards after 1975. † Estimates.
‡ Average 1981–3.
Source: Le Khoa *et al.* 1979, p. 136; General Statistical Office, 1980, p. 59; 1985, p. 97.

The condition of South Vietnamese agriculture in 1975 was therefore very different from that of the North in 1954. Not only was there no large class of very poor peasants demanding land redistribution and access to means of production, but the relatively high level of capitalization and existence of a growing output surplus meant that the advantages of collectively organized labour-intensive hydraulic projects were not immediately apparent to the majority of peasants. Moreover, the efforts of the new government to intervene in the established market system of the South, in combination with acute shortages created by withdrawal of the US aid prop, made the transition period after April 1975 very difficult (see below). As in the urban areas, the regime's transitional program was met by passive resistance which culminated in the generation of a national economic crisis by the late 1970s.

The Crisis of Socialism in the South

In contrast to some American expectations, there was no bloodbath in South Vietnam following the communist victory—in spite of the fact that relatively few Vietnamese collaborators or anti-communists had been able to evacuate (see Snepp, 1980, for an eyewitness account of the US failure to evacuate most of its 'at risk' personnel). As in the North two decades earlier, the regime pursued a policy of economic restoration prior to beginning the transition to socialism. Therefore, only those enterprises whose owners refused to cooperate with the new regime were nationalized at first. Most small and medium-sized businesses remained in private ownership. Even foreign businesses were allowed to continue operating, though few took advantage of the offer in view of the regime's interventionist approach to the market economy and the US trade embargo imposed in May. There was some effort to bring the economy under state control via monetary policy, although most locally-owned banks stayed open, while other measures were taken to halt currency speculation (Nyland, 1981, p. 439). In September there had already been raids on homes and offices of some of the wealthiest Cholon families as part of a campaign against speculation and black marketeering. In agriculture some rich officials and landowners had their property confiscated and redistributed to poor peasants, but it was not until mid-1976 that a more *dirigiste* approach—fixing prices for compulsory quota sales and for state supplied inputs—began to be applied.

One of the key platforms of the development strategy pursued in the South after 1975 was the creation of New Economic Zones (NEZs). These were designed to fulfil a dual function of boosting the area of land under cultivation (including recovery of former agricultural areas which had been damaged and abandoned during the war) and absorbing surplus labour from the swollen southern cities and overcrowded northern deltas. Given the wartime legacy of very high unemployment in the South, the NEZs were seen as a way of rapidly expanding the productive labour force and output with a minimum of capital expenditure. Volunteers were given tools, basic housing materials and six months' food supply and expected to carve out an existence in the zone to which they were assigned. NEZs were slated to contain highly specialized farms producing rice in the Mekong delta, but cash crops for industry and export in the foothills and mountain provinces. Large numbers of state farms were established, as well as cooperatives.

From the beginning, the NEZ program ran into serious problems in retaining labour. Conditions were very harsh, especially for former urban dwellers with no previous farming experience. In spite of substantial state investment in the state farms, the remuneration to workers was low, living conditions difficult and productivity disappointing. Large numbers of *émigrés* began to drift back to the cities—a move in itself entailing a considerable degree of economic insecurity. But in response to the situation the authorities began to use the armed forces and 'youth brigades' to carry out the initial work of clearing land and building infrastructure (schools, clinics, roads, canals, etc.) and once this had been done the zones began to be more successful in holding people. A further boost came with the introduction of economic reforms (Chapter 11), which enabled those living in the NEZs to improve their incomes greatly. By 1985 about 2 million people had moved to the zones, more than half from the North, and 600–700,000 hectares were in production.

In 1976, with economic recovery proceeding well, those in the leadership who favoured a fairly rapid move to the 'socialist transition' stage began to press for more radical measures. They were strengthened in their determination to proceed on this path by the continued activity of private capitalists in undermining the government's grain purchase policy through hoarding and speculation. From now on, more stringent efforts were made to control the bourgeoisie by pressuring them to enter joint-ventures with the state (including provision for worker participation in management) (Nyland, 1981, p. 441). In early 1977 the government also turned towards collectivization of agriculture. The feeling that this should be hastened was reinforced by a succession of poor harvests and in 1978 it was announced that the collectivization of southern agriculture should be completed by 1980. This more radical turn after 1976 was in keeping with the decision to proceed with formal political reunification of the country in July 1976.

By 1978, however, an atmosphere of crisis hung over Vietnam. For the second year in succession harvests were poor and state procurement of grain had fallen in the South. Escalation of war with Pol Pot's Cambodia was causing a flood of refugees from the border regions—only about half the estimated 750,000 refugees came from within Cambodia itself; the rest were Vietnamese fleeing from artillery bombardment and cross-border raids by

Pol Pot armies. Two important South Vietnamese cities, Chau Doc and Tay Ninh were badly damaged and the settlement of New Economic Zones was severely disrupted.

In addition, the activities of the predominantly Chinese private business-men had not been curbed by regulatory measures so far introduced and the temptation for the more orthodox leaders to respond by bringing in even tighter measures was great. In fact the ability of Cholon-based rice merchants to undermine the government's grain purchase policy by pushing up free market prices through hoarding and speculation was a key element in the decision to accelerate the nationalization and collectivization of the southern economy. So in March 1978 a campaign of repression against large private traders was launched.[2] Small traders were allowed to remain in business until employment in production could be found for them, but only if they traded in goods not controlled by the government. Guards were placed on private premises until government stocktakers had completed inventories and removed goods. These measures were followed by a currency reform establishing a single nation-wide currency and setting a fairly low ceiling on the amount of old currency which could be exchanged unconditionally.

While these reforms succeeded in giving the government greater control over trade in the short run, they were instrumental in bringing about the exodus of 'Boat People'. During 1978 and 1979 an estimated 150,398 and 270,882 persons left the country (Thrift & Forbes, 1986, p. 134), a dispropor-tionate number from the southern Chinese community. Moreover, it is not at all certain that the immediate economic impact was that desired by the government. Many people's cash holdings were converted to gold and hidden (as is evidenced by the vast amounts of gold paid to Singapore-based shipowners and corrupt Vietnamese officials engaged in the refugee traffic (Wain, 1981; Grant *et al*., 1979). In 1978, following the campaign against private traders, the level of government grain procurement fell still further from its already low levels, while complaints intensified that grain and other 'state-controlled' goods were being diverted to the black market. Critical shortages of pesticides, fuel and other key agricultural inputs meant that when bad weather and insects threatened, farmers were unable to save their crops. Farmers concentrated on ensuring adequate food for their own families and in any case lacked incentive to produce marketed surpluses because they could not buy manufactured goods in exchange. The acute shortages in state trade networks meant that goods were not delivered, or were of poor quality, while the very high prices prevailing in uncontrolled markets were an obstacle to all but the richest farmers. There was a general reduction in economic activity. No firm evidence is available as to the extent to which the nationwide fall in state procurement (Table 10.3) occurred in the south, but there are plenty of indications that this is where the main problem occurred. In 1976, only 50 per cent of the state purchasing target for the Mekong delta had been met. In 1977 the procurement rate was 'even lower' and in the first three months of 1978 the rate was less than half that of the same period of the previous year. This was the situation prior to the 1978 clampdown on private trade, but it should be noted that after the reform, national procurement continued to decline (Table 10.3), in spite of a recovery in output levels due to better weather in 1979. It was only after the socialization measures were relaxed in the economic reforms of September 1979 that state procurement was able to rise.

Table 10.3 State grain procurement, 1975–84

Year	State grain procurement (million tonnes)				
	Total	Agricultural tax	Quota sales	Negotiated sales	Per cent of crop
1975	1.69				15%
1976	2.03				15%
1977	1.84	1.18	0.66	0	14%
1978	1.59	0.52	1.06	0	12%
1979	1.40	0.67	0.69	0.04	10%
1980	2.01	0.90	0.86	0.24	14%
1981	2.50	0.91	0.86	0.73	17%
1982	2.90				17%
1983	3.75	*	3.37	0.38	22%
1984	3.86				22%

* Included under 'Quota sales'.

Sources: IMF, 1982, p. 13; General Statistical Office, 1980, p. 61; 1985, p. 159; *Far Eastern Economic Review*, 10 February 1983, 2 February 1984.

In the meantime, the consequences of falling agricultural output and procurement in 1977–8 included widespread food shortages as well as crucial shortfalls in the supply of agricultural exports (needed to finance imported machinery, fuel, etc.) and raw material supplies. This soon began to affect industrial production in both halves of the country, especially as workers in state-owned enterprises were forced, by rising free market prices, to devote most of their energy to work outside the state system in order to survive. The productivity of industry was thus affected by both raw material shortages and by low labour productivity. Managers of state and joint state–private enterprises often resorted to the black market themselves in order to sustain production and the government increasingly lost control over the economy. Plans were drawn up, but they no longer counted for anything more than an exhortation to produce.

The effect was further exacerbated by rising tension with China and with the ethnic Chinese minority within Vietnam, which increased the refugee exodus. The Chinese invasion along the North Vietnamese border in February–March 1979 severely affected chemical fertilizer production (the main phosphate ore mine was destroyed), coal and other important industries (e.g., the anise oil plant at Lang Son was totally destroyed).

By 1980 less than half the country's industrial capacity was in use and output of key industrial commodities like steel, cement, coal, chemical fertilizer, water pumps, insecticides, diesel motors, machine tools, cloth, bicycle tyres and tubes, porcelain, paper, glass products, salt, cigarettes and fish sauce had tumbled from their 1978 or 1979 levels (General Statistical Office, 1980, pp. 32–3; 1983, pp. 32–3; 1985, pp. 44–5).

While many of these problems can also be ascribed to the conditions of the North Vietnamese economy described in Chapter 9, a large portion of the difficulty must be allocated to the policies pursued in the South. Again this is due to the fact that the transition model followed in the South was much the same as that employed in the North two decades earlier and which had already led to problems there. But if the model was no longer appropriate for the North itself, an even greater difficulty was caused by the special conditions of the South which were not very well understood by the leadership at the time it had taken over from the Thieu regime.

The key to understanding these special conditions is the much higher level of commercialization of the southern economy prior to 1975 compared to the North in 1954. Whereas the northern economy had been over-whelmingly agrarian and technologically backward at the time of the Communist victory, the southern economy in 1975 comprised a large market-oriented farm sector, an even larger tertiary sector and a tiny import-dependent manufacturing sector. In fact all areas of the southern economy were locked into a market system which had been sustained by American aid-financed imports. When this aid was cut off in May 1975 and stocks were run down, the southern economy naturally underwent severe dislocation and shortages of goods which people had become accustomed to using were acute.

The hiatus in supply was to some extent filled by an influx of goods from the DRV (which, however, served to intensify the shortages experienced in the North) and this did probably help ameliorate a potentially explosive political situation in the South. Nevertheless, the shortages persisted in the South and in this case the application of a system of official administrative prices based on those prevailing in the DRV was bound to aggravate the situation.

It is worth remembering that during the early transition period in North Vietnam the imposition of state-controlled grain prices had been carried out in a situation where grain supplies were adequate to meet the needs of the population. Official prices were, at first, above the rather low prices prevailing in the free market and so the state had little difficulty in acquiring whatever it needed (White, 1985). In the South, on the other hand, there was a grain shortage from the outset in 1975, in spite of the much higher proportion of output normally marketed. This shortage existed mainly because of the much greater non-agricultural population, which had to be supported. Over a third of the population lived in urban areas and many of those still living in the countryside either were no longer engaged in agricultural occupations (possibly as much as 5 per cent of the rural population (Tran Huu Quang, 1982, p. 32)), or, as agricultural wage labourers (23 per cent), had to resort to the market for food. In all, the marketed grain surplus of the South was required to support well over half the population. In the North, only 11 per cent of the population was urbanized in 1975 (Thrift & Forbes, 1986, p. 89) and possibly another 3 per cent were in the armed forces, which were only partially self-sufficient in food, but all agricultural workers (65–70 per cent) were remunerated in kind under the collective system. In spite of this lesser dependence on marketed (or procured) grain, the regime still found it necessary to import substantial quantities of grain each year, owing to the low productivity of northern agriculture. Before 1975 the southern cities had been largely supplied by US PL 480 imports. After 1975 the cost of importing grain had to be met from scarce foreign exchange resources, which were thereby diverted from other uses. But more importantly, the prices fixed by the state for grain were the same as those currently prevailing in the North of the country (White, 1985), and bore no relation at all to market conditions in the South. In fact these prices were well below prevailing market prices and so, with private trade channels still undisturbed, the government could not hope to gain control over the market. Even after the campaign against the Cholon rice merchants in 1978 the system of price incentives still in operation mitigated against peasants selling to the state and in favour of the rapid re-emergence of a strong black market.

Prices of industrial goods were similarly established without regard to their actual scarcity value and thus with an in-built temptation for corrupt cadres and others to divert them to the black market. Even the fact that the official terms of trade of agricultural and industrial goods had been drifting in agriculture's favour did not help farmers because returns to the sale of grain at official prices were often insufficient to cover costs of basic inputs and consumer goods. In theory, a system of two-way contracts was in operation whereby grain purchases by the state would be matched by inputs sold to peasants at low state prices. In practice, the government usually did not control enough quantities of these inputs and even though peasants signed contracts, they did not receive the fertilizer, fuel, insecticides, etc. they required in exchange in time. The attempt to implement a system of administrative pricing was therefore counter-productive to the procurement goals of the government.

The collectivization campaign, which was stepped up in 1978, was also affected by these developments. At the time, the low rate of voluntary collectivization in the South and the poor performance of collectives that were established were attributed to lack of adequate preparation and inexperience of cadres ('subjectivism, voluntarism and hastiness' in the jargon of the regime). But a number of more fundamental problems also existed. In the first place, under the administrative system which the regime was attempting to institute, most peasants would actually suffer a decline in income by joining collectives. This was because (a) the price received for the marketed surplus was low compared with the free market price and yet, because of the shortages, collectives would still need to resort to high-priced non-official channels or go without necessary inputs and consumer goods; (b) peasants could no longer determine the proportions of their output retained for own consumption and investment—instead the consumption share became a residual allocated only after taxes, obligatory sales quotas and investment, etc., funds had been met; (c) the gains from collective irrigation schemes rarely offset or outweighed losses to productivity caused by misapplication or shortage of collectively owned means of production and state supplied modern inputs which had previously been the mainstay of middle peasant productivity. This is because such irrigation schemes were often dependent upon prior completion of much larger state-funded water storage schemes (e.g., the Dau Tieng scheme in Tay Ninh) or dike building to reduce saline intrusion. Moreover, construction of collective hydraulic schemes was carried out by increased labour inputs from peasants. The returns to such extra labour for the collective were often insufficient to offset the decline in income from family plots caused by the reduction of labour there. Family plots were larger in the South than in the North and frequently contained more lucrative cash crops, whereas only rice land tended to be collectivized. Faced with such choices, many peasants either refused to join collectives or withdrew after one or two seasons. Many other collectives remained collective on paper only.

By July 1979, there were only ninety-seven cooperatives and 9,737 lower-level production collectives in the nine provinces of the Mekong River delta, compared with 1,104 cooperatives and only 1,564 collectives in the central coastal provinces.

The reasons for this difference may be partly that, like the North in 1954, central Vietnam had a high proportion of communal land. This was also a cause of the failure of the Thieu's regime's Land To The Tiller program in this region: there were too many disputes over who, if anyone, should benefit from freehold title to formerly communal lands. The distribution of social classes in this area had not changed as radically over the preceding two decades as it had further south, since most landlords were themselves quite small farmers cultivating their own land and had been subjected to rent reductions rather than expropriation by the NLF. The central region was also much poorer and the cultivated areas more densely populated than the Mekong delta. Few families had been able to acquire modern means of production and there was a much larger class of poor peasants, eking an existence from minuscule plots of land.[3] Crop losses due to floods, droughts and frequent typhoons were another important factor—collectivization could cushion peasants against the devastating impact of these. Trung Bo also had a long revolutionary tradition and had been more heavily affected by the war. Collective effort to restore abandoned and damaged land could be an advantage. In other words, the conditions applying in central Vietnam in 1975 were in many ways similar to those which had made collectivization initially successful in the North between 1960 and 1965, namely, widespread poverty with opportunities for big productivity increases via labour accumulation projects (irrigation, land reclamation).

The relative success of the collectivization program in the southern Trung Bo region was also reflected in rapidly rising grain output. For the years 1975–80, Quang Nam Da Nang, Nghia Binh, Phu Khanh and Thuan Hai provinces averaged a 12 per cent per annum growth of foodgrain production (by comparison with 4.9 per cent for the Mekong delta provinces).[4]

But although the Trung Bo provinces (both north and south of the 17th parallel) contain approximately 25 per cent of Vietnam's population, they produced just about 20 per cent of its grain output in 1976–84. The Mekong delta plain, on the other hand, with 23 per cent of the population, produced 36 per cent of the country's foodgrain in 1976, a figure which had risen to

40 per cent by 1984 (Beresford, 1987, p. 265). The failure of collectivization in this key rice-bowl region was therefore all the more urgently requiring a solution.

At the 6th Plenum of the Party Central Committee, held in a mounting atmosphere of crisis in August 1979, Vietnam's leaders agreed upon a number of reforms to the economic system. They thus began a process of rejuvenation which has been extended and deepened, despite some conservative reaction, up to the present.

The reforms were designed to stimulate production, especially in those areas of the economy which were not covered by the state plan. Since earlier in the year (June) the number of products to be controlled by this plan had been increased, it can be seen that this first approach to economic reform was very limited in scope. The caution embodied in the reforms was a reflection of the still considerable political power wielded by conservatives.

The measures announced in September 1979 allowed enterprises wanting to produce products not covered by their plan to use their own initiatives to find raw materials and to sell those products on the free market. Handicraft cooperatives, for example, could send teams of workers to collect raw materials from forest areas or buy them directly from producers without having to wait for state supplies. Also, fallow or virgin land belonging to cooperatives could be allocated to individual households to clear and, as an added incentive, those utilizing such land would receive a three to five-year tax exemption. Output produced by cooperatives over and above obligatory quota sales to the state could be sold on the free market and the state would compete for a share of this above-quota output by a system of two-way exchanges (i.e., inputs for outputs) at negotiated prices. These were to be close to, though normally a little below, free market prices. The main incentive for peasants to utilize this channel of distribution rather than the free market was price stability: this would be of advantage to peasants needing to sell right after the harvest when prices in the unorganized market are usually low. Secondly, the state could make available extra fertilizer, pesticide and fuel at the relatively low official prices (however, the success of this system depended very much upon the state's ability to control the supply of these inputs). Family pig-rearing and production of basic consumer goods (basketry, processed food, etc.) was also encouraged under the reforms.[1] Highway checkpoints were closed down, in order to encourage the free flow of goods carried by small traders between city and countryside. This last measure was particularly important in the Mekong delta where the clampdown on private trade in

1978 had caused a severe disruption to the trade between urban and rural areas: the shortage of consumer goods reaching the delta provinces had been cited as a major cause of the drying up of marketed agricultural surpluses.

A leading cause for concern in the agricultural crisis of 1977–8 had been the poor performance of exports and a mounting debt problem. In the 1979 reforms enterprises producing for export were given priority in the supply of raw materials, including imported ones and special allocations of food were made available to their workers. This was at a time when the rice ration to government workers in Hanoi had been reduced to 6–7 kg. per head per month and in Ho Chi Minh City to 2–3 kg. per head (Far Eastern Economic Review, *Asia Yearbook*, 1980, p. 302) compared with the 13–14 kg. considered to be the normal subsistence requirement. Exporting enterprises were permitted to sign contracts directly with foreign importers after obtaining approval of the Foreign Trade Ministry. This meant that industrial cooperatives in Ho Chi Minh City, for example, could independently seek export orders from overseas buyers and make arrangements to import the necessary raw materials. A number of garment manufacturers visited by the author during December 1979 were already operating under these new arrangements: their raw materials were supplied directly by their Hungarian and Japanese customers.

Grain production showed renewed growth in 1979 and 1980 and state procurement also began to improve after the reforms were introduced. But at first it was not clear whether the better performance was due to the reforms themselves or to other factors like favourable weather or a return to relative peace after the brief wars with Cambodia and China in 1978 and early 1979. Official explanations of the very poor harvests of 1977–8 still tended to focus on the weather and the alarming decline in livestock numbers (cattle numbers were reported to have dropped by 20 per cent in 1978) was said to be the result of flooding. Moreover, concern was expressed by prominent Vietnamese leaders during 1980 that a tendency towards 'individualism and excessive attention to personal interests' might arise as a result of the turn to market forces (Nyland, 1981, p. 446).

Nevertheless, the reform process was extended over the next few years. Most importantly, from January 1981 a new contract system in agriculture was introduced all over North Vietnam. (It did not become widespread in the South until 1982.) Known as the product contract system (*khoan san pham*), it had already operated in a *de facto* fashion in a number of areas since 1978 and was first tried officially on an experimental basis in the suburbs of Haiphong. The adoption of this system represented a virtual revolution in official thinking on collective agriculture.

Under the new system, many of the existing production teams, based on specialization of tasks, were broken up and individual households (or in rare cases, work teams) were allocated plots of land by the collective. On these plots, each household or team is responsible for sowing, transplanting, cultivation and harvesting of the crop. Cooperatives themselves remain responsible for those areas of production which involve the use of collectively owned means of production or more advanced techniques—ploughing, insecticide spraying, irrigation, seed propagation and selection and supply of chemical fertilizer.[2] Households sign individual contracts with the collective (or directly with the state in the case of the remaining private land in the South), under which they are to receive any inputs and services they require in return for a fixed quantity of grain, pork, etc. The prices at which these goods exchange are determined by the state (some examples: 1 kg. urea = 3 kg. paddy, 1 kg. phosphate fertilizer = 1.5 kg. paddy, 1 litre diesel fuel = 0.8 kg. paddy (Lam Thanh Liem, 1985, p. 387)). Any output produced over and above the contracted amount may be retained by the household for its own use or sale. Above-contract sales could initially be made either in the free market or to the state at negotiated prices, but in more recent years, the state has attempted to gain full control over the grain and pork markets, so that above-contract sales should all be made at negotiated prices.[3]

The product contract system was immediately successful. It enabled a much greater utilization rate of labour in the collectives by abolishing the artificial division of labour which had prevailed under the old management system and creating a system of incentives in which individual incomes were directly related to labour expenditure. Every cooperative household was allocated a piece of land (including those of cadres and members of specialized teams) according to its available labour force. A system of allocating land according to the number of mouths to feed was explicitly rejected as (a) encouraging a high population growth rate as families tried to acquire more land and (b) encouraging the re-introduction of wage-labour as households with large numbers of dependants would be unable to farm all the land themselves.[4] Cooperatives continued to plan their crop structure, providing seed, ploughing services, water, fertilizer and pesticides to households for their contract land, while households retained full control over the family plots (the so-called '5 per cent land') as before.

Contracts are fixed according to the average productivity of the land over the preceding three years and are set for a 2–3 year period so that increases in output will not immediately be siphoned off by the state. Some effort is made to ensure land of differing fertility is equitably allocated and provision is also made to have periodic redistributions (every three years). However, it is doubtful whether these are carried out so frequently in practice, as frequent redistribution might discourage investment by peasants in improving the land.[5]

In October 1981 a major change in the official price structure was announced. The price of most agricultural goods was raised by 300–400 per cent, but those of major inputs were raised by approximately 1,000 per cent. This was designed to bring the official prices of most goods much closer to their prevailing free market prices and reduce incentives to divert state resources to the black market. Prices of most goods were raised higher in the South than in the North, in keeping with existing price differentials in the unorganized markets. Although these reforms marked a turn in the official terms of trade against agriculture for the first time in many years, it is also possible to argue that the *effective* terms of trade faced by farmers improved under the reforms, given a greater availability of state-supplied inputs at the new prices, which were still some way below free market prices.

In 1981 the foreign trade sector was also decentralized further. The four major cities of Ho Chi Minh City, Hanoi, Haiphong and Da Nang were permitted to establish their own import–export (IMEX) corporations. Ho Chi Minh City, for example, had about a hundred municipal-level enterprises producing for export and receiving imported raw materials and spare parts in exchange. Enterprises and local authorities producing for export were permitted to retain a 25 per cent share of foreign exchange earnings which they received in the form of imported goods.

In industry, the Council of Ministers decided to establish a new system of enterprise management. Their decision, embodied in a decree of 21 January 1981 and reinforced by the Political Bureau in November 1981, was that wages should be paid wherever possible according to a piece-rate system and that enterprises should be given greater independence in production, trade and finance. Enterprises outside the state system (i.e., collective and private enterprises) would use the product contract system.

Intense debate over the reforms delayed the holding of the 5th Party Congress by several months. Originally scheduled for late 1981, the Congress was not in fact held until March 1982. One of the difficulties would appear to be that although the reforms had caused a spurt to production, they had been accompanied by some undesirable side-effects. In the South, in particular, there had been a renewal of the inflationary spiral after a brief lull when the reforms were first introduced (Lam Thanh Liem, 1985), there had been a resurgence of the free market in luxury imports leading to fears of the re-emergence of capitalism and, moreover, the problem of cadre corruption seemed to have become worse. Even in the North, the 'southern diseases' of corruption, inflation and unemployment were becoming a major issue for the first time.

These problems were largely due to the use of market-type reforms, particularly price reform, in a situation in which acute shortages continued to prevail in the sphere of production. The Third Five Year Plan, which was ratified by the 1982 Party Congress, took an important step towards overcoming the latter difficulty by beginning the process of restructuring investment. In drawing up the new Plan, the leadership had recognized that the development strategy pursued by the DRV since the inauguration of the First FYP in 1961 had been a major cause of imbalances in the economic structure. In the first place, agriculture had been starved of investment funds so that the growth rate of marketed surpluses had been correspondingly stunted. In the second place, industrial investment had been too heavily concentrated in large heavy industrial products with long gestation periods and few production linkages to the rest of the economy. Scarce capital resources had been tied up in these construction projects, which in themselves created new demands for wage goods, raw materials, etc. without any commensurate short-term increase in production. A very high proportion of imports was devoted to capital goods for these heavy industry projects and this was a factor further exacerbating the shortages of raw materials and consumer goods. Because of this, many plants were an inordinately long time in construction. When new plants *were* completed, they could not be used to full capacity because of the failure to invest in production and transport of inputs and worker productivity was low (see Chapter 9). In the late 1970s it was estimated that only 40–50 per cent of existing industrial capacity was in use.

The Fifth Party Congress set about correcting some of the more acute imbalances. This is an inherently difficult and long-term task because the nature of such large-scale projects is that through depreciation they continue to absorb a large proportion of investment funds. Moreover, two decades of pursuing this type of strategy had seen the growth of a formidable bureaucratic, managerial and employee group with vested interests in preserving the rate of constructing new large-scale projects. The problem of finding employment for workers and cadres displaced by the stoppage of inessential construction or closure of non-profitable plant is a particularly difficult one in an economy already characterized by high levels of unemployment.

Nevertheless, the task was begun by switching priorities to five key areas during the 3rd FYP. These were energy (which alone absorbed 30 per cent of industrial investment in the 1981–5 Plan), agriculture, transport and communications, exports and consumer goods. Although the priority to heavy industry was not abandoned, its development was expected to be much more closely linked to the development of these key sectors. Of industrial investment, for example, a further 18 per cent was reportedly devoted to industries producing inputs and machinery for agriculture. A policy of halting the construction of inessential projects and slowing the rate of new starts was adopted, though, from the self-criticisms made at the Sixth Congress held in December 1986, this policy was widely resisted within the bureaucracy and little was achieved.

In early 1983 the first phase of economic reform drew to a close and measures were taken to curb what many Party leaders saw as undesirable side-effects. Some new directives were issued in an attempt to slow the rate of inflation and the resurgence of private trading. Very steep taxes were imposed upon private enterprises operating in areas considered inessential to the growth of production. Private traders were a particular target because the leadership felt that the problems of unemployment and poor growth of the economy would be better solved by increased production rather than by an increase in the numbers of traders and middlemen. Cloth merchants in Ben Thanh market in Ho Chi Minh City were, according to one report, taxed at the rate of 40,000 Dong (about US $100 at the black market rate of exchange, around US $4,000 at the official rate) per square metre of stall space; restaurants had to pay 50,000–70,000 Dong per month. Many were forced to close or were taken over by the state (Lam Thanh Liem, 1985, p. 400).

In March 1983 a new system of taxation of agriculture was introduced. Land was divided into seven categories, according to its average yield over the previous five years. Taxes were fixed at 10 per cent of this average yield (instead of 15 per cent under the previous system), though taxes on land still privately held would appear to have been higher.[6] The new system ensured that increased yields would not lead to a proportionate increase in taxes and was designed to encourage intensification of cultivation effort in the collective sector.

In industry, the freedom of enterprises to buy and sell outside official channels was revoked in 1983. In July, the 4th Plenum of the Central Committee attacked the slow pace of socialist transformation in the South. The collectivization drive, in abeyance since late 1979, was renewed and a target date of complete collectivization by the end of 1985 was announced.

Initial Results of the Reform Process

In the South, economic growth appears to have benefited greatly from these reforms. In particular, the introduction of the product contract system and discriminatory taxation system appear to have encouraged a more successful collectivization of agriculture. Although many of the production collectives and cooperatives may not yet be fully operational—the setting of collectivization targets by a fixed deadline always contains a strong element of artificiality—the 1983-5 collectivization of the South was not marked by declining output and procurement in the way that the earlier campaign was. Paddy output in the nine provinces of the Mekong delta reportedly rose at an average of 9.7 per cent per annum between 1979 and 1984 (the last year for which relevant data are available). In spite of the renewed collectivization campaign, the new taxes on private enterprises and renewed effort to attain state control over the distribution of goods, output rose by over 10 per cent in 1984.

There is also a good deal of evidence that industrial activity in the South has accelerated in the 1980s. Some of this evidence is indirect—for example, reports in 1986 that Ho Chi Minh City had been declared a model for emulation by other industrial centres. Other evidence comes from data on the relative growth rates of heavy and light industrial production during the Third FYP. Ho Chi Minh City, which has a concentration of consumer goods industries (both for the domestic market and for export), had undoubtedly benefited from the higher growth rate of the consumer goods sector since 1979 (Table 11.1). The city now accounts for about 30 per cent of total industrial production in Vietnam and its industrial growth rate of over 26 per

Table 11.1 Growth Rates of Industry*

Years	Producer goods (Group A)	Consumer goods (Group B)	Central management	Local management	Total
1975-9	4.7	6.3	4.4	6.7	5.7
1979-82	7.2	9.8	0.2	14.2	8.9
1982-4	9.0	12.3	11.2	11.0	11.1

* 1975-82 — 1970 constant prices; 1982-4 — 1982 constant prices.
Source: General Statistical Office, 1985, pp. 40-2.

cent in 1980-1 and 1983-4 (the years for which figures are available), probably accounts for a high proportion of the growth of the consumer goods sector (Group B) nationally.

Export growth has also received a substantial boost from the reforms. Between 1979 and 1985 the annual growth rate of exports (measured in US$) was 7 per cent while imports grew at only 3 per cent per annum. However, there was a marked difference in reported trade with Western and socialist countries. Exports to the convertible currency area grew at 22 per cent per annum, in spite of the Western blockade, which was supposedly extended after Vietnam's invasion of Cambodia in 1979, and imports grew by only 1 per cent. Exports to the non-convertible area, on the other hand, grew at only 2 per cent per annum compared with a 4 per cent growth of imports.[7] This means that Vietnam now pays for over 70 per cent of its imports from the West by exports, compared with 24 per cent in 1979. Exports in 1985 covered 45 per cent of total imports (1979 = 37 per cent) (IMF, 1983; *Far Eastern Economic Review*, 13 November 1986, citing IMF). One consequence of the large trade deficits in the past has been a burgeoning growth of external indebtedness: at the end of 1982 the IMF reported Vietnam's total debt in convertible currencies as being US$ 1.46 billion out of a total $5 billion, with a total debt service ratio of 72 per cent. Arrears in payments caused friction with the IMF and Western creditors in the mid-1980s. The vastly improved export performance thus serves a dual function: on the one hand it reduces the cost of Vietnam's external debt by concentrating trade deficits, and loans to cover them, within CMEA and avoiding the commercial interest rates of Western credit. On the other hand, the growing trade relationship with the West will in the longer term help undermine the political opposition, which intensified after the Cambodia invasion, and assist Vietnam to return to its more independent trade and foreign policy stance of pre-1978. Southern cities and provinces appear to be the main sources of exports.

The good performance of the economy of the southern region in the 1980s can largely be attributed to a better balance of industrial and agricultural output than that prevailing in the North. At a time that many northern leaders still clung to the notion of 'heavy industry priority' (Le Duan made a speech at the Central Committee's 6th Plenum in July 1984 in which he claimed that there 'will be neither heavy industry nor socialism without steel and engineering' (Le Duan, 1984, p. 11)), the priorities of those in charge of industrial development in the South were quite different. Development thinking in the South has tended to stress the importance of supplying light industrial goods to peasants as part of developing the division of labour between agriculture and industry, both to modernize agriculture and to increase the supply of consumer goods and export income for the expansion of industry itself. Since the South lacks the large mineral and coal deposits of the North, the Vietnamese leadership has never really been tempted to try to establish a heavy industry base in the South. Instead, it has looked at development of the southern region in terms of its agricultural and light industrial potential. Where the administrative planning system transferred from the North after 1975 failed to achieve its objectives, the economic reforms, through a better mixture of price incentives and encouraging greater local initiative in adjusting output mix to meet changes in demand, have provided the mechanism that was needed to boost growth. The reforms have also helped increase the ability of state and collective institutions to mobilize marketed agricultural surpluses, hence to promote social rather than private appropriation and given the collectives themselves a better chance to work successfully.

In the North, on the other hand, the industrial structure, in spite of some changes since 1982, remains concentrated in heavy and large-scale industrial capacity. While this might not be detrimental in the longer run, the long gestation periods and teething problems of many of the industrial projects means that an increase in the supply of commodities to the rural areas has been very slow to eventuate. Electricity supply has been identified as the most crucial bottleneck and Hanoi, for example, experiences frequent blackouts while all available supplies have to be diverted to prevent agricultural disasters (flooding, etc.). But the investment in new power generation has been concentrated in giant projects (like the Da River scheme which, when it is completed in the 1990s, will treble Vietnam's electricity supply) and significant increases in output cannot be expected in the short term.

Shortages of such basic goods as fuel and fertilizer severely hamper the expansion of North Vietnamese agricultural output.[8] A remedy could be found in increased imports, but rapid growth of exports to pay for this is hampered by lack of large marketable surpluses and continued over-concentration of export earnings in importing capital requirements for heavy industry. The self-reinforcing nature of a continuing 'goods famine' and low marketed agricultural surpluses in the North has lessened the impact of economic reforms on the rate of growth of the region.

This was starkly brought out by a price and currency reform introduced in September 1985. As mentioned in Chapter 9, the low wages of state sector employees in a situation of food shortages and rapid price inflation of the free market had contributed to low labour productivity of industry. Moreover, subsidized food prices to urban workers under the rationing system had, by the 1980s, become the single most important item of state expenditure and a major factor in the growing budget deficits that were being financed by inflationary methods (IMF, 1983). In an attempt to remedy this, the government (possibly following IMF recommendations (IMF, 1982)) abolished the food subsidy and raised urban wages to take into account the prevailing non-ration rice price. At the same time, a currency reform was introduced in an effort to gain greater control over the retail market and curb private capital accumulation. The State Bank introduced a new Dong into circulation (equivalent to 10 old Dong) and strictly limited the quantities of old currency which could be converted. Designed to wipe out large holdings of private wealth, it also succeeded in creating acute problems for many state enterprises, which had been in the habit of keeping large amounts of cash on hand in order to be able to by-pass official state trade channels in purchasing scarce inputs.[9] As in previous reforms of a similar nature, the sudden drying up of cash holdings served only to disrupt the circulation of goods, further exacerbating the already acute shortages. The increased shortages, when combined with salary increases of urban workers (some cadres, for example, went from salaries of 150 old Dong per month to 200–300 new Dong—a thirteen- to twenty-fold increase) provided a massive boost to inflationary pressures and precipitated a renewed economic and political crisis. A partial reversal of the reforms and re-implementation of the food rationing system was undertaken as soon as the effects became apparent (*Far Eastern Economic Review*, 10 April 1986), but in 1986 inflation continued to spiral—with reported rates ranging from 50 per cent to 1,000 per cent.

The experience of other socialist countries has shown that price reform is inevitably accompanied by some inflation. One lesson from the Vietnamese experience of 1985 is that price reform cannot be undertaken in the absence of simultaneous changes in the sphere of production. It therefore needs to be a gradual process, linked to the rate of change in output which in turn depends upon the kind of investment strategy being implemented (cf. Liu Guoguang, 1986). The difficulty for countries like Vietnam in embarking upon a process of reform stem from (a) the long-term nature of carrying out adjustments to the industrial structure to achieve a better input–output balance, especially in view of (b) resistance by both bureaucrats and employees to the attempt to wind down large-scale, but low productivity and loss-making, enterprises. Where unemployment is already a problem, as it has been in Vietnam generally since the end of the war, it is politically very difficult to achieve such changes (see *Far Eastern Economic Review*, 23 April 1987, for similar problems facing China).

Nevertheless, the regime has resumed the reform process. The 8th Plenum of the Central Committee in August 1985, which had decided on the failed price reform, also shifted the emphasis towards changes in the industrial management system. Steps have been taken to try to increase the managerial prerogatives of enterprise directors, to enable them to carry out production without excessive interference from above and to ensure both financial independence and accountability. One such move has been to extend the ability of firms to trade directly with other firms—even to include products within the state plan. Whereas in 1979 it was reported that to transport a relatively insignificant product like umbrella stands from Tay Ninh to Ho Chi Minh City, it was necessary to 'go through 17 agencies, obtain 15 seals, sign 5 contracts and pay many different types of tax' (JPRS 75471, p. 55), the measures introduced by mid-1985 included provisions to allow large consumers of coal to obtain it directly from the mine, while smaller consumers need go through only one intermediary link. Such measures were aimed both at reducing delivery delays and at eliminating the favouritism and corruption which has plagued state distribution networks under administrative allocation systems.

A great deal of stress has also been laid on introducing the system of 'economic accounting and business management' (which is the same as the Soviet *khozraschet*). In reality, the enormous shortages experienced by firms and their inability to operate at full capacity have meant that planned costs of production do not reflect actual costs and planned profits are often non-existent. Firms in the state sector have therefore become increasingly dependent upon state subsidies in order to continue in operation. In effect, the enterprise managements are not responsible for the financial success of their operation. State Planning minister, Vo Van Kiet, in an important speech made in October 1985 pointed to the cleft stick that managers are held in:

By issuing orders, higher level agencies usually avoid responsibility for setbacks. All setbacks and their consequences are shouldered by the primary installations. Never has an order-issuing agency been punished for issuing a wrong order or for taking time to fulfil the urgent demands of lower echelons, no matter how much damage this may cause. However, there are many types of punishment for production installations. For example, if higher echelons assign plan norms without securing the necessary conditions for implementing them or if they set forth incorrect prices, those who comply suffer losses while the higher echelon agencies are not held responsible for anything. This leads to the practice of deliberately issuing orders in order to avoid responsibility. [Vo Van Kiet, 1985, p. 8]

A major aim of the reforms has been to reverse this situation and to give the state-run enterprises a better chance to operate at a profit. However, reform of enterprise management suffers from many of the same problems identified in relation to price reform. Enterprise managers can hardly be held responsible for profits and losses of their firms if they continue to be subject to administrative plans, on the one hand, and shortages over which they have no control, on the other.

A process of overhauling wage payments has also been extended. The 1982 Fifth Party Congress had reported that, in general, wages of state-employees were below average income levels of the population, poor health was affecting productivity and longevity of workers, and higher remuneration outside the state sector was leading to absenteeism, low motivation and low productivity in industry. In artisan cooperatives, accumulation funds were said to be too high, leaving insufficient for distribution (JPRS 75945, p. 20) and in many state-run industries it would appear that wage differentials hardly existed (JPRS 75456, p. 37). This meant that the principle adhered to by the government, that under socialism income distribution should be carried out according to labour, was not being applied.

Piece rates had begun to be applied in industry in 1980, in order to improve the relationship between remuneration and work effort, but by 1982 the system had reportedly spread to only nineteen factories. One reason for this failure may have been resistance to the reorganization of the labour process away from job specialization towards product-based systems, but there were also indications that piece-rates were unable to solve the basic problem of continuing shortages of food and consumer goods.[10] Workers on piece rates were able to earn higher wages than time-rated colleagues, but the rate of inflation ensured that incomes remained insufficient for both groups. More recently, there have been calls for the application of the contract system in industry wherever possible, in order to ensure that rising incomes of workers are closely linked to increases in output. However, there are considerable difficulties with applying this idea to more advanced technology industries where fully integrated production processes mean that the labour expenditure of a single individual cannot be linked to final output.

The Sixth Party Congress

The economic crisis induced by the ill-thought out wage and currency reform of late 1985 caused a dramatic shake-up in the Vietnamese Communist Party. On the political front, a number of ministers, including Vice-Premier in charge of the economy Tran Phuong and Political Bureau member To Huu, were dismissed from their ministerial positions,[11] though the latter retained his high Party position until the 6th Congress later in the year. In mid-1986 a 'criticism and self-criticism' drive was launched at all levels of the Party apparatus, resulting, in the run up to the national Congress, in replacement by local Party meetings of a large proportion of the membership of existing executive committees. At the National Congress, which was held in December after several months' delay caused by intense debate over the political report (chiefly concerning economic issues) to be delivered by Secretary Truong Chinh,[12] there was now a sizeable majority in favour of continuation and extension of the reform process. Both the political report and the economic report, given by the head of the State Planning Commission, Vo Van Kiet,[13] were strongly critical of the progress made so far in correcting the imbalances in the economic structure and in implementing new forms of economic management—although the reports did record an average annual growth rate of national income of 6.4 per cent in 1981–6 compared to 0.4 per cent for the 1976–80 period and annual growth in industrial output of 9.5 per cent compared with 0.6 per cent for the earlier period (Truong Chinh, 1986, p. C1/2). While a large number of construction projects were completed and productive capacity of the economy greatly enhanced, capacity utilization remained at only half, the state enterprises were unable to play the 'leading role' assigned to them in a socialist economy, shortages had become more acute, inflation was rampant and 'negative manifestations in society', such as abuse of power and corruption, had gone unchecked (p. C1/4).

Blame for this state of affairs was largely placed on the failure to correct economic imbalances brought about by the investment programs of the 1976–80 FYP, in which, Truong Chinh said, 'we set too high targets for capital construction . . . laying much stress on building heavy industry and large-scale projects, failing to pool efforts on solving basically the food problem, on boosting the production of consumer goods and goods for exports' (p. C1/5). Secondly, 'we laid stress on changing the ownership of the means of production, but overlooked the settlement of problems relating to management organization and the system of distribution. We often resorted to campaign-like, coercive measures running after quantity, but neglecting quality and efficiency' (p. C1/5).

The economic objectives of the 6th Congress differed markedly from those of earlier congresses chiefly in the references made to transformation of the relations of production. Both the 1976 and 1982 congresses had stressed the need to complete the socialist transformation by the end of the current Five Year Plan. The report of the 6th Congress, by contrast, stated that the relations of production should be in conformity with the need for enterprises to earn a profit and with the level of productive forces. Transformation of the relations of production should proceed according to the principle of increasing production, raising economic efficiency and increasing working people's incomes. This was followed by an admission that there were still many areas of production in which collectivization was not likely to yield good results, so household production should be encouraged for its ability to supply essential consumer goods and as a source of funds for accumulation and expanded reproduction. Small private enterprises would also be allowed to operate in certain areas of production.

In commerce, all private capital was to be eliminated except for joint ventures between the state and some 'medium-sized' businesses. However, this restriction is also contradicted later in the same report by the assertion that it is impossible to abolish private trade by 'wishful thinking' and it should be used where the state and collective trade networks are not yet able to fulfil their role properly. Ultimately, the ability of the state to dominate commerce depends on its pricing policy and mode of operation, as well as the ability to eliminate the shortages.

The basic tenets of the development strategy outlined by the 6th Congress are similar to those of the 1982 Congress, but are stated with greater force. For the first time, there is an unambiguous statement of priority to the development of agriculture for the coming period. It is to receive priority in supplies of investment goods and labour and will be complemented by investment in processing plant, transport and storage facilities.[14] In industry, production of consumer goods is also given a high priority for the Fourth FYP and a number of requirements for rationalizing production and improving quality of output in this area are outlined in the report—including carrying out of market research to link production to demand, closure of firms which fail to thrive, inviting tenders before placing orders and mobilization of the resources of overseas Vietnamese.

Exports of agricultural and light industrial goods and the development of transport and other infrastructure are also mentioned as key areas for development, but heavy industry and infrastructure should only be developed, according to the Report, in so far as they serve the priority areas of agriculture and consumer goods or national defence. Fertilizer, pesticides and veterinary medicines (products of the chemical sector) are specifically mentioned in this context.

It is stressed that all industrial development programs should be both realistic and aimed at overcoming autarky in production. On the first point, the yardsticks of investment effectiveness will be low capital intensity, high employment creation and rapid completion of the construction phase. Priority will be given to 'in depth' investment in existing installations rather than commencement of new projects. On the second point, the aim is to get rid of local self-sufficiency as well as provincial rivalries and unnecessary duplication of productive capacity by encouraging an intensification of the social division of labour and increased commoditization of the economy. Payments in kind are to be replaced by cash payments; there will be increased use of economic levers in planning, while legally binding plan targets, the hallmark of administrative planning systems, are to be abolished except in 'a few essential areas', for example where foreign trade commitments are involved; prices are to correspond to actual production costs and should take account of supply and demand conditions; there should be a single price system applied to all commodities (although multiple prices may persist in the short run for some commodities in order to avoid problems like those which arose with the attempted abolition of the food subsidy in October 1985); wages are to be reformed to get rid of payment in kind and also to take better account of subsistence requirements.

In 1987 a new foreign investment law is under consideration. Unlike the earlier law which offered fairly restrictive conditions and has not been very successful in attracting foreign investors, the new law is likely to allow up to 100 per cent ownership by the foreign company, full remittance of profits and other income accruing to the company or its personnel (subject to certain provisions set out below), full repatriation of capital upon sale or dissolution. The company tax rate is set at 20–25 per cent subject to exemption for the first two profit-making years and 50 per cent reduction for the following two. Losses may be offset against profits of the next five years and any reinvested profits are entirely exempted from the tax. A 10 per cent withholding tax on dividends is proposed and a reserve fund of 5 per cent of net profits, but not exceeding 25 per cent of capital value of the enterprise. Exemption or reduction of import and export duties are also proposed, depending upon their nature and volume. While these conditions, if they are eventually approved, are likely to prove more attractive to potential investors than those set out in the foreign investment law of 1977, the likelihood of substantial Western investment in Vietnam depends on a more favourable international climate, particularly a reduction in Cold War tensions in the Southeast Asian region.

The major foreign investor and aid donor in Vietnam since the signing of a Treaty of Friendship and Cooperation between the two countries in 1978, is the Soviet Union. Because it is Vietnam's largest trading partner and the major source of investment funds for development projects, it has been in a position to influence the direction of the economic reforms to a considerable extent. The main changes in the pattern of Soviet assistance since the early 1980s have been the setting of priority investment projects in line with the goals of the 1982 plan and a shift towards greater specialization of trade between Vietnam and the other CMEA countries—with Vietnam attempting to raise its exports of tropical products (fruit, rubber, coffee, tea) and light manufactures, while imports from the Soviet Union have shifted towards fertilizers and industrial inputs. It appears that pricing policy in relation to foreign trade has also attempted to encourage Vietnam to reduce food imports and increase exports (Fforde, 1985). Some authors have tended to suggest that the Vietnamese reforms are the result of Soviet pressure, seeing that the changes occurred soon after Vietnam joined CMEA and considering the poor economic returns to Soviet aid programs in the country. While this is probably an important factor, and while Vietnamese authors do not always consider Soviet policy to be in Vietnam's national interest (Fforde, 1985, p. 207), it should be clear from the arguments of preceding chapters that the reforms were initially prompted by domestic pressures. The SRV continues to have a certain amount of political leverage over the Soviet Union because of the latter's desire not to cede strategic ground in Southeast Asia and the Pacific Rim to China and the United States. Moreover, there are many precedents in Vietnamese debates and practice, dating back to the 1960s, for the type of reforms which have been implemented. It seems unlikely, then, that Soviet pressure has been decisive.

Conclusion

In response to the economic crisis generated by the attempt to integrate the southern economy into an already weakened socialist system after 1975, the regime has embarked upon a series of fundamental reforms since 1979. In spite of some manifest opposition from the more traditional socialists within the Party and from those within the bureaucracy having a vested interest in maintaining the previous system—particularly evident in a partial reversal of the reforms during 1983—the reforms have been gradually deepened and extended over the past eight years. On the whole, the Vietnamese regime has proceeded with greater caution compared with the Chinese economic reforms: it has refused, for example, to de-collectivize agricultural production; persisted with the attempt to achieve state control over the commercial sector; taken a wait-and-see attitude towards adoption of more relaxed foreign investment laws.

The disastrous currency and wage reform of late 1985 remains the only aberration in this pattern of caution. Although there were rumours of possible sabotage, the cause is more likely to have been a severe lack of judgement by decision makers acting under pressure from a number of quarters. These quarters included: (a) the IMF and creditor nations anxious for a reduction in inflationary deficit financing to help control the burgeoning balance of trade deficit and ease the country's debt problem; (b) the Soviet Union, anxious to create a more efficiently working economy in which the large quantities of Soviet development aid would be more effectively utilized; and last, but not least, (c) those elements within the Party who were anxious about a revival of capitalist tendencies. These pressures were to some extent contradictory, and the reforms (abolition of subsidies and currency reform) had different goals. But their combined effect was to create severe hardship for urban workers and to shake popular confidence in the Party and government. The new Party leadership clearly hopes that a resumption of the more gradual reform process will restore that confidence.

Part V
The Regime's Policies

The revolutionary victory in the South in 1975 and steps taken to accelerate political and economic reunification of the country have created a plethora of new problems for the regime, quite apart from those of the economy discussed above. In Vietnam's external relations there have been armed conflicts with Democratic Kampuchea and China as well as continued pressure from the Western powers (mainly limited to the economic and diplomatic spheres) and in the domestic sphere there have been new challenges in education, health, ideology and cultural policies posed by the absorption of the capitalist South and the crisis of economic development that this produced.

Given the enormous significance to Vietnam and to the trajectory of Vietnamese socialism of its external relations, it is inevitable that the greater share of this Part of the book should be devoted to an analysis of the external environment and Vietnamese responses to it. In this section the fundamental continuity in the ways that Vietnamese leaders analyse and react to changes in their external environment can be seen, despite the common Western perception that since 1975 there has been a basic shift in alignment by Vietnam, even a new 'neo-colonial' relationship with the Soviet Union.

In domestic affairs, education policy is an especially important area of concern to the regime and serious efforts at reform are currently being made. A persistent theme of efforts in this direction has been to relate the 'outputs' of the education system much more closely to the needs of an economically backward socialist society and to break down some of the dysfunctional legacies of traditional Confucian and colonial systems. Similarly, in health, culture and other social policies, the attempt has been to produce realistic programs based on local and national conditions, eschewing mindless imitation of foreign 'models'. However, Vietnamese policies are not iconoclastic. They seek to combine the very practical and nationally oriented approach with appropriate borrowings from older traditions and overseas influences. While they are revolutionary, they also seek to keep close to the needs and aspirations of the masses, a task which is hardly simple and which often produces conflicting objectives.

12   Domestic Policies

Education

Mass education has always been seen by Vietnamese Communist leaders as one of the most important revolutionary goals. This may be partly a result of the deep literary traditions of the Vietnamese which were badly disrupted and broken down by French colonial rule.[1] But it is also attributable to the Party's concept of the need for a 'triple revolution' in Vietnamese society, not only in the relations of production, but in culture and ideology and in science and technology, with the last-named being the 'kingpin', the key to successful industrialization and creation of a genuinely proletarian state.

Early education policy concentrated on the acquisition of basic literacy skills by every member of the population over the age of eight. This campaign was begun even before 1945 and was followed in 1949–50 by the creation of a universal general education system using the Vietnamese language and romanized script (Quoc Ngu) for the first time in Vietnamese educational history. In 1975 a new literacy campaign was launched among the estimated 1.4 million illiterates of working age in the South and by 1978 the government claimed that 94 per cent of these could read and write (Woodside, 1983, p. 406).

The spread of education has been one of the truly major achievements of the Vietnamese revolution. In the period from 1945 to 1970 the number of students in the general education system in the DRV rose from 190,000 to 4.7 million (*Education in Vietnam*, 1982, p. 37). Since unification in 1975 roughly doubled the number of children in the system, the total has risen to 11.7 million studying in eleven grades (in the North) or twelve (in the South). According to the World Bank (World Bank, 1986), the percentage of the appropriate age cohort enrolled in primary school in Vietnam is 114 per cent, compared with the average for low income countries of 91 per cent.[2] The percentage attending secondary school is 48 per cent, compared with the low income country average of 31 per cent. Indeed, in terms of its commitment to secondary education, Vietnam is well ahead of some of its wealthier neighbours: figures on secondary school enrolment in some of them are: China 35 per cent; Thailand 29 per cent; Malaysia 49 per cent; Indonesia 37 per cent (World Bank, 1986).

In spite of the impressive achievements, the Vietnamese have identified a number of serious faults with their education system in recent years and in 1979 began a far-reaching overhaul. The main problem to be focused on is the lack of relationship between the type of education received by students and the labour-force requirements of the economy. The curriculum has concentrated overwhelmingly on the study of theoretical and classical subjects, particularly Vietnamese (primarily classical literature) and mathematics, and, in spite of a policy emphasis to the contrary, has tended to ignore or underrate practical experimentation and subjects which could give students technical competence in future careers. There has also been a persistence of Confucian rote learning methods and 'encyclopaedism' (Rubin, forthcoming), which equates learning with knowing everything rather than making use of students' creativity and capacity to reason. Moreover, most students see the educational system, as in olden times, as a means of achieving upward social mobility through a position in the bureaucracy. There is strong resistance to undertaking vocationally oriented courses and a preference for continuing with general education which opens the door to the university and the bureaucratic career. Only a tiny percentage of general school graduates are, however, accepted by the universities and, consequently, unemployment among high school graduates is high. The other side of the coin is that over-emphasis on general education causes many students who have no hope of proceeding further in this direction to see schooling as increasingly irrelevant to their needs and the drop out and failure rate is high. During 1980–1, for example, the estimated drop out rate among primary children varied from 5 per cent in the North to 15 per cent in the South and as high as 33 per cent in Ha Tuyen province in the mountainous north-west. The number of students repeating grades at primary and lower secondary level in the same years was thought to be 7 per cent (Rubin, forthcoming).

A further difficulty is that technical education is geared to non-rural occupations in the modern sector and is therefore of little benefit in modernizing the most backward sector, i.e., agriculture. In the early 1970s, fewer than 10 per cent of cooperative managers had graduated from lower secondary level and only 1 per cent of the graduates of agriculture colleges were actually working in cooperatives (Woodside, 1983, p. 412). But several authors have also observed that not only do young people desire to move out of farming work, those in charge of allocating employment within the cooperatives usually regard people with an education as no longer belonging. This is partly due to a lack of occupational diversification in the villages and it may not be possible to overcome the problem in the absence of further economic development. But it is also possible to change the method of educating villagers to provide more on-the-job training, which can increase skill levels and technical capability without separating them from the mainstream of economic life. At the No. 1 Agricultural University in Hanoi, for example, the administration hoped (when I visited it in 1985) to establish a mobile education unit, which could be used to travel into the villages and give farmers short, practically-oriented courses on new techniques. But they lacked funds and basic equipment, such as bicycles and slide projectors, for the project.

One aim of the 1979 reforms is to bring about a more vocationally oriented education process, which will more nearly match the aptitudes of students with the possibilities of employment. Vocational guidance is to be introduced into schools based on assessment of local and national labour force requirements and more emphasis is being given to the teaching of handicraft skills and on engagement in productive work as an integral part of education. Education outside the formal structure is also being encouraged to foster a demand for learning and skill enhancement continuously through-out life (Pham Van Dong, 1985, p. 5). But against this tendency to reduce the theoretical content of the curriculum is the goal of offering all students a full twelve years of education in primary, middle and upper secondary schools[3] and the introduction of compulsory education for nine years from ages 6 to 15, where traditionally formal education has not begun until 8 years and many rural students did not begin attending until they reached 10 or 11 years of age. Such policies will be hard to implement in a difficult economic climate where the demand to maximize family labour is high. Moreover, there have been warnings from some Vietnamese commentators that the new twelve-year curriculum may be overloaded and will actually reduce the amount of time students have to pursue their own interests and talents (Rubin, forthcoming).

Health

In the DRV health policy was based on a strategy of making simple medical treatment widely available and concentrating on prophylactic measures, to make optimal use of the extremely limited resources available. Clinics were established in every village during the collectivization movement. These were mainly staffed by people who had received partial medical training and combined Western medical techniques with the use of traditional medicines (often the only ones available) for simple complaints. More complicated cases could be referred to hospitals at the district or provincial town, where fully qualified personnel would be available. By 1970 the DRV had one physician for every 5,454 inhabitants and a medical assistant for every 1,093 people (DRV, 1975, p. 116).

But it was in the area of prophylactic medicine that the DRV health policy achieved its greatest recognition and success. Intestinal parasites, which provide perhaps the major source of poor health in the Third World, were tackled by campaigns to separate sources of drinking water from those used for washing, sewage and livestock. The introduction of double compartment septic tanks with their dual function of containing the spread of disease and providing organic fertilizer was a major aspect of this campaign. The DRV was largely successful in its campaign to stamp out malaria—through mass movements to help eradicate mosquitoes and DDT spraying—and a number of other major diseases like small pox, cholera, typhoid, trachoma, tuberculosis and leprosy (McMichael, 1976).

The regime inherited a truly enormous set of health and social problems when it took over the South in 1975. Hundreds of thousands of people were affected by the legacies of war, either as invalids, orphans and widows, or as a result of the breakdown of urban and rural infrastructure which led to serious health problems—a resurgence of malaria, malnutrition and other diseases. In addition, the high living of the Saigon rich combined with extreme poverty of many new urban dwellers had led to the rise of prostitution (with serious attendant problems of venereal disease), drug addiction and criminality. The socialist regime saw all these people as victims of war and neo-colonialism and adopted an approach based on rehabilitation, job training and integration into the productive work-force as soon as possible. These programs posed a huge drain on scarce medical resources and government finances in the first few years.

Two of these rehabilitation programs have attracted considerable attention outside Vietnam: these were the treatment of drug addicts and rehabilitation of prostitutes. The drug treatment combines the use of acupuncture (mainly to relieve withdrawal symptoms) with physical education, political education and the learning of handicraft skills in the later stages. The success rate is said to be rather high, but with an estimated 100,000 drug addicts in the South by the end of the war, the process of eliminating the problem is necessarily prolonged. The main centre, in Ho Chi Minh City, can handle only a tiny percentage of the victims at any given time and each treatment takes about three months.

In the case of prostitutes, neighbourhood committees were mobilized to persuade women to enter the rehabilitation centres, where they underwent medical treatment, some political education and training in handicraft techniques such as basketry, weaving and embroidery. They also participated in community activities, organizing drama and musical shows for people living in the vicinity of the centre. At the end of their course the ex-prostitutes were returned to the community from whence they came, the idea being that social pressure from their neighbours would keep them on the straight and narrow. In fact most of those entering the centres were probably doing a poor trade anyway and, in the straitened economic circumstances of the city, there would be few reasons to return to their old occupation.

These are two examples of the general approach of the regime to tackling some of the less mundane social health problems of the South. Others, like water and sewerage, roads and electric power, improved housing stock, etc., are also long-term projects that will have to await economic development for their solution. But by adopting an interventionist rather than a *laissez-faire* approach, and by making use of the available resources, the regime can at least ensure that the social problems of the South (or for that matter the North) do not reach the horrific proportions of some other Third World cities, in spite of the extraordinarily difficult base it has had to build upon.

A number of factors have combined, however, to ensure that, in spite of these strenuous efforts, the health situation in Vietnam today remains very poor. One is that no such campaigns as were responsible for the elimination of major diseases in the North were ever carried out by the South Vietnamese regime, with the consequence that many remained endemic. Even in the North, the effects of war greatly exacerbated the problems—the millions of bomb craters, for example, providing a breeding ground for mosquitoes. With growing mosquito resistance to DDT and shortages of pesticides, diseases like malaria began to return in more virulent strains and, with the destruction of infrastructure, stagnation of the economy and rise of food shortages after the war, the health situation deteriorated. The system of village clinics could no longer cope with the load, especially in the virtual absence of Western medicines. Hospitals were understaffed and lacked all kinds of facilities: many professionally trained southerners had emigrated as well. A survey carried out in 1977 among schoolchildren in North Vietnam showed that no less than 97 per cent suffered from between one and three diseases (not counting worms) (Rubin, forthcoming). Those are very alarming statistics and one of the most damning indictments of the Western economic embargo of Vietnam. Yet improved food availability and general economic climate, as well as the gradual loosening of aid and trade restrictions in the 1980s provide the possibility that the health authorities will be able to alleviate the situation to some extent.

Culture and Ideology

Cultural policy has provided the regime with some of its most vexed questions. On the one hand, the origins of the Vietnamese communist movement as an anti-colonial movement have led the Party to emphasize the need for a specifically *national* Vietnamese culture. On the other hand, it has never been very clear how this national culture is to be developed in a modern industrialized society or how it is to be manifested in the creation of new socialist individuals.

Vietnamese cultural identification has in the past been backward-looking. In fact at the core of Vietnamese nationalist ideology has been the conscious linking of contemporary struggles with the stories of past heroes in the fight against foreign occupation. Some Vietnamese writers have tended to identify foreign cultural borrowings (such as Confucianism) with reactionary tendencies, which are pitted against a progressive indigenous village-based culture (Duiker, 1983, p. 117) and this has been especially true since the growth of tension with China. Great stress has also been laid on recent archaeological finds indicating the existence of a highly developed agrarian civilization in present-day Vietnam long before the Chinese conquest in the second century BC. This somewhat xenophobic approach to defining and promoting a national culture is understandable, given the prevalent tendency in non-Vietnamese scholarship until recently to dismiss Vietnamese culture as basically Sinitic. Vietnam was often referred to in the colonial period as 'Little China'.[4] The words Annam and Annamite, names commonly used for the whole country (as well as its central region) and its people, come from the Chinese meaning 'pacified south'. Even the term Indochina disguises the indigenous elements of the three countries' cultures beneath the Indianized and Sinicized cultures of their old ruling classes. The digging up of this indigenous culture and its inculcation into the consciousness of the Vietnamese people was therefore a very important part of the process of reconstituting the nation as an independent entity and unifying it in the fight against the French, the Americans and the Chinese.

However, the description of foreign borrowings as 'reactionary' is hardly accurate, even in terms of the Vietnamese communists' own interpretation of historical events. Many among the pantheon of national heroes who defeated Chinese invasions, such as the fifteenth-century scholar-general Nguyen Trai, were themselves Confucian in outlook and training. Moreover, while aspects of the Confucian tradition are indeed seen as reactionary in present-day Vietnam—such as the alleged practice of 'Mandarin-like' behaviour by bureaucrats (meaning favouritism, corruption, arrogance)—others are seen as worth preserving, for example, the emphasis on education and promotion by merit, the system of moral values that stresses respect for parents and older people, and a spirit of serving the community.

The difficulty of defining a specifically national culture becomes even more acute when the question of looking towards the future and creation of a socialist society arises. What happens, for example, when instead of the relatively autarkic society of pre-colonial days, Vietnam becomes integrated into the international commodity economy? In other countries, the process of industrialization has tended to internationalize certain aspects of culture and, in the age of satellite communication, it is increasingly difficult to isolate national communities from such international influences. So far the Vietnamese have not given any clear indication of an attitude towards this problem. Rather they have tended to avoid it by cultural borrowing from China and/or the Soviet Union while continuing to emphasize the past as a source of 'national culture'.

A certain amount of confusion was shown over the policy adopted towards the 'neo-colonial culture' of the South, illustrating the fluid state of policy after 1975. On the one hand, there was a definite tendency among northerners to regard the cultural preferences of many southerners, especially urban dwellers, with hostility. Individualism, sexual licence and mysticism were singled out for attack as the most undesirable cultural accretions and books or films expressing such points of view were to be replaced by those reflecting 'a genuine spirit of the people' (Duiker, 1983, p. 133). Along with pornography and drugs, such cultural adaptations as rock and roll, long hair and jeans were often regarded by cadres (though not in official policy) as neo-colonial 'noxious weeds' and as essentially 'un-Vietnamese'. To be sure, many of these cultural products came into the category of luxury consumer imports which could not be afforded by the post-war economy. Many others may have run directly counter to the sort of collectivist culture which the new regime was attempting to promote. But others may also have been simply part of an increasingly internationalized commodity culture. Part of the problem arose therefore because commodity relations were deeply entrenched in southern society in a way which had not yet occurred in the North. What northerners often saw as 'un-Vietnamese' or decadent behaviour was no more than a cultural difference, produced in many cases by prolonged exposure to international capitalism, which the northerners had not experienced. The greater openness and lack of a strong communal ownership tradition in southern villages is an example that comes to mind, as is the fashion consciousness of urban youth. In some ways, then, the decades of separate development have led to greater cultural hetero-geneity in Vietnamese society and it is no longer very clear what constitutes the 'genuine spirit of the people'.

This poses difficult questions for the idea of a socialist national culture, especially one that looks forward into a more industrialized future, rather than backwards to the traditions of classical literature and scholar-generals. The problem is not just one of how much outside influence and what sort should be permitted, but whether values and morality systems which originated in technologically backward and autarkic rural societies are appropriate for the modernization process that the Party leadership feels it must pursue.

Defence

Vietnam is one of the most highly mobilized societies in existence. A continuing perception of threat to national security is the main reason for this, but it also stems from the nature of the Vietnamese Communists' military theory of armed *political* struggle. The concept of 'people's war' involves everyone in the defence of the nation—in addition to the regular armed forces, therefore, there are civilian militia forces in every village, made up of part-time volunteers. During the Vietnam War and again during the short 1979 war with China, these militia forces were a vital part of the defence strategy. But the origins of the armed forces as an arm of the *political movement* are also important. The People's Army was founded as an Armed Propaganda Unit in 1944 and since then it has been a highly politicized body. A significant comparison between the Vietnamese army, which developed as an instrument of a revolutionary movement, and the Soviet army, which grew out of revolutionary capture of the existing state apparatus, has been made by William Turley (Turley, 1975, p. 136). This means that where the Party in the Soviet Union had to concentrate on politicizing and ensuring the loyalty of the army itself, especially its tsarist officers, the Party in Vietnam has been able to use the army to politicize and mobilize the society as a whole. Thus there has never been a really clear distinction of functions between army and Party in Vietnam, in spite of a growing trend towards professional-ization of the armed forces as the Vietnam War moved out of its guerrilla stage. Because of this blurring of functions, the army has not emerged as a separate interest group in Vietnamese political life. There is no identifiable 'army faction' within the Party, although the army does contain a high proportion of Party members. Debates on military strategy or on the appropriate type of armed forces for Vietnam in each new stage of war or peace have involved divisions of opinion within the army as much as outside it. The army, as such, does not play a major role in domestic politics.

Defence policy formation is in the hands of the Party, primarily the Political Bureau. Currently this body contains two active army officers—Generals Le Duc Anh and Doan Khue—though at least one other holds high military rank (General Dong Si Nguyen whose recent career seems to have been more in government than in the army). There is also a Central Military Party Committee, which is responsible for generating and refining policy. In 1985 the military were more heavily represented on this committee, with seven out of ten places (Pike, 1986, p. 151). (Membership changes since the 1986 Party Congress are not known at the time of writing.)

The National Defence Council is the other major state body concerned with military affairs. This body, which is elected by the National Assembly, is not concerned with defence policy formation, but with mobilization of human and other resources for defence purposes, in accordance with Party policy (Pike, 1986, p. 94). In 1987 its membership comprised the Chairman of State Council (Vo Chi Cong), Prime Minister (Pham Hung) and Ministers of Defence, Interior and Foreign Affairs—all are members of the Political Bureau and all except the Minister of Defence are civilians.

Implementation of Party policy within the army is vested in the General Political Directorate. It is responsible for political education activities and for motivating the troops as well as proselytization among civilians. Until 1980, the army had a dual command structure in which the professional officer corps was paralleled by a political command structure. This system was borrowed from the Soviet Union and seems inappropriate for Vietnam where the officer corps has been highly politicized from the outset. The unwieldiness of the structure resulted eventually in its abolition and replacement by a single command system in which officers are expected to combine military and political skills. Though the implementation of the new structure was for long resisted by the Political Directorate (Pike, 1986, p. 170), this may have been for internal bureaucratic reasons—the Vietnamese Party as a whole has never accepted the Chinese distinction between 'red' and 'expert' and most leaders would find little to fear in the rise of a more 'technocratic' officer corps. In the army, as in other organizations that were developed as instruments of the political movement, the command structure has always been dominated by Party members.

Given that the Vietnamese military is effectively controlled by the Party, the question arises as to what extent Party policy has been consciously directed towards militarization of Vietnamese society in order to detract attention from domestic problems and sustain nationalist sentiment. This assertion has frequently been made by Western commentators, who further argue that militarization has been at the expense of economic development.

The Vietnamese regular armed forces have been estimated to number about 1 million men, making them the fourth largest in the world. In addition, there are paramilitary regional defence forces, local militias and armed youth brigades, possibly totalling as many as $2\frac{1}{2}$ million persons. The regular army alone has more than doubled in size since the end of the Vietnam War according to these (Western) estimates. In my view, however, this is neither the result of a deliberate militarization policy, nor has it been a fundamental constraint on economic development. Defence mobilization has been carried out in a way that ensures minimum economic costs and maximum political mobilization of the population in accordance with well tried and tested Vietnamese practices.

The Vietnamese army is very labour intensive and considerable efforts have been made to reduce costs by making it self-sufficient. Since most members of the army are peasants, this is not difficult, especially when they are not engaged in combat. Vietnamese troops stationed along the border with China, for example, have established army farms to provide themselves with food—often in areas abandoned by local residents after the border war. Vietnamese troops on garrison duty in Cambodia also grow their own vegetables. Other sections of the army are engaged in the construction of basic infrastructure such as roads, canals and public buildings in New Economic Zones. The high level of mobilization does not necessarily imply, then, that maintenance costs of a large army are a net drain on economic development. In a country of high unemployment, the productive activities of the army may in fact constitute an economically effective way of absorbing labour and simultaneously providing a greater degree of defence readiness.

As far as equipment is concerned, costs are mostly borne by the Soviet Union. The Stockholm International Peace Research Institute (SIPRI) estimated that between 1982 and 1986 Vietnam received 2.6 per cent of Soviet supplies of major weapons to Third World countries (well under 2 per cent of its total exports), though at the time of the Chinese invasion in 1979 this share had risen sharply before falling off again—in other words, supplies are purpose-related rather than continuously high. In spite of having the fourth largest army in the world, Vietnam did not rank among the twenty largest Third World importers of major weapons during this period (SIPRI, 1987, pp. 187, 201).[5] In this respect, then, Vietnam's army continues to be labour-intensive and relatively low cost (notwithstanding a trend over time towards modernization and professionalization (Turley, 1975)).

Another way of trying to find the cost of the armed forces to the economy is via state budget expenditure. It is often assumed that Vietnam spends a third to a half of its budget on defence and that this must be a major source of inflationary pressure. Again, however, there is little evidence to support this hypothesis. Official data supplied to the IMF suggest that economic construction is the largest single budget item, at 31 per cent, with subsidies on wages and salaries, education, health and social allocations a further 35 per cent. Defence expenditure is not listed separately, but is included in the remaining 34 per cent along with such items as administration and debt service.

China, in the late 1970s, spent 17.5–18 per cent of its state budget on defence, though by 1985 this had dropped to 12 per cent under the impact of economic reforms (SIPRI, 1986, p. 235). According to SIPRI estimates, the ASEAN countries spent between 5 and 6.5 per cent of GDP on defence budgets and in Thailand, Malaysia and Singapore real expenditure was rising faster in 1980–5 than in Indochina. In 1985 Thailand spent approximately as much on the military as the three Indochinese countries taken together (including Soviet and East European aid); Singapore, with only 3 million people, spent nearly half as much; and Malaysia with less than a quarter of the population of Indochina spent an amount equal to 80 per cent of the Indochinese military budget (SIPRI, 1986, p. 235). Compared to the other countries of the region, then, Vietnam would not appear to be excessively militarized, especially given that its security has been repeatedly threatened in recent decades.

As we shall see in the next chapter, the primary reason for the rapid expansion of the Vietnamese armed forces since 1975 has been the persistence of external threats to national security. Military build-ups did occur in the immediate aftermath of the wars with Democratic Kampuchea and China, but these do not represent a permanent militarization policy. The Vietnamese army underwent a rapid increase in numbers after 1976 and although the high levels of defence mobilization of the population must have some negative economic effects, these cannot be quantified with any level of certainty, given that they are partially offset by self-sufficiency and development projects in a society with high unemployment. Rapid demobilization, even if a more secure environment could be achieved, may also have awkward economic side-effects. Much will depend upon how economic recovery proceeds and the development of Party priorities as the difficulties with China and ASEAN begin to recede.

It is sometimes suggested that the Vietnamese regime has no scope to carry out an independent foreign policy, its actions being determined by more powerful external forces. Certainly the options open to it have been severely constrained by the actions of foreign powers, probably far more so than has been the case in recent times for any other nation of equivalent size and level of development. But within the narrow confines offered by the 'clash of elephants' in the Southeast Asian region, the Vietnamese 'grasshopper'[1] has shown a remarkable ability to manœuvre successfully and to achieve the goals it has set for itself. These goals are only partly determined by the external environment. They are also largely a product of the nature of the Vietnamese revolution and domestic developments in the course of that revolution. In what follows I will outline what I consider to be the main factors determining Vietnamese foreign policy and, keeping in mind the framework thus established, I will then discuss three areas of major interest in Vietnam's external relations today, namely, relations with China, the Soviet Union and with neighbours in the Southeast Asian region. Vietnamese ties with the Western countries, most particularly the United States, are intimately bound up with these and cut across all three areas.

Nationalism and Foreign Policy

Most Western discussions of Vietnamese foreign policy have focused around a single major area of disagreement between those, on one side, who defend the view that Vietnam has been little more than a surrogate (willing or not) for its more powerful socialist benefactors (Buszynski, 1986, is a recent example) and those, on the other side, who argue that Vietnamese policy has been determined above all by the *nationalism* of the VCP (Rowley & Evans, 1984). The 'nationalist' arguments essentially look at Vietnamese foreign policy from the point of view of ideological and political determinants and tend to ignore or underrate the very important material foundations of that policy.[2] The 'surrogate' school on the other hand, tend to focus on Vietnam's economic dependence on Soviet (or earlier Chinese) material assistance to the exclusion of any consideration of Vietnamese ideological premises (though some do admit a difference between what the Vietnamese would like to do and what they actually do). Neither approach in my view is very helpful in understanding the totality of Vietnamese foreign policy, though each contains elements of an explanation. A more satisfactory approach is one which links Vietnamese ideological premises to the historical trajectory of the revolution and to developments in contemporary political economy.

We have already seen that the Vietnamese revolution was rooted in the social conflicts engendered by the impact of French colonial rule on almost the entire Vietnamese population. The class struggle was therefore, as in other colonial countries, inevitably bound up with the question of national self-determination and the creation of a sovereign national state. Revolutionary movements in the Third World, including that in Vietnam, have all developed according to the way their leaders and participants perceived the nature of the oppressive forces in their society. Each movement has a basic motivating vision of a liberated society and this is formed, not as an abstract ideal, but as a direct response to the material conditions facing it. In each case, external intervention by the colonial powers has been an important, if not always decisive, factor. But in Vietnam external intervention has been carried to extraordinary lengths and, the Vietnamese revolutionaries have largely defined their goals in response to this intervention. Patriotism, a desire for national independence and to create a modern nation-state accepted on equal terms with others have thus formed an important part of the Vietnamese revolutionary impetus. This 'nationalism' of the Vietnamese communists does, however, need qualifying.

Firstly, Vietnamese leaders have clearly understood, much better than some Western writers, that 'national independence' is a relative concept, something that is always constrained by the external environment within which a nation-state resides. Since even superpowers are limited in this way, it is hardly surprising that a small, underdeveloped country would be so constrained. Vietnamese policy is accordingly aimed at extending the limits of its action where possible and at maximizing its scope for independent action within these limits.

Secondly, Vietnamese communists have always seen the achievement of a socialist society as a necessary prerequisite for national self-determination (i.e., self-determination by all the people, rather than the sort of independence in which a new ruling class continues to collaborate with imperialism). Socialism itself came to be defined by Communist Parties in China, Laos and Cambodia as well as Vietnam, as their response to the impact of foreign occupation and/or dismemberment. The egalitarian goals of socialism were attractive to those excluded from influence in governing their own country and the launching of mass-based revolutionary movements was also seen by certain leaders as the only viable means of overthrowing an intractable imperial power. Indeed it was precisely this acceptance of and reliance on mass participation in the revolution and the Party's ability to respond to the *social* demands of peasants and workers that gave the nationalist project its formula for success. The nationalist and socialist tendencies were thus inextricably linked in the thinking of Southeast Asian communists. It is a mistake to accord one or the other primacy in analysing Vietnamese Party policy because the survival and development of the Vietnamese state continues to be seen as both a product of and a prerequisite for the development of socialism.

While the Vietnamese revolution did unmistakeably incorporate nationalist goals, the socialist ideology of the Party has also been strongly laced with internationalism. Western writers often find it difficult to reconcile the apparent internationalism of the world's Communist Parties with the nationalism that is of such clear importance in inter-state relations. But the Vietnamese themselves have generally seen no contradiction between the two. From the Vietnamese point of view, internationalism has been an important benefit to the goal of national liberation.

In early days, for example, Ho Chi Minh launched an appeal to the French labour movement to support the struggle of the Indochinese peoples and he joined the Comintern on the basis of his reading of Lenin's views on the international movement and the 'national question'. Ho's appeal to the French workers was based on a graphic description of colonialism as a necessary outgrowth of capitalism, which also exploited workers in the metropolitan country:

Capitalism is a big leech with two suckers, one sticking to the proletarian class in the metropolitan country, and the other to the proletarian class of the colony. To kill the monster, one must cut off both its suckers at the same time. If one is left, it will continue to suck the blood of the proletarian class, the monster will remain alive and a new sucker will grow out to replace the one which has been cut off.[3]

While this appeal sought to exploit anti-colonial sentiment within France and help isolate enemies of the revolution, membership of the Comintern proved useful in lending international prestige, education and training facilities as well as sanctuary to Vietnamese communists (though, as we saw in Chapter 2, this was not an unmixed blessing). From the beginning of the Vietnamese communist movement, then, internationalism was seen as a means, indeed a necessary means, to achieve the national goals of the revolution. In more recent times, with the growth of economic reformism in the socialist bloc, there has also been a rising awareness of the possibilities offered by international cooperation and division of labour within the framework of CMEA. This is not just the result of Soviet pressure for such integration, but is also due to a realistic appraisal of the economic problems caused by autarkism practised in the past. The benefits of internationalism are seen as accruing to individual *states*, rather than to the working class of the world as a whole.

This attitude towards internationalism, as a means to attain national goals, is not in itself contradictory. Given that class struggle in the real contemporary world is carried out within the confines of nation-states, it is actually the only basis upon which internationalism is a viable concept. Marx's own internationalism was based upon the presumed common material interests of workers in throwing off the capitalist yoke and *not* on any moral or ideological premises about what workers ought to do, still less upon the idea that some should sacrifice their interests for the betterment of others. The major problems have arisen because the interests of proletarian-led movements within nation-states have diverged, or at least been perceived by nationally-based Communist Parties to diverge. Communist Parties which have succeeded in gaining power are also subject to material constraints, the relevant one here being that they can only to a limited extent influence revolutionary development outside their national boundaries. Defence of the revolution and creation of external conditions favourable to further development of socialism within those national boundaries therefore becomes paramount.

Conflicts which have arisen between socialist states must, therefore, be explained not only by reference to the ideological nationalism of the parties concerned, or by great power chauvinism, but as the product of differences of perception by nationally-based communists concerning the need to defend revolutionary achievements at home and to advance the longer-term goal of world-wide socialism. In practice, socialist revolutions have developed out of very complex socio-economic conditions—the role of peasants in the revolutionary movements of Asia, for example, has rendered any simple version of Marxism (in which workers and capitalists are the only actors) irrelevant. Communist Parties have found their mass base, not only among the urban working class, but among peasants and intellectuals in varying proportions and in countries with vastly differing cultural traditions, levels of economic development and degrees of foreign influence or control. These complex material circumstances have led to widely differing revolutionary paths—ranging from terroristic regimes to paternalist personality cults, from charismatic leadership to grey bureaucracies or military dictatorship, from highly centralized to decentralized or market-based economies, from collective, politicized leadership to personalized dynastic regimes. Different states have also found themselves in widely varying relationships with the two largest socialist states. For those regimes without the ability to mobilize mass support, or facing very stiff resistance (possibly with foreign assistance) from former ruling classes, or at a low stage of economic development, the opportunities to adopt independent policies are likely to be more limited. Even for China and the Soviet Union, foreign policy options are constrained by the perceived need to maintain allies, secure border areas, etc. In view of the enormous complexity of actual socialist regimes, something which has led them to evolve highly individual solutions to the often quite similar problems facing them, it is not at all surprising (except to the most vulgar interpreter of Marx) that serious conflicts of interest have arisen between them.

It is primarily the requirements of the socialist *state* which form the basis of foreign policy in countries like Vietnam and determine whether this will move towards international cooperation or conflict. These requirements are in turn determined by the Communist Party as the outcome of a domestic political process drawing on its historical traditions, its links with the population and with various interest groups in society, its analyses of external pressures and opportunities as well as its vision of the future development of socialism.

Sino-Vietnamese Relations Since 1975

The relationship between China and Vietnam is a case in point. There are many respects in which these two countries and their communist movements have much in common, but the interaction between nationalism and socialism has evolved quite differently. Some of the historical similarities and differences have already been canvassed in Chapter 6; here I will concentrate on developments since 1975.

The Sino-Vietnamese dispute had been simmering for some years before the end of the Vietnam War—at least since Richard Nixon's visit to China in early 1972 and Mao's advice to Pham Van Dong on his subsequent visit that the DRV 'broom' was too short to reach Saigon.[4] In the aftermath of the Vietnamese victory in 1975, China withdrew much of the commodity aid (mainly food) which had sustained North Vietnamese living standards during the previous decade, but it was not until 1978–9 that the conflict broke into the open, culminating in a brief war during February–March 1979.

The pretext for the fighting was territorial. At issue are both the land boundary established by treaty between France and China and areas of the South China Sea for which no boundary has ever been set down.[5] The question has acquired importance largely because of the recent interest in the likelihood of oil and gas deposits being found in the sea-bed.

The real causes of the conflict do not lie in territorial disputes, however. At the root of the Sino-Vietnamese differences lies the Sino-Soviet split which both colours Chinese policy towards Vietnam and Vietnamese responses.

Chinese leaders had already recognized their ability to influence the strategic balance in the Southeast Asian region at Geneva in 1954, when they were able to pressure the DRV into accepting division of Vietnam at the 17th parallel. After Sino-Soviet antagonisms surfaced in 1960, Mao Zedong sought to establish China as an alternative leader of the world socialist movement to the Soviet Union and as a leader of the Third World in general. The Vietnamese, on the other hand, sought to create a balanced relationship between the two socialist powers in order to maximize their own freedom of action. While acknowledging the importance of Maoist ideas for national liberation movements in the Third World, then, they rejected China's proposal for a Beijing-based Communist International, floated in 1963, and refused to join in furious Chinese attacks on Soviet 'revisionism' and 'restoration of capitalism'.

While Vietnamese ideology drifted further away from the Chinese after the launching of the Cultural Revolution by Mao, both China and the Soviet Union continued to supply important quantities of aid to Vietnam until the end of the war. Even after 1971, when China's leaders had clearly decided to cooperate with the Nixon–Kissinger strategy in order to isolate the Soviet Union and gain ground on the Taiwan question, aid to Vietnam did not fall off significantly. Although Khrushchev had, at one stage, apparently considered abandoning effective support for Vietnam on the grounds that escalation of the war would threaten his 'peaceful coexistence' strategy and that Vietnam fell into a natural Chinese sphere of influence anyway, the idea was never carried through by his successors. Both China and the Soviet Union evidently considered Vietnam important as a symbol of their leadership of the world socialist movement and as a strategic antidote to each other's influence, as well as that of the United States, in the Southeast Asian region. Neither was, therefore, prepared to leave the field to the other and the rivalry thus worked mostly to Vietnam's advantage.

Nevertheless, this was not always so. Chinese sabotage of Soviet arms shipments to Vietnam which had to pass through Chinese territory during the Cultural Revolution (Funnell, 1978, pp. 149–50) and Chinese signals to

Washington that it would limit its support of Vietnam (CIA, 1983) created difficulties for the Vietnamese. Vietnamese foreign policy at this time can be seen largely in terms of an effort to stay afloat in a volatile environment rather than something initiated by Hanoi itself.

By 1976, however, a significant change had taken place within the Chinese leadership with the death of Mao and defeat of the so-called 'Gang of Four'. The shift towards accommodation with the United States, which had originated with a desire to isolate the Soviet Union and gain concessions on Taiwan, was now greatly reinforced by those in the Chinese leadership favouring rapid modernization of agriculture, industry, technology and the military. By improving relations with the West, the Chinese hoped to gain access to modern technology and loans for investment. The period after 1976 also saw a strong push to establish links with wealthy overseas Chinese and encourage them to invest in China. On the diplomatic front, this involved greatly improved relations with Japan and the ASEAN countries, as well as the United States and Western Europe, and on the political front, cancellation of effective aid for national liberation movements, particularly the Southeast Asian Communist Parties.

In the space of five years from 1971 to 1976, then, an important shift in the international balance of forces had taken place. An essentially triangular relationship between the United States, China and the Soviet Union had been replaced by a bi-polar one with China in essence allied to the West against the Soviet Union. From the Vietnamese point of view, this realignment was a serious blow, since it meant that China now joined with the United States in attempting to apply military and economic pressure on Vietnam. The pressure was all the more intense as a newly reunified Vietnam, undergoing peaceful economic construction and maintaining friendly relations with the Soviet Union, constituted a potentially independent source of influence in the region, which could neutralize China's diplomatic initiatives.

Between 1975 and 1978 the Vietnamese attempted to maintain their neutrality *vis-à-vis* the two socialist powers, both refusing Chinese demands that they condemn the Soviet Union and resisting Soviet pressure to align themselves by joining CMEA. In May 1978, however, a sudden deterioration in relations with China was initiated by the latter's defence of ethnic Chinese businessmen being subjected to socialization measures by the Vietnamese (in virtual imitation of the policies carried out in China itself twenty-five years earlier) (Buszynski, 1986, p. 163). Chinese manipulation of the ethnic issue became the pretext upon which all remaining economic and technical assistance to Vietnam was withdrawn, while simultaneously aid to Democratic Kampuchea was stepped up, enabling Pol Pot to intensify his attacks on

Vietnamese territory using Chinese-supplied artillery. Sporadic fighting also broke out along the border of China and northern Vietnam.

In the context of an economic embargo imposed by the United States and lack of interest by other Western countries in increasing aid, investment or trade with Vietnam, rising pressure from China forced the Vietnamese to rely on the Soviet Union and Eastern Europe. Only the Soviet Union could now supply the technology which the Vietnamese wanted for their industrialization program or the military equipment they needed to counter the threats to their two borders. A month after the breakdown with China, in June 1978, a Treaty of Friendship and Cooperation was signed with the Soviet Union and Vietnam formally acceded to the Council for Mutual Economic Assistance (CMEA), on which it had had observer status since 1961.

As tension rose, the situation of ethnic Chinese living in Vietnam became very awkward. This community, numbering over a million persons, lived mainly in the South where, as we have seen, they were already somewhat disaffected with the regime. In North Vietnam, the much smaller community of ethnic Chinese were predominantly working class and urban. Under an agreement between China and the DRV signed in 1951, these people had been allowed to retain Chinese nationality and, where applicable, membership of the CCP. The Chinese community as a whole, then, fell under suspicion of collaborating with China to undermine Vietnamese security. Reports of sabotage, seeming to confirm these suspicions, mingled in 1978 with accounts of severe harassment of ethnic Chinese living in North Vietnam and, as rumours of impending war circulated, many Chinese tried to leave the country. While the Chinese made substantial propaganda use of the plight of the Vietnamese Chinese community, they were noticeably silent about similar difficulties being created for their compatriots living under the xenophobic Pol Pot regime.

War did break out in February 1979, when China attacked along the length of its border with Vietnam in an attempt to 'teach Vietnam a lesson' for its invasion and overthrow of the Democratic Kampuchea regime. Several hundred thousand troops of the People's Liberation Army were used in the invasion[6] and, because Vietnam had not anticipated the timing of the attack, most of the defence was carried out by local People's Militia forces.

It is not very clear what the strategic objectives of the Chinese offensive were. The 'human wave' tactics used proved disastrous and led to heavy casualties. After a change of tactics and some bitter fighting several large towns were captured, but Chinese losses remained high due to constant guerrilla harassment in the rear and the necessity to fight house by house.

After a month the Chinese withdrew as Vietnamese regular reinforcements were brought up, blowing up everything as they departed.[7] The poor performance of the PLA in this war caused recriminations within the Chinese leadership, while the Vietnamese loudly proclaimed that it was they who had given the lesson. If a Chinese objective had been to force a change in Vietnamese policy,[8] it failed badly. By the massive destruction they wrought, they merely increased the price Vietnam would have to pay for its independence.

Certainly the Chinese have not made a second attempt at invading Vietnam, despite frequent threats to the contrary and numerous border clashes. The 1984–5 dry season offensive in Cambodia in which Vietnamese troops wiped out the military bases of the Khmer Rouge passed by without a significant response from China. Since that time Vietnam has dropped much of its anti-Chinese rhetoric in an effort to aid the resumption of negotiations (Truong Chinh, 1986). Of ultimately greater importance, however, has been a move by China and the Soviet Union to resolve their own dispute. If Sino-Soviet relations continue to thaw, the Vietnamese will have more scope to resume a more balanced relationship between the two powers. Chinese reasons for seeking a reduction in tension with the Soviet Union go beyond a desire to split Vietnam from its Soviet ally and isolate it, as some commentators have suggested. A much more important consideration from the Chinese point of view, is that having consolidated relations with the West and ended years of externally imposed isolation, Chinese leaders now feel in a strong enough position to restore more triangularity to the international balance by 'playing the Soviet card'. Moreover, rapid modernization of the economy has placed downward pressure on the military budget and increased the need to enhance national security by diplomatic means (Blecher, 1986, pp. 202, 205). In other words, domestic considerations of economic strategy are just as important in determining the Chinese position as foreign policy objectives.

Soviet-Vietnamese Relations

Vietnamese links with the Soviet Union have developed since 1975 largely as a by-product of the deterioration in relations with China and the failure of Vietnam's earlier policy of maintaining a careful distance from both socialist powers. Between 1975 and 1978 Vietnam had resisted Soviet and East European pressure for integration into CMEA (Chanda, 1986, pp. 185–6) in the hope of improving relations with China and the West. But the events of

1978 in South Vietnam and Cambodia, coming on top of open hostility of the US Congress,[9] left Vietnam with no further options.

Greatly increased dependence by Vietnam on Soviet economic and military assistance after 1978 has inevitably led to more Soviet pressure to 'coordinate' policies in trade and diplomacy, but this has not been all a one-way street. Considerable differences of policy goals have continued to surface, often reflecting the global orientation of the Soviet Union versus the essentially regional and national concerns of the Vietnamese.[10] An example of this is the Soviet use of naval docking and repair facilities at Cam Ranh Bay. Although the Soviet build-up at Cam Ranh Bay may have been voluntarily limited (Buszynski, 1986, p. 206), the enhanced access and mobility in the southern Pacific Ocean area which it gives is clearly of lasting strategic importance to the Soviet Union. For the Vietnamese, on the other hand, continued Soviet use of the facility is equally clearly contingent upon continued Soviet support for their regional objectives, primarily the security of Indochina and the northern border with China. Vietnam has not awarded the Soviet Union a permanent base at Cam Ranh Bay, or made any open-ended commitment so that Soviet use of the facilities is subject to periodic renegotiation.

In 1978, at the time of the signing of the Soviet–Vietnamese Treaty, the Vietnamese continued (rather unsuccessfully) to seek links with Western powers to offset their dependence on the Soviet Union. A month after the Treaty was signed Vietnam offered to normalize relations with the United States without preconditions, dropping an earlier demand for payment of the $3.25 billion reconstruction aid promised by Henry Kissinger at the time of the Paris Peace Accords. But the Carter administration was more interested in developing its relations with China. Nevertheless, these efforts have persisted whenever fresh opportunities arose and do appear to be bearing more fruit in the late 1980s as trading links have begun to be restored with Japan, Australia and ASEAN, while previously cold diplomatic relations with several countries in the region have thawed somewhat. Negotiations with the United States have also resumed.

The Vietnamese have managed to limit their commitment to the Soviet alliance in other ways as well. The Treaty itself commits the two countries to no more than immediate consultations in the event of an attack (Buszynski, 1986, p. 169)—which is hardly more than had been taking place since the 1950s in practice anyway. There is no mention in the Treaty of Soviet proposals for a collective security arrangement (such as is found in the Soviet–Afghan treaty of December 1978) and Vietnam is not a member of the Warsaw Pact or any equivalent. In so far as Vietnamese policy does contain a global element, it emphasizes membership of the Non-Aligned Movement on at least equal terms with membership of the socialist camp (Nguyen Kien, 1985, pp. 33–4). The Vietnamese see themselves as having a distinct role to play in this movement as among the leaders of a socialist group of not very powerful, economically underdeveloped former colonies of the Third World.

Besides the differences, however, the Soviet Union and Vietnam have also had a number of common goals and, to the extent that the policies have moved closer together since 1978, it is extremely difficult to ascertain the degree to which Vietnam is responding to Soviet or to domestic pressures. Some combination of these seems to be the most likely explanation.

Perhaps the most outstanding area in which the policies of the two countries have become coordinated is in the economic sphere. Vietnam embarked upon a series of economic reforms in 1979, soon after the shift towards the Soviet Union, and it has been argued (Fforde, 1985, p. 202) that this was in response to Soviet pressure, particularly due to concern over the way in which Soviet economic aid had been used in the construction of large-scale projects, which had failed to make an effective contribution to growth of the economy. Certainly, the introduction of reforms in Vietnam coincided with a similar process in the Soviet Union (and also China), but there is no reason to suppose that the Vietnamese would not themselves have arrived at the same conclusions. Domestic economic and political considerations in 1978–9 had given leverage to Vietnamese economic reformers whose criticisms of the existing system had already been voiced much earlier, even before the end of the War (White, 1982a). Vietnamese economic growth theory had long stressed the need for a balance between industry and agriculture and between heavy and light industry, although little of practical effect had been achieved in this direction because of the conflicting desire among Party leaders for priority to heavy industry and rapid modernization. There is every reason why in the early 1980s, especially given the chaos in the southern economy caused by the attempt to impose the northern administrative planning system, the reformers led by Nguyen Van Linh and Vo Van Kiet would themselves have wanted to renegotiate the terms and, more particularly, the content of Soviet aid.

Vietnamese integration into CMEA is another area often cited as leading to greater Vietnamese dependence on the Soviet Union, notably via the growing proportion of trade in non-convertible currencies (up to 90 per cent by 1983, compared to 77 per cent in 1980) (Buszynski, 1986, p. 186) and the new concentration of Soviet investment aid into expanding exports of tropical products rather than industry. This, it is asserted, will not only force

Vietnam into a position of dependence on primary commodity exports, but will result in the organization of the economy such that it will be more difficult to develop strong trading links with the West in future. The new strategy within CMEA, however, coincides very well with the Vietnamese desire to restructure their economy so as to place more emphasis on agriculture and light industry and to achieve a rapid expansion of exports, which is necessary to overcome heavy external indebtedness. While the Vietnamese are aware of the possible unequal distribution of benefits from trading in CMEA (Fforde, 1985, p. 207), they see economic integration primarily as one means of building a stronger socialist national economy. They have also continued their efforts, along with other CMEA countries, to extend the international division of labour to the West—since 1980 exports to the convertible area have in fact grown much faster than those to the non-convertible area (see Chapter 11), while imports (and borrowings to finance them) have shifted towards the socialist bloc. Membership of CMEA has thus assisted the Vietnamese to make economic adjustments which might otherwise have proven much more costly.

Whatever the origins of the pressure for greater economic integration and division of labour within CMEA, the Vietnamese have a further incentive to take up the idea with enthusiasm. As part of their concern with the contribution of Laos and Cambodia to Vietnamese security, they have talked of the inherent rationality of integrated economic development of the three Indochinese countries.[11]

Vietnam's Relations with its Southeast Asian Neighbours

The dominating issue in Vietnamese relations with Southeast Asia since 1975 has been the 1979 invasion of Cambodia. Indeed very few nations outside the Soviet bloc have supported Vietnamese actions to resolve their conflict with Pol Pot's Democratic Kampuchea,[12] but the reasons have less to do with an appreciation of the reasons and justifications for events by the parties involved than with the wider implications of the dispute for the regional balance of power. The Cambodian issue has been overshadowed (though not wholly determined) by the Sino-Soviet dispute and its ramifications for Vietnamese policy and by the strategic responses of the Western powers and their regional allies.

Background to the Cambodian Conflict

On the surface, the conflict between Vietnam and Democratic Kampuchea (DK) was territorial, arising from the establishment of formal boundaries (where none had previously existed) by the French colonial regime for its own administrative purposes. As in the case of Vietnam's border dispute with China, the sea boundary assumed particular importance in view of the prospects of oil and gas discoveries in the Gulf of Thailand. Armed conflict broke out on 4 May 1975 when forces from Democratic Kampuchea attacked Tho Chu Island, carrying away 500 Vietnamese residents who were never heard of again (Chanda, 1986, pp. 12–13). Vietnam retaliated in June, but while the Vietnamese tried persistently to reach a negotiated settlement, Pol Pot continued to escalate the fighting each year until 1978.[13] Cross-border raids which resulted in the massacre of thousands of Vietnamese civilians in early 1978,[14] and artillery bombardment of important Vietnamese towns (Chau Doc and Tay Ninh) added to the flow of refugees from Cambodia itself towards Ho Chi Minh City and to the severe disruption of economic life in the region.

The territorial dispute, however, was only one facet of a deeper conflict which had its roots in the parallel development of the two Communist Parties (Kiernan, 1985; Vickery, 1984). Fighting between Khmer Rouge and Vietnamese NLF troops had broken out as early as 1971 as part of a struggle within the Khmer communist movement for political supremacy as the Pol Pot group attempted effectively to exclude Prince Sihanouk, whom the Vietnamese at that stage supported, from any position of real power in a liberated Cambodian state. Anti-Vietnamese sentiment within the Khmer Rouge was primarily fuelled, as Kiernan (1985) has shown, by the desire of the Pol Pot group to increase and consolidate their power in the Cambodian Party over the older elements who had fought with the Viet Minh in the struggle against the French and many of whom had gone into exile in Hanoi after the Geneva settlement of the First Indochina War. For their purpose, this group of younger Paris-educated intellectuals revived traditional fears of Vietnamese domination (based on Vietnamese expansionism in pre-colonial days, but given some credence by cross-border attacks and depredations by the Thieu regime in South Vietnam) and territorial irredentism, based on a reconstitution of the Khmer nation along purely ethnic lines. This anti-Vietnamese policy of the Pol Pot group was at first only one element of its struggle for supremacy over other tendencies within the Khmer Rouge, but as Cambodian society increasingly disintegrated during the four years from

1975 to 1978 and, finally, after a number of key figures had been helped by the Vietnamese to form a Front for National Salvation in late 1978, it became the dominating element.

During 1978 the attacks on Vietnamese territory grew in intensity and by December a decision had been taken in Hanoi to try to capture the whole east bank of the Mekong, at least to push the problem away from Vietnamese territory where it was creating serious problems. The offensive was launched at the end of December. Victory proved surprisingly easy and the Vietnamese commander waited for a day or two outside Phnom Penh while Party leaders in Hanoi decided to go for control of the entire country (Chanda, 1986, pp. 343–7). By April 1979 the Pol Pot regime was ended, its army reduced to a force of some 20,000 guerrillas confined to remote parts of the country, mostly the mountains along the Thai border. The National Salvation Front under the leadership of a former Khmer Rouge deputy commander of the eastern zone of the country, Heng Samrin, was installed in the capital.

Since 1979 both Vietnam and the Soviet Union as well as some Western non-governmental agencies have provided extensive aid towards the recovery of normalcy in Cambodia. This has involved not only the supply of food, basic consumer goods and machinery, but the re-establishment of an education system and training of professional and technical staff for virtually every area of social and economic life. It has called for a massive effort, particularly from the Vietnamese with their already stretched resources (most Western aid by contrast being devoted to the support of comparatively small numbers of Khmer Rouge fighters and civilian refugees in camps strung out along the Thai border). Later we will see why the Vietnamese consider the burden a worthwhile investment.

It follows from what has been said above that the Vietnamese invasion of Cambodia was essentially a defensive reaction, in spite of their own oft-repeated assertion of the internationalist character of their intervention to save the Cambodian people from genocide. The initial invasion was formally justifiable under international law and was also received with considerable relief by most Cambodians. What has made continued Vietnamese military occupation necessary, however, has been the ability of the Khmer Rouge to maintain guerrilla activity in the country by courtesy of aid supplied by China and refuge by Thailand, to name just the principal actors. To proceed further with the analysis of Vietnamese policy, then, we now need to examine the policies of China, the ASEAN countries, and the United States in response to the Vietnamese invasion.

The Role of China and the Capitalist Countries

Unlike the other allies of the Khmer Rouge, China has never accepted that the group was guilty of genocidal attacks on its own people. Chinese motives for providing sustenance to the deposed regime have been based on a desire to limit Vietnamese influence in the Southeast Asian region, simultaneously promoting their own interests. While the Chinese leaders may have thought the Khmer Rouge policies excessive, the strategic situation of Cambodia as a socialist country sandwiched between Vietnam and capitalist Thailand was of far greater importance in their calculations. Their support for Pol Pot has thus been based primarily on Vietnam's refusal to be drawn into an anti-Soviet alliance in the region.

The policies of Thailand and the other capitalist countries have rather different origins. Pol Pot's non-communist allies have all accepted that the regime was probably the most murderous the world has seen since World War II. In view of this and in order to try to lessen Khmer Rouge influence while maintaining it as an effective armed opposition to the Vietnamese, the ASEAN countries constructed a coalition consisting of the Khmer Rouge, a much smaller right-wing group (KPNLF) led by a former Sihanoukist Prime Minister, Son Sann, and an even smaller group (Armée Nationale Sihanoukiste) led by the Prince himself. It is this coalition, with Sihanouk as its titular head,[15] which retains the Cambodian seat at the United Nations, although it has not controlled any significant area of the country since 1979.

For the United States, support for the Khmer Rouge-dominated coalition has been a means to continue its policy, pursued consistently in the region since 1945, of destabilizing and, if possible, dislodging socialist regimes in Southeast Asia. US policy at first favoured the overthrow of the DK regime, but after 1979 the emphasis changed as the United States perceived the formation of a Vietnamese-dominated Indochinese bloc to be more threatening to its interests than an internally divided Indochina. However, developments in strategic priority areas like the Middle East have prevented the Americans from devoting many resources to this part of the world and they have been content to leave most of the running to Thailand and the other ASEAN countries.

For the ASEAN group as a whole, the conflict in Cambodia represents a front line in the struggle against communism. While many of them have seen the threat to internal stability recede with the withdrawal of Chinese support for local communists, the possibility of a Vietnamese or Soviet-backed movement emerging is still a worry. ASEAN states also share a wider

Western concern about any dilution of US military domination of the Pacific Basin.

Within ASEAN, however, there are significant differences in policy emphasis towards Indochina, which have given the Vietnamese more room to manœuvre. Thailand, as the frontline state, has been the most resolute in its opposition to the Vietnamese intervention. Its hard line has historical as well as contemporary roots. Like the ancient Vietnamese dynasties, the Thai also laid claim to rule the peoples of present-day Cambodia and Laos. But unlike the Vietnamese communists, the Thai have asserted territorial claims to parts of these two countries in recent times as well.[16] One cannot, therefore, assume that Thai efforts to unseat Heng Samrin are entirely divorced from these considerations. Secondly, the large ethnic Chinese business community in Thailand benefit from China's current policy of wooing overseas Chinese and the prospect this offers of lucrative market and investment opportunities provide a strong incentive to maintain good relations by supporting Chinese policy on Cambodia. There is also a minority business group anxious to develop trade and investment with Vietnam and who see the continuing conflict as detrimental to the stability of the Thai economy, but these are outweighed for the time being by the pro-Chinese group and by military leaders for whom the fighting provides a justification for taking a larger slice of the state budget, increased supplies of US hardware and enhances their otherwise declining domestic political profile.

Malaysia and Indonesia have shown greater willingness than Thailand to come to terms with Vietnam, a stance which is related to greater suspicion of Chinese motives. Both these states are anxious to reduce ethnic Chinese domination of their business sectors and see a stable and prosperous Vietnam as a useful counterweight to excessive Chinese regional influence. Indonesia is particularly wary of China and has only recently moved tentatively towards re-establishing relations broken in 1965 after the massacre of Indonesian communists and ethnic Chinese by the Indonesian military. While so far refusing to break publicly with other ASEAN countries on the Cambodia question, Indonesia has in fact moved quite rapidly to improve relations with Vietnam and renew trading links. Singapore, in spite of its uncompromising political position, Australia and Japan have also made a number of moves towards breaking the economic blockade of Vietnam, which was tightened after the 1979 invasion. These changes since 1984 have come alongside gradual moves towards a negotiated settlement, which should eventually involve recognition of the Heng Samrin regime, as I shall argue below.

Vietnamese Policy

A recent article surveying Vietnam's external relations from the Vietnamese point of view (Nguyen Kien, 1985) stressed the overriding concern with regional questions. Besides its commitment to socialism and non-alignment, the article stressed two salient factors in Vietnamese foreign policy. Firstly, it argued that Vietnam has 'special relations' with Laos and Cambodia arising from the fact that they can and have been used as bases for foreign powers to attack Vietnam and vice versa. Here the author is referring to American use of Laos as a staging post to launch attacks on Vietnam, Chinese aid to Pol Pot to serve its own hostile purposes as well as US use of South Vietnam as a base for attacking Cambodian territory. Secondly, the article emphasizes Vietnamese independence from Soviet strategic considerations and the need to develop good relations with its Southeast Asian neighbours. It thus continues a strand in Vietnamese foreign-policy thinking that has always been present—namely, that Vietnam seeks a wide range of openings to the non-communist as well as communist countries, but that this must also coincide with Vietnamese perception of its independent state interests. Both the United States and China have recently tried to compel the Vietnamese leadership to alter this perspective with notable lack of success. It seems less than likely, then, that anyone else will be able to achieve the same goal.

Prior to 1978 Vietnamese policy towards Cambodia was essentially moderate. The time-honoured strategy of 'fighting while negotiating' was pursued: while meeting the DK challenge by force of arms, Vietnam outwardly maintained a conciliatory tone, offering to negotiate a settlement of the border dispute with Pol Pot. Conscious of Chinese backing for the DK regime, the Vietnamese military response was also restrained until 1978 when China had provoked a more serious breach in relations and the military alliance with the Soviet Union was sealed. The December 1978 invasion took place as political instability in South Vietnam reached a peak due to rising tension with the ethnic Chinese community, mounting economic problems and the difficulties of dealing with some three-quarters of a million refugees from the devastated regions on both sides of the Cambodia–Vietnam border. The invasion became one among a number of measures attempted to restore economic and political order and the likely long-term costs probably weighed far less in the minds of Vietnamese leaders than the immediate problems caused by diversion of resources to the border war and its consequences.

Since the invasion, however, the Vietnamese government has moved as quickly as possible to 'Cambodianize' the conflict, as well as normalize the economic and social life of the country. Formation of a Cambodian army to meet the Khmer Rouge challenge was impossible at first owing to the lack of experienced soldiers and an urgent need to keep able-bodied males for economic reconstruction (in the immediate aftermath of the Pol Pot regime females were an estimated 60 per cent of the population). By 1987, however, the PRK army was reportedly taking on about half of the garrison duty, the more experienced Vietnamese units being held in reserve for important military operations. A similar process has taken place in government and other areas of economic life, of placing newly trained Cambodians in key positions as they become available (Vickery, 1986).

As the analogy with 'Vietnamization' implies, however, 'Cambodianization' of military and government does not necessarily mean independence and there are clearly limits beyond which the Vietnamese are not prepared to allow Cambodian independence to go. These limits are set out in the notion of a 'special relationship' mentioned above. In any settlement of the conflict the Vietnamese will be concerned to ensure that no future regime in Cambodia will adopt policies detrimental to Vietnamese security interests. In practice this means that they could live with a wide variety of regimes including, for example, one which adhered to Sihanoukist neutrality, although given the success of their strategy of propping up the avowedly socialist Heng Samrin regime, it seems unlikely that they will need to make such concessions. The regime that seems to be emerging in Cambodia, while socialist in aim, also incorporates many elements from earlier (pre-DK) governments and the economic policy pursued (ownership and tax regimes, for example) is rather liberal. In spite of the massive Vietnamese presence in economic and administrative life up till now, a distinctive Cambodian style seems to be emerging, as much a result of the traumatic experiences under Pol Pot (which did much to damage popular acceptance of collective and state socialism) and proximity to Thailand as of Vietnamese influence.

The more the Heng Samrin government is able to consolidate its rule over Cambodia, the greater are the foreign policy options open to Vietnam in relation to its ASEAN neighbours. We have already seen the gradual erosion of the Western economic embargo of Vietnam as it came into conflict with wider strategic goals of some of the smaller regional powers. Since Vietnam carried out a successful offensive during the dry season of 1984-5 against the main base camps of all three coalition partners, the ability of ASEAN to rely on Khmer Rouge military operations to destabilize the Phnom Penh regime has been severely curtailed and this has led to several new initiatives towards a negotiated settlement. Vietnam has announced that its troops will be withdrawn by 1990 and has made other concessions—such as accepting the Malaysian proposal to hold a 'cocktail party' to establish informal contacts between the coalition partners and the PRK as a prelude to negotiations. So far the Thai have resisted these initiatives, as have the Chinese. Developments since 1985 are, however, a good illustration of the Vietnamese strategy of combining military, diplomatic and political means. Real concessions are made only once it is considered that the balance of these three has tipped decisively in Vietnam's favour so that its fundamental goal is not compromised.

A thaw in the Sino-Soviet dispute may also enhance the conditions for a settlement of the Cambodian conflict. A lessening of Sino-Soviet rivalry and restoration of greater distance between China and the United States may also lead to reduced tension in Sino-Vietnamese relations, allowing Vietnam to resume its more balanced policy towards the two socialist giants. Presently, China makes it a condition of further improvements in its relations with the Soviet Union that the latter abandons its support for Vietnamese policy in Cambodia. But there are equally pressing issues between the two sides which may eventually make for a settlement independently of this issue. Such an outcome will be all the more likely if ASEAN support for the Khmer Rouge collapses, effectively isolating China and Thailand. So far the Soviet Union has shown no inclination to pressure Vietnam to withdraw ahead of its own timetable, nor is it absolutely clear that Vietnam would respond to such pressure. Continued access to Cam Ranh Bay is one incentive for the Soviet Union to continue supporting Vietnam in Cambodia.

In summary, then, it was the divergent trajectories of the Cambodian and Vietnamese revolutions which led to the emergence of armed conflict in the 1970s, culminating in a Vietnamese decision that the Pol Pot regime constituted a fundamental threat to national security and the further development of socialism in Vietnam. The decision to invade Cambodia was taken as an essentially defensive measure, but the strategy pursued since then has been one of combining military, political and diplomatic efforts to achieve a settlement that does not compromise the basic goals of the regime. By and large they have pursued this strategy successfully and, eight years after the invasion, have succeeded not only in consolidating a sympathetic regime in Phnom Penh, but in gradually widening their foreign policy options in the region and opening gaps in the Western economic embargo.

The Vietnamese revolution was part of a world-wide revolutionary upsurge in the era immediate following the Second World War, in which nationalist and communist groups took advantage of the faltering power of European colonialism to stake their claim for national independence and often for far-reaching social reform. However, the period from 1954, when the French colonial power was defeated, to 1975, when the Vietnamese independence movement reached its final success, saw profound changes take place, both in the nature of Vietnamese economy and society and in the relationship of communist theory and practice to the society. An analysis of these changes provides some important lessons about the conditions giving rise to and sustaining revolutionary movements in the Third World.

A comparison of the Vietnamese revolution with that of neighbouring Thailand may be helpful to illustrate this point. In the early 1970s the Communist Party of Thailand (CPT) had, like the Vietnamese CP, organized a vigorous peasant-based guerrilla movement. Yet unlike the VCP, the CPT-led revolution subsequently collapsed, in spite of an infusion of urban radicals into the movement following the 1976 military coup in Thailand. The most obvious difference between the two countries, that Thailand had never been a colony, can, I think, be dismissed as of relatively minor significance in explaining this. The Thai economy was effectively managed by European interests (mainly British) between 1856 and 1932 and in any case the rule of absolute monarchy in Thailand was no less oppressive than French rule in Vietnam. Thailand had, however, had a civilian-military revolution in 1932 which overthrew the absolute monarchy and allowed nationalist elements to assume a role in government. Thus the Thai left was deprived of a potentially powerful ally until after the 1946 overthrow of nationalist leader Pridi Phanomyong by the military. In the 1950s and 1960s the repressive policies of the Thanon dictatorship and its strong pro-American leanings attracted many Thai intellectuals to the left and greatly strengthened the ideological base of the peasant guerrilla movement which subsequently arose. In principle then, the conditions in Thailand seemed ripe for a repeat performance of the sort of peasant-based and Communist-led revolutions which had taken place in China and Vietnam two or three decades earlier.

However, a number of developments occurred in the Southeast Asian region at the time which, as we have seen earlier in this book, had a profound effect on the course of the Vietnamese revolution after 1975 and proved fatal to the CPT. Foremost among these was the rapid development, particularly in the 1970s, of the social division of labour. In the case of South Vietnam, as I have pointed out, this was a wholly international division of labour in which the prosperity of Vietnamese agriculture and the consumption standards of inflated urban populations depended upon American aid-financed imports of manufactured goods. For Thailand, this development was also partly a domestic division of labour, which saw rising incomes from agriculture being ploughed back into the development of a substantial manufacturing and services sector in Bangkok and several provincial towns. Instead of 'the countryside surrounding the cities' as in classic Maoist guerrilla warfare doctrine, the octopus tentacles of the city—in both countries—reached out and drew the rural areas into a rapidly growing commodity economy.

As in South Vietnam, the Party in Thailand began to lose touch, not only with the urban areas, but with the fast-changing rural environment of the peasantry. By the late 1970s the CPT was operating in increasingly remote areas and by the mid-1980s it could no longer be regarded as a serious threat to the Thai state.

In South Vietnam, on the other hand, the speed of development in Thailand was not matched. Not only did the war hamper economic progress before 1975, but loyalty to the Communist Party had taken much deeper roots among the population over a period of nearly fifty years of fighting against foreign invaders and local oppressors. There remained a strong core of support for the VCP, which, combined with the armed forces of the successful socialist regime in the North, enabled the Vietnamese revolution to retain sufficient momentum to carry it to victory.

The Vietnamese revolution occurred, therefore, under conditions which cannot be repeated anywhere in Southeast Asia today. This assessment includes the Philippines where it might be argued that the Communist New People's Army (NPA) pursues a similar strategy to that of the CPT and VCP. Although the NPA is able to operate quite easily in the more remote and less developed areas of the Philippines, it has been far less successful in mobilizing sustained popular support in the more developed regions and in the industrial centre of Manila. Because they appeared on the scene rather recently, in reaction to a set of economic and social conditions which are gradually (if unevenly) disappearing, neither the CPT nor the NPA have really developed an ideological apparatus which is capable of embracing the newly emerging conditions. Instead they tend to rely on the tried formulae of the Vietnam era and it is for this reason I feel that they will prove unable to adapt and survive. Paradoxically, it is the Vietnamese struggle itself which contributed most to the ending of the era of successful Communist-led peasant revolutions in Asia: the enormous expenditures which American leaders felt were necessary to defeat the revolution have been a prime factor in industrialization and the rise of rural capitalism in the region.

Finally, something needs to be said about the impact of these changes on the course of the Vietnamese revolution after 1975. A major argument of this book has been that it was the unification process after 1975 which brought about a serious economic and political crisis and eventually led to economic reforms being set in train from 1979 onwards. The cause of the unification crisis can, in turn, be traced directly to the types of economic and social changes outlined above. The inappropriateness to the South of a socialist development strategy designed for a relatively autarkic social system became starkly apparent in the face of this crisis, while the lack of dynamism of the Northern economy contrasted with the superior economic performance of several neighbouring capitalist regimes.

Vietnamese leaders therefore embarked upon the hitherto uncharted course of creating a new sort of development strategy which could bring about a rapid advancement of the social division of labour, a nationally integrated market and rising standards of living. Similar efforts of the Soviet Union or China to revitalize their economies may encourage and assist this process, but the problem faced by Vietnam, in having to integrate the two very different socio-economic structures of North and South, is so far unique. Moreover, compounding the challenge posed to the Party leadership by unification is the very low level of development compared with other socialist countries. Under these circumstances, the economic experiences of capitalist neighbours like Thailand or South Korea may seem to have as much relevance for Vietnam as the models of the much larger and more industrialized socialist countries. If this is so (and some prominent Vietnamese have suggested it), then it will be an even greater challenge for the Party to maintain a vision of a socialist future which can inspire the same sort of loyalty that sustained the thirty-year independence struggle.

Notes

Chapter 1

1. The Communist Party in Vietnam has been known by a number of different names: (1) from February to October 1930 it was the Vietnamese Communist Party; (2) from October 1930 to November 1945 it was the Indochinese Communist Party and included Khmer and Lao revolutionaries in its membership; (3) from November 1945 to February 1951 the Party was formally dissolved; (4) from February 1951 to December 1976 it was the Vietnamese Workers' Party; (5) in December 1976 it was named once again the Vietnamese Communist Party. During the 1960s and 1970s the southern regional branch was also known as the People's Revolutionary Party.
2. In Tonkin, for example, Francis Garnier was able to capture Hanoi with only a handful of men in 1873, though he later lost it. Henri de la Rivière repeated the feat in 1882.

Chapter 2

1. Although land tax varied according to classification of land quality, there were frequent cases where villages had to pay tax on land which they did not have (*khong thu*)—e.g., land washed away by flood, uncultivated forest land—and village councils sometimes resorted to the method of reclassifying all land as Grade 1 in order to meet the tax (Truong Chinh & Vo Nguyen Giap, 1974, pp. 49–50). Abuses of other taxes were also common, e.g., through the forced sale of alcohol to villagers (Truong Chinh & Vo Nguyen Giap, 1974). Many of the taxes were in fact continuations of the pre-colonial tax system, but the way they were implemented by the new 'dynasty' intensified rather than ameliorated the social problems generated under the old, corrupt dynasty (see previous chapter).
2. Seasonal migration by peasants seeking agricultural labouring work during slack periods in their own areas was a common phenomenon (Gourou, 1965), but it did not involve stepping outside the familiar rural environment.
3. Ho Chi Minh was born Nguyen Sinh Cung in 1890 according to his official biography, but was renamed by his parents, in keeping with a fairly common tradition, at the age of 11 as Nguyen Tat Thanh. He adopted a large number of pseudonyms through the course of his political career—the two best known being Nguyen Ai Quoc (Nguyen the Patriot) which he used in the 1920s and 1930s, and Ho Chi Minh (Ho who enlightens) which he adopted in 1942

(Lacouture, 1968; Huynh Kim Khanh, 1982). For the sake of simplicity I have used the name Ho Chi Minh throughout this book.

4. The alleged appearance of a Maitreya Buddha in Nam Bo in 1912 and subsequent movement to establish Phan Xich Long as Emperor in 1913 was the first of these. Later, more widespread religious movements among the peasants included the Cao Dai and Hoa Hao.

5. However, Phan Boi Chau, whose life spanned the whole period from the Can Vuong (Aid the King) movement up to the formation of the ICP and after, was able in the end to see the importance of this.

6. There is little documentary evidence to support a direct conection, but given the attacks launched by the Bac Bo activists on 'petty bourgeois intellectuals' in Thanh Nien it does seem likely. It is not clear whether Ho Chi Minh supported or opposed the move to form a Communist Party, but Huynh Kim Khanh makes a convincing case that he *was* opposed to the 1928 Comintern policy (Huynh Kim Khanh, 1982, esp. pp. 179–86).

7. Note the coincidence in time of this movement with the much larger and longer-lived Jiangsu Soviet in China (1930–4).

8. A subsequent self-criticism suggests that the failure of the Party to criticize Daladier's appeasement of Hitler at Munich and the lack of real reforms in Indochina by the French Popular Front government tended to weaken the ICP's ideological appeal at the time (Vietnam Workers' Party, 1960, pp. 57–61). The ICP had adopted the Popular Front tactics of the Comintern.

Chapter 3

1. Both Huynh Kim Khanh (1982) and Duiker (1981) say that Ho was in Moscow during the 1930s. The official Party history of 1960 (Vietnamese Workers' Party, 1960, p. 52) puts him in China during the Popular Front period of 1936–9. However, the 1980 version of Party history (VCP, 1980) has him in Moscow from 1933 (p. 43) and in China in about 1937 (p. 52). Others say he did not leave Moscow until 1938 (Kolko, 1986; Chen, 1969, p. 333). Vagueness in the written texts on points like these reflects both the absence of documentation of these early activities and the vicissitudes of Vietnam's relations with China. Thus the 1960 version of Party history stresses Chinese assistance to the ICP from 1927, though the evidence to support this is rather weak. When he first went to China in 1925, Ho worked under Mikhail Borodin. He returned to Moscow in 1927 after the smashing of the Canton Commune and then went to Siam, returning to Hong Kong in 1930 where he was detained by the British in 1931–2. Managing to escape, he returned to Moscow in 1933. Indeed Comintern influence seems to have been dominant during the 1930s on all the ICP's activities (at a time when Ho Chi Minh himself was possibly out of favour in Moscow—see Huynh Kim Khanh (1982)). After Hitler's attack on the Soviet

Union in June 1941, the ICP seems to have been thrown more on its own resources and it was not until the Chinese revolution in 1949 and the establishment of a common border between China and the liberated zones of the DRV that Chinese assistance, and Maoism in particular, seem to have become a major influence though this was reduced again after 1964 (see also Chapter 6).

2. For the story of US involvement with the Viet Minh in 1944–5, see Patti (1980).

3. Interestingly, they did not choose Prince Cuong De, a close relative of Bao Dai who had lived in Japan for many years (after having been encouraged to form an anti-French 'government-in-exile' by Phan Boi Chau). Cuong De had received support for his claims from the Japanese earlier in the war as part of their encouragement of anti-Western and anti-communist nationalists, including the Cao Dai and Hoa Hao religious movements.

4. Note that, contrary to recent Chinese and Democratic Kampuchea (Pol Pot) propaganda, the idea of an Indochinese Federation was French, not Vietnamese. Ho Chi Minh consistently supported national solutions to the problems of colonialism and social inequality in the three Indochinese countries.

5. Though even as late as 15 December Ho Chi Minh apparently still hoped to postpone war by appealing to the new government of Leon Blum to order a French return to their positions of 20 November. Apparently Blum did not get the message, due to failure by the Saigon authorities to transmit it, until too late (Duiker, 1981, p. 124).

6. Duiker (1981), p. 122. The 1953 map of French commander General Navarre (reprinted in Kahin & Lewis, 1967, p. 34) confirms that the Viet Minh continued to hold most of the southern countryside until the end of the war.

7. During the early 1940s at Pac Bo, Ho Chi Minh had translated the Chinese classic on military thought (Sun-tzu) and written two books on guerrilla warfare based on Chinese experiences of Yenan (Woodside, 1976, pp. 223–4).

8. Meanwhile, the United States also began to establish independent links with the Bao Dai government.

9. See Michael Vickery (1986) for a discussion of the debate over the founding date of the Communist Party in Cambodia. Pol Pot's supporters have tried to argue that the Communist Party was not founded until 1962, at what most scholars regard as the Party's Second Congress, held in the year before Pol Pot became Secretary.

10. In November 1956 Party Secretary Truong Chinh accepted responsibility for the mistakes that led to these excesses and resigned.

11. The motives of the Soviet government in seeking to make concessions to France would appear to have been a desire to persuade the French to stay out of the proposed European Defence Community.

12. China had lost an estimated half million men in the Korean War (Kolko, 1986, p. 64).

13. In the case of the other two Indochinese countries, the solutions arrived at were

also advantageous to the Chinese and detrimental to local communist organizations. In Laos the communists were given two provinces bordering on China and North Vietnam as a regroupment zone. The Khmer communists were ceded nothing, the French having granted formal independence to Prince Sihanouk in 1953. Most of the Cambodian communists fled into exile in Hanoi while a handful stayed on to try to work legally under Sihanouk's regime or to form a tiny and largely ineffective guerrilla force. Both Cambodia and Laos were 'neutralized' under the Geneva Accords, though this meant their effective domination by anti-communist regimes.

Chapter 4

1. France had signed the Geneva Agreement on behalf of the Bao Dai government which was not then independent. But during the talks at Geneva, France had signed a separate agreement with Bao Dai promising independence from 1 January 1955. Technically, then, the State of Vietnam inherited the legal obligations of France under the Geneva Agreement on becoming independent, but in practice Bao Dai's regime had opposed the Geneva settlement, with US encouragement, and used this as a reason not to abide by its provisions. Ultimately, the French were responsible for this state of affairs and it is clear that they never had any intention of seeing the Agreement fulfilled.

2. This Front was from its inception openly dominated by the Party (Turley, 1986, pp. 18–31), the southern branch of which became known as the People's Revolutionary Party. While this party (branch), as before, showed considerable local autonomy, it was subject to the central Party offices in Hanoi. The name change of the southern party merely reflected the requisites of the united front policy, just as the name of the Vietnam Workers' Party in 1951 reflected the emerging shift towards class-based politics. The actual party structure remained unified while the two names accorded with the different needs of the two regions.

3. This is reflected in the analysis of the South presented in the Political Report to the 4th Party Congress in 1976. The problem of the transition to socialism in the South was treated there with extraordinary brevity compared with the space devoted to a critical analysis of developments in the North of the country (VCP, 1977). The lack of a deep analysis of the southern social system in the latter years of the war is contrasted, however, with the very sophisticated analysis of the weak points of the RVN regime, of the possibilities of exploiting differences among the DRV's allies in the socialist camp and, above all, of the constraints operating on American policy—as Gabriel Kolko makes abundantly clear (1986).

4. HES was an American attempt to apply quantitative criteria to political and military control of villages. However, information gathering was poorly carried out and dishonest and the system was unable to grasp the symbiotic relations of

the NLF and RVN structures—which are very well described by Douglas Pike (1969, pp. 18–30). As the United States escalated its involvement in 1965 to stave off imminent defeat of the RVN, the HES rated only 24 per cent of the South as 'NLF-controlled' (Kolko, 1986, pp. 240–1).

5. Kolko (1986) provides an interesting account based on the different assessments of Generals Van Tien Dung, whom he describes as a technocratically oriented military officer, and General Tran Van Tra, a southern leader who continued to advocate a close relationship between politics and armed struggle. It was on the basis of a *political* analysis of conditions in the south that Party leaders there pushed for an offensive in early 1975. In fact a study of the history of the Vietnam War makes it clear that purely military factors were *never* decisive. This is a point which is of relevance to subsequent attempts by American authors to suggest that, if not for the 'treacherous' activities of the Peace Movement, the United States could have achieved a military victory.

6. Snepp (1980) offers a graphic account, from the point of view of an Embassy official (CIA), of the final days.

Chapter 5

1. Involving up to 100,000 workers by the end of the 1930s (Murray, 1980).

2. Le Khoa *et al*., 1979, pp. 124, 126–8; Tran Huu Quang, 1982, p. 32. In the 1978 survey lower-middle peasants (57 per cent of households) owned 56 per cent of the land or 0.35 ha. per capita. Upper-middle peasants (15 per cent of households) owned 25 per cent of the land or 0.57 ha. per capita. The former are defined by their household self-sufficiency with regard to labour supply and output levels; the latter earn most of their income from family farming, but may also own machinery which they rent out to others.

3. The Vietnamese officially define their society at the time of independence as 'colonial and feudal' (see, for example, VCP, 1980, p. 133), hence a distinction is made for political purposes between the 'feudal' landlords and the 'capitalist' rich peasant farmers, who hire wage-labour and use more modern technology, for example. It should also be noted, however, that the Vietnamese have debated among themselves whether their society could ever have been characterized as 'feudal' or whether Marx's concept of the Asiatic Mode of Production might be more suitable to explain the processes of the pre-capitalist society. In contrast to other socialist countries, where this topic has only recently, if at all, been revived, there has been a substantial school of thought in Vietnam favouring the Asiatic Mode concept for some years. The nature of the mode of production in underdeveloped societies has been debated rather extensively in the literature (notably in the debate on Indian agriculture carried out chiefly in the pages of *Economic and Political Weekly*) and it is not proposed to canvas the issues here.

4. Though owing to the contract labour system in the plantations and mines, the number who had worked in industry at some time was much greater.

5. In 1955, for example, Hanoi had, according to one source, eighteen industrial establishments employing 1,369 workers and 496 privately-owned workshops and handicraft enterprises with about 5,000 workers. In 1983 the city accounted for 14 per cent of national industrial output and had 100,000 factory workers and another 130,000 handicraft workers (Hanoi, 1986, p. 175). For the DRV as a whole, modern industry accounted for 29 per cent of industrial gross output value in 1955 and 73 per cent in 1973 (Vickerman, 1985, p. 228).

6. Primarily because land distribution was carried out by the state and there was no political campaign.

7. Many ethnic Chinese also left the North after 1978 as tensions between Vietnam and China rose and the Vietnamese authorities became suspicious of possible Chinese infiltration and sabotage. Chinese communities overseas do tend to retain strong links with China, even after several generations, and many of those in North Vietnam were members of the CCP under the terms of an agreement between the DRV and PRC in the 1950s. In the South, the Chinese community was organized into self-governing *bangs*, based on province of origin with China, and tended to retain close links with Taiwan. The Taiwan government had, for example, intervened to try to protect the *bang* system against Ngo Dinh Diem's attempts to dismantle it (Chen, 1969), but Thieu had left the Chinese alone. The Chinese population of Vietnam fell from 1,228,000 in 1976 to 935,000 in 1979 (General Statistical Office, 1985, p. 20) and may have fallen further since then, given the high level of anti-Chinese feeling as a result of the February 1979 war. The rate of departure has, however, slowed dramatically in recent years and may be offset by natural population growth.

8. For example, the Ho Chi Minh City Food and Agriculture Department which, under the management of Mrs Nguyen Thi Thi has actively and successfully competed with private traders and, after much debate, has won the approval of Hanoi (*Financial Times*, 11 May 1987).

9. An estimate by unnamed 'Vietnamese economists' given to the *Far Eastern Economic Review*, correspondent Murray Hiebert (*Far Eastern Economic Review*, 23 July 1987, p. 29). A radio Hanoi broadcast mentioned a figure of 65,000 for Hanoi alone. If this were multiplied up for the entire urban population it would come to about 400,000, which can be taken as a conservative estimate.

10. The decline in the share of unproductive employment and stagnation of industry's share may also be due to the fact that state employees in Vietnam receive insufficient remuneration and usually have to take up other employment. According to the article cited in the previous note, over 2,000 school teachers, or a fifth of Ho Chi Minh City's teaching staff, resigned to take up other employment during the first five months of 1987 because of the inadequacy of government salaries.

11. This is a 1985 figure.

12. The extent of this depletion of the male labour force in the countryside can be seen in the fact that in 1976 women still formed over 52 per cent of the

population and were more than this in seven of North Vietnam's provinces (over 54 per cent in two of them) and in eight South Vietnamese provinces. By 1984 this imbalance had been reduced to six provinces (all in the South) and women were 51 per cent of the population as a whole (General Statistical Office, 1985, pp. 15–16).

13. White (1982b and n.d.) discussed this in relation to agriculture. I am indebted to Irene Norlund for the information on women in industry taken from her as yet unpublished research.

Chapter 6

1. Indigenous Lao and Khmer membership of the ICP was negligible before the Second World War when a recruitment drive was launched. Kiernan (1985), for example, was only able positively to identify one such individual in the 1930s. Ethnic Vietnamese working on plantations and mines in the two countries were far more numerous at first.

2. The pre-1960 Central Committee had only thirty-one members. That elected in 1960 had forty-five full members and twenty-eight alternates. That elected in 1976 had 101 full and thirty-two alternate members and that elected in 1982 had 116 full and thirty-six alternate members.

3. E.g., Pike, 1969; Fall, 1960; Chen, 1969; Thai Quang Trung, 1985; and see also recent journalistic attempts to understand the economic debates of the 1980s in terms of factional disputes between 'ideologues' and 'pragmatists'.

4. Elliott (1975, p. 41) describes the changes in factional alignments as 'kaleidoscopic'.

5. Zhou Enlai reportedly met Ho Chi Minh in Paris in 1922 and described him as already a mature Marxist, in contrast to himself (Chen, 1969, p. 21).

6. Mao strongly opposed the Comintern call for a radical land reform in 1927 (Chen, 1969, p. 214). For the Vietnamese position see Chapters 2 and 3 and Huynh Kim Khanh (1982).

7. It is perhaps significant, however, that the title of the book was *Guerrilla Warfare: Experiences of the Chinese Guerrillas, Experiences of the French Guerrillas*.

8. The Chinese claim that the battle of Dien Bien Phu was directed by a Chinese general and that Chinese officers were present at every level of command. Chen (1969) refers to unspecified Chinese sources on this and the claim was confirmed to me by CCP historian Hu Hua in 1986. This claim has been repeated by (or originated from?) John Foster Dulles, when he was US Secretary of State, and Gen. H. Navarre, the French commanding officer (see Chen, 1969, pp. 296–7), both of whom may have wanted to see the hand of 'International Communism' behind the Vietnamese revolution. Whether the claim is true or not, however, hardly alters the legitimacy of the Viet Minh regime in the eyes of the Vietnamese people, or the ultimate independence of the Vietnamese Party in

deciding its course between domestic and international pressures and opportunities. Chinese stress on this sort of claim, in the light of the present conflict between the two countries, smacks of a more traditional relationship between the two countries (which operated rather like a protection racket—in return for protection, or non-aggression, you are supposed to pay tribute) than communist internationalism in which mutual assistance is based on mutual interest in the outcome.

9. The idea of 'uninterrupted' revolution, i.e. one proceeding straight from a bourgeois to socialist stage because of the weakness of the bourgeoisie had also been raised by Marx in 1848 and by Lenin in 1917.

10. This episode has also contributed to the identification of Truong Chinh as a Maoist, but an equally plausible explanation is that his resignation showed a willingness of the senior leadership to accept some responsibility for errors which had led to a serious loss of public confidence in the Party. Thirty years later, Truong Chinh and other top leaders underwent a similar process of self-criticism in accepting responsibility for errors in economic management which had led to a renewed loss of public confidence (Truong Chinh, 1986). Ironically, the mistakes identified in this case—bureaucratism, over-centralization of decision-making, over-emphasis on heavy industry, voluntarism and conservatism—could just as easily (if not more easily) be applied to the 'Soviet model' as to Maoism. Moreover, Truong Chinh had maintained and even increased his influence in the Party at a time of severe conflict with China between 1978 and 1986, temporarily becoming Party Secretary again after Le Duan's death—a factor which scarcely points to his adherence to Maoist or pro-Chinese sentiments, especially at a time when Vietnamese theoreticians argued that Maoism was incompatible with Marxism.

11. Vietnamese leaders have even been known to describe Mao Zedong as 'the brilliant sun of the Asian people' (Chen, 1969, p. 327) in deference to the sensitivities of their ally, though it must be noted that the statements cited by Chen were all made in Beijing for Chinese consumption.

12. The construction of an elaborate tomb and the re-creation of Ho as a sort of saintly 'uncle' are consistent with traditional family-oriented and patriarchial Confucian ideas. Mao's tomb in Peking is a far grander affair, however. In the entrance hall a large marble statue sits before, and seemingly above, a vast mural panorama representing the whole of China. The contrast in symbolism (whether intentional or not) is marked: Ho as a greatly respected member of the family, Mao as a Son of Heaven.

13. The three revolutions are the revolution in the relations of production, the scientific and technological revolution and the cultural and ideological revolution. Among these the scientific and technological revolution is considered the 'kingpin' which creates the material basis for the other two.

Chapter 7

1. This primacy of the legitimation function is implicitly recognized in the preamble to the 1980 Vietnamese constitution: 'The Socialist Republic of Vietnam needs a constitution institutionalizing the current line of the Communist Party of Vietnam in the new stage, namely a constitution for the period of transition to socialism on a national scale. . . . the present constitution sums up and affirms the gains of the revolutionary struggle of the Vietnamese people over the past half century, expresses the will and aspirations of the Vietnamese people and guarantees the successful development of Vietnamese society in the coming period.' (*Constitution* . . . , p. 10.)

2. Cf. Article 6 of the Soviet constitution which states that 'The leading and guiding force of Soviet society and the nucleus of its political system, of all state organizations and public organizations is the Communist Party of the Soviet Union.' (Reproduced in Lane 1985.)

3. The Vietnamese constitution describes the SRV as a proletarian dictatorship (in contrast to the Chinese 'people's democratic dictatorship'). However, where both Vietnam and China place the 'worker–peasant alliance, led by the working class' at the core of the class power structure, the Soviet constitution merely states that 'all power belongs to the people'.

4. In China this role is fulfilled by the Standing Committee of the National People's Congress. The Vietnamese National Assembly also elects a Standing Committee to facilitate examination and drafting of bills, but its functions are quite distinct from those of the Council of State.

5. In the Soviet Union it is by meetings of citizens held at places of work and by a show of hands.

6. It may be significant that amidst rising tension with China in mid-1978, two prominent minority leaders, Generals Chu Van Tan and Le Quang Ba were unofficially reported under house arrest (Duiker, 1983, p. 8).

7. This is closer to the Chinese wording ('helps, guides and supervises') (Wang, 1985, p. 321), though other aspects of the economic chapter are markedly dissimilar.

8. Cf. also the debate in the letters column of the *Far Eastern Economic Review* in July and August 1987 concerning the assertion that Laos and Cambodia have 'ready-made' constitutions borrowed from Vietnam.

9. A major example of political intervention in administrative appointments occurred with the redeployment of military personnel after the War. The high levels of political consciousness in the PAVN plus the desire to reward soldiers by finding civilian employment commensurate with their military levels of responsibility were the Party's motives. One provincial director of agriculture whom I met was a former artillery commander trained in electronic engineering. While I am in no position to judge the competence of this person in his new

field, there does seem to be a high probability of such mismatches producing an inexpert bureaucratic structure.

10. At the purely formal level, the powers of the Vietnamese Assembly are wider here than their Soviet or Chinese counterparts. The latter may only ratify appointments made by the executive to ministerial positions.

11. Vietnamese practice here contrasts with that in China where only the lower level councils are directly elected: at provincial and central levels they are indirectly elected, by deputies from the level below. Until very recently this was also true of county, though not commune, level in China.

Chapter 8

1. Much larger numbers of workers are involved in artisan manufacturing organized into collectives. These may suffer from some, though not all the problems experienced by salaried workers.

2. Poor health of working mothers and shortages of milk for babies were the reason for the extension of the leave period. The debate was not so much over this as over how to cope with the need for replacement labour, whether women should lose seniority and promotion prospects, etc.

3. Since 1975 a number of prominent intellectuals, formerly closely associated with the NLF or Third Force, and even with the DRV regime (such as the economist Vo Nhan Tri) have left legally.

4. In 1978 the paper had run articles on suicides among people 'deported' to New Economic Zones and some highly critical articles on the then economic policy by a US-trained economist who now holds a high advisory position.

5. Based on population data and estimated growth rates between 1976 and 1979, it is possible to estimate that approximtely 400,000 ethnic Chinese left the country by the latter date. No figures are available for subsequent years.

6. Paris-based refugee sources put the figure as high as 700,000 to 800,000 around this time. An anonymous 'Hanoi-based diplomat' also made an estimate, of 50,000.

Chapter 9

1. With adequate irrigation and drainage, land which previously depended on rainfall for one crop a year could be sown with two, three and even four successive crops. Total sown area in North Vietnam rose from 2.5 million hectares in 1955 to about 2.9 million hectares in 1961 and 3.1 million hectares by 1964 (Nguyen Tien Hung, 1977, pp. 118, 127). (Sown area is measured by multiplying the cultivated land area by the number of crops it bears per annum.)

2. Although women were entitled to own and inherit land in Vietnam (in contrast

to the traditional position of Chinese women), effective economic control over the land was held by men as heads of households. Women were also excluded from village political affairs in traditional Vietnamese society because the village councils were open only to registered males. During the war many women not only participated in collective bodies, but rose to management positions, though in peacetime they tended to be displaced by returned soldiers.

3. Some industries, e.g., garments, are essentially updated handicraft industries in which workers also retain a high degree of control over their labour process (except that supervision is easier, because of spatial concentration, than in agriculture). In more technically advanced industries, however, the individual skills of the worker are increasingly replaced by the precision of a machine which dictates the speed and quality of the operation.

4. Loosely identified with Marx's Department I, or industries producing means of production.

5. By 1982 external debt had risen to an estimated US$5,000 million. A minority of this was owed to the West, but Vietnamese requests for a moratorium on payments caused a breakdown of relations with the IMF by 1985. Vietnam's debt service ratio with the convertible area was estimated to be 150 per cent, while its overall debt service ratio was 76 per cent. Better export performance in recent years has enabled a re-opening of negotiations with the IMF, however.

Chapter 10

1. This is graphically illustrated by the fact that South Vietnamese spent more on imported cosmetics and beauty aids than the country's entire export income.

2. This followed the sacking of Nguyen Van Linh from his post as Chairman of the Committee for Transformation of Private Trade and Industry in the South. Linh resumed his political rise after the 1979 reforms and became Party Secretary in 1986.

3. Even 'middle' or 'rich' peasants who had owned draft animals had often lost them during the war. American soldiers often used buffaloes for target practice, and deliberate slaughter was carried out if a village was suspected of harbouring the NLF—a frequent occurrence in a region with a strong revolutionary tradition. See Trullinger, 1980; Ngo Vinh Long, 1984.

4. These figures are based on calculations from General Statistical Office, 1985, pp. 90–1; 1983, pp. 56–7; 1980, pp. 56–7.

Chapter 11

1. Household production has typically gone through a number of vicissitudes under the socialist regime in Vietnam. While it has always had some nominal

status as a 'complementary' system of production to the collective and state enterprises, it has only received active encouragement in phases of economic reform such as that begun in 1979. The policy of active encouragement of household production was re-affirmed even more strongly in 1986 than in 1979. A *Nhan Dan* editorial of 1 December 1986, for example, stated that: 'While the sources of capital of the state and the collective are still not sufficient, the sources of capital left among the people are virtually spent only for covering personal expenses, kept in reserve, or used to buy goods for hoarding. This situation requires an integrated policy by which the state must join with the labouring people to create more jobs, encourage the people to make capital investments in production and business, foster traditional trades and develop more new trades in small-industry and handicraft production and support services' (SWB, FE/ 8432/B/8, 3 December 1986).

2. Some exceptions to this general rule are made, however, chiefly where soil preparation involves the use of draft animals or where small means of production are not already collectively owned in the South. In these cases households can use their own animals for ploughing.

3. Needless to say, a free market in grain still exists, but chiefly for the higher quality strains of rice (i.e., the low-yielding, traditional varieties which are valued for their superior taste and texture), which no longer form the staple diet of the bulk of the population.

4. However, the system at least sometimes comes close to a land-for-mouths one. In one cooperative visited by the author near Ho Chi Minh City, land had been allocated according to the following formula: 0.15 hectares per full-time adult labourer (aged between 16 and 65); 0.075 hectares per 'additional' labourer (e.g. able-bodied people with full-time jobs or high school students able to work part-time on the land) and 0.05 hectares for 'supplementary' labourers (e.g., small children or the aged who could tend animals and fruit trees). But it was pointed out that this allocation had been made in order to ensure that all existing family members of cooperators could be fed and future redistributions would not be made in a way which encouraged growth of families. There may also have been a more overtly political element in the allocation of land by this cooperative: before the introduction of the product contract system the cooperative had all but disintegrated and the allocation of land according to family size may have acted as an incentive to adhere to the cooperative.

5. In China, which also has a system of contracting land to peasants, the period of tenure has recently been extended to fifty years and is transferable from one generation to the next.

6. Lam Thanh Liem (1985) reports a range of tax rates from 14 per cent on Category 1 land (the best) to 10 per cent on Category 7 land (the worst) and argues that because yields were actually lower than those calculated by the authorities, real rates of tax were as high as 28 per cent on the best land. My visits to a number of cooperatives in both northern and southern Vietnam in October

1985 revealed that they were all paying effective rates of about 6 per cent, though the nominal rate was 10 per cent and that on family land was reported to be 11–12 per cent. By this time most southern rice land had been, at least nominally, collectivized.

7. The relatively fast growth of imports from the CMEA countries is probably accounted for by a change in sourcing of oil imports (Fforde, 1985).

8. Reported foodgrain output of the northern provinces averaged only 246 kg. per capita (of paddy equivalent) in 1984, compared with the national average of 304 kg. and 511 kg. in the Mekong River delta (Beresford, 1987, p. 266).

9. In theory, all transactions of enterprises carrying out their plans were conducted via the State Bank. But the frequency with which firms were ignoring official channels and engaging in illegal transactions meant that most had large cash holdings.

10. This was brought out in a speech by Pham Ngoc Bich, director of the Nam Dinh Textile Mill at the 5th Congress (see JPRS 81347, p. 64).

11. To Huu had been seen as a rising star in the political hierarchy after his elevation to the Political Bureau by the 5th Congress in 1982 and to the No. 2 position in the Council of Ministers. His rise coincided closely in time with the second temporary eclipse of Nguyen Van Linh (see Chapter 10 for the earlier one in 1978). After 1982 To Huu had been given economic responsibilities, but see Kolko (1986, p. 24), who quotes him as saying that he could not understand Marx's *Capital*.

12. In the opening of his speech Truong Chinh referred to the 'outspoken suggestions to the draft' and 'many heartfelt proposals' which had been received (Truong Chinh, 1986, p. C1/1).

13. In 1982 the Economic Report had been given by Prime Minister Pham Van Dong. Dong retired from his Political Bureau position at the 1986 Congress, but remained Prime Minister until the National Assembly meeting in June 1987. Kiet is widely regarded as pro-reform and his delivery of the Economic Report in 1986 reflected his promotion within the Political Bureau to the No. 5 position. However, the Economic Report is couched in much more orthodox language than the Political Report, possibly it was less intensely debated.

14. In the ministerial reshuffle which took place early in 1987, the old ministries of Agriculture and Food were amalgamated as part of the move to achieve more vertically integrated production for this sector. The Ho Chi Minh City Food Corporation has been cited as a model in this area (*Financial Times*, 11 May 1987). The Vietnamese have shown considerable interest in the East German vertically integrated industrial trusts.

Chapter 12

1. Buttinger (1972, p. 66) estimates that some 80 per cent of Vietnamese were functionally literate prior to the French conquest, but that by 1939 only 15 per cent of school-age children received any form of schooling. Woodside (1983, p. 404) says that just over 2 per cent received a 'pinched and rudimentary' schooling under the French.
2. The fact that the number is over 100 per cent reflects wide age disparities within the Vietnamese system, due to a high drop-out rate and large numbers of students repeating grades.
3. Prior to the reforms the northern system had ten years and the southern system (still based on the colonial one) had twelve years.
4. See, for example, A. H. Brodrick, *Little China: The Annamese Lands*, Oxford University Press, London, 1942.
5. Thailand did rank, at number 20. Between them, these twenty countries account for 80 per cent of all Third World imports of major weapons.

Chapter 13

1. This is a reference to Ho Chi Minh's speech at the 1951 Party Congress: 'Today it is the grasshoppers that dare stand up to the elephants. Tomorrow, it's the elephant that leaves its skin behind.' Cited in Wilfred Burchett, *Grasshoppers and Elephants: Why Vietnam Fell*, Urizen Books, New York, 1977.
2. Rowley & Evans (1984), for example, state quite correctly that Vietnamese foreign policy cannot be understood independently of domestic economic developments, but (for reasons of space) they then proceed to ignore this, focusing instead on a mainly political explanation of nationalism as a movement for the creation of a modern state.
3. From his 'Indictment of French Colonialism' (1925), cited in Nguyen Kien (1985).
4. The analogy was with the sweeping of spiders' cobwebs (capitalist enclaves) out of the house. Mao told the Vietnamese that since China's broom was too short to reach Taiwan, the Vietnamese should be content to leave the Thieu regime in charge of Saigon for a relatively prolonged period—they could hardly hope to do better than the Chinese themselves.
5. Both Chinese and Vietnamese claims are based on dynastic records of doubtful geographical accuracy and not recognized in current international law of the sea. In terms of modern law, all claims are complicated by conflicting principles which can be used to justify the cases of both sides. See the essay of Davenport & Woodward in Keith (1986).
6. Estimates of the numbers used range from 225,000 (Chanda, 1986, p. 350) to the

Vietnamese figure of 600,000. Chinese casualty estimates were 20,000 of their own troops as against about 10,000 Vietnamese (including civilians) (Chanda, 1986, pp. 360–1).

7. In December 1979 I visited Lang Son, one of the towns captured just 18 km. from the Chinese border. The town had been completely flattened: everything from the kindergartens to the museum of Ho Chi Minh's Pac Bo days and the French-built anise oil factory was reduced to rubble. The population were living in makeshift shelters in the town and strung out along the road towards Hanoi.

8. The Vietnamese themselves apparently believed the Chinese goal was to hold a slice of Vietnamese territory to use as a bargaining chip to obtain Vietnamese withdrawal from Cambodia (Chanda, 1986, p. 358).

9. The US House of Representatives had passed an amendment on 4 May 1976 forbidding payment of reparation to Vietnam (after ten minutes' debate). In June 1977 ninety out of a hundred Senators voted for an amendment banning either aid *or* reparations (Ton That Thien, 1983, p. 697).

10. China's attack on Vietnam in 1979 did not provoke any Soviet retaliation because the United States acted to shield China by linking Soviet 'good behaviour' with the signing of the SALT II agreement (Chanda, 1986, p. 353).

11. The same idea was floated by the World Bank in the early 1970s, also including Thailand as a Mekong basin country, and a committee was set up to begin planning the process.

12. Kampuchea is the romanized transliteration chosen by the Pol Pot regime to represent the Khmer word normally rendered in English as Cambodia. The Heng Samrin regime has retained the new spelling in its official title, but I have used Cambodia here except where using the official name (for the same reason I do not use Zhongguo for China). As a phonetic rendering there is not a great deal to chose between the two versions.

13. Supporters of Pol Pot have argued that since attacking the larger, more powerful Vietnam would be irrational, it cannot be true that DK initiated the fighting. If this were the case Argentina would not have attacked the Falklands. The motivations for such attacks are not based on the likelihood of success, but on the need to distract attention from domestic problems.

14. In 1979 I visited Ba Chuc in An Giang province, the scene of one such raid during April 1978, and was shown the wreckage of buildings, scars of survivors and a lot of extremely grisly photographs taken some time after the event. Ba Chuc and surrounding districts have a large number of ethnic Khmer residents.

15. In 1987 the Prince took a year's 'leave of absence'. He has never got on well with the Khmer Rouge, who kept him under house arrest between 1975 and 1978 and killed several members of his family. By distancing himself from them now he may be opening the way for an accommodation with the Heng Samrin regime. The Vietnamese would probably be prepared to see Sihanouk take a nominal role in the government. Several authors have argued that his absence from political life inside Cambodia for over seventeen years has greatly eroded

his former popularity and ability to mobilize significant support, so he may be considered unlikely to pose an effective threat to the regime. Much, however, will depend on the attitude of the Chinese, who have been Sihanouk's financial and political patrons since his overthrow by Lon Nol in 1970.

16. During World War II, their alliance with Japan enabled them to force France to hand over two western provinces of Cambodia (including the main rice growing region around Battambang), though these were restored to French rule after the Japanese surrender. Parts of Laos were also affected. In 1962 the World Court awarded Cambodia an important temple in the border region which was also claimed by Thailand. In 1983 the Thai invaded and occupied three villages on the Laotian left bank of the Mekong. Although they have now withdrawn they have not renounced their claim to the whole left bank of the Mekong which were assigned to Laos under the 1904 treaty between France and the then Kingdom of Siam.

Selected Bibliography

This bibliography contains the main secondary sources used in compiling this book, concentrating on those written in English which are fairly readily accessible to students. Other valuable sources of material in English are the British Broadcasting Corporation's *Summary of World Broadcasts, Far East*, the United States Congress Joint Publications Research Service's *Translations on Vietnam*, succeeded by its *Vietnam Report*, and also the US Foreign Broadcast Information Service/JPRS *Southeast Asia Report*. Various Vietnamese language sources have also been used, but only a few of the main ones are cited here.

Abbreviations: DRV, Democratic Republic of Vietnam; FLPH, Foreign Languages Publishing House; IMF, International Monetary Fund; JPRS, Joint Publications Research Service; SWB, Summary of World Broadcasts; VCP, Vietnamese Communist Party (also Parti Communiste du Vietnam); VWP, Vietnamese Workers' Party.

Appleton, Judith, 1983. 'Socialist Vietnam: Continuity and Change' in David A. M. Lea & D. P. Chaudhri (eds), *Rural Development and the State*, London, Methuen.

Asian Development Bank, 1971. *Southeast Asia's Economy in the 1970s*, London, Longman.

Beresford, Melanie, 1985a. 'Household and Collective in Vietnamese Agriculture'. *Journal of Contemporary Asia*, Vol. 15.

—— 1985b. 'Agriculture in the Transition to Socialism: the Case of South Vietnam' in Mats Lundahl (ed.), *The Primary Sector in Economic Development*, London, Croom Helm.

—— 1987. 'Vietnam: Northernizing the South or Southernizing the North?', *Contemporary Southeast Asia*, Vol. 8.

——, Catley, R. & Pilkington, F., 1979. 'America's New Pacific Rim Strategy', *Journal of Contemporary Asia*, Vol. 9.

Bernard, Paul, 1934. *Le Problème économique indochinois*, Paris, Nouvelles Editions latines.

Bhaduri, Amit, 1976. *Agricultural Cooperatives in North Vietnam*, International Labour Organization, Rural Employment Policy Research Program, Working Paper WEP 10/WP/6, Geneva.

Blecher, Marc, 1986. *China: Politics, Economics and Society*, London, Frances Pinter.

Burchett, W., 1966. *My Visit to the Liberated Zones of South Vietnam*, Hanoi, FLPH.

Burr, J. M., 1976. 'Land to the Tiller: Land Redistribution in South Vietnam 1970–1973', doctoral thesis, University of Oregon.

Buszynski, L., 1986. *Soviet Foreign Policy and Southeast Asia*, London, Croom Helm.

Buttinger, Joseph, 1967. *Vietnam: A Dragon Embattled* (2 vols), New York, Praeger.

—— 1972. *A Dragon Defiant: A Short History of Vietnam*, Melbourne, Wren.

Callison, C. Stuart, 1974. 'The Land to the Tiller Program and Rural Resource Mobilization in the Mekong Delta of South Vietnam', *Papers in International Studies, Southeast Asia Series*, No. 34, Ohio University, Athens, Ohio.

Casella, Alexander, 1978. 'Dateline Vietnam: Managing the Peace', *Foreign Policy*, No. 30, Spring.

Catley, R. & McFarlane, B. 1974. 'The Vietnamese Social Model', *Australian Quarterly*, Vol. 46.

Chaliand, Gerard, 1969. *The Peasants of North Vietnam*, Harmondsworth, Penguin.

Chanda, Nayan, 1986. *Brother Enemy: The War After The War*, San Diego, Harcourt Brace & Jovanovich.

Chen, King C., 1969. *Vietnam and China 1938–54*, Princeton, N.J., Princeton University Press.

Chesnaux, Jean, 1966. *The Vietnamese Nation: Contribution to a History*, Sydney, Current Book Distributors.

CIA, 1983. 'Memorandum, June 9, 1965', *Journal of Contemporary Asia*, Vol. 13.

Coedes, G., 1966. *The Making of South East Asia*, Berkeley, University of California Press.

Constitution of the Socialist Republic of Viet Nam, 1981. FLPH, Hanoi.

Dobb, Maurice, 1967. *Papers on Capitalism, Development and Planning*, London, Routledge & Kegan Paul.

DRV, 1975. *The Democratic Republic of Vietnam*, FLPH, Hanoi.

Duiker, William J., 1980. 'Vietnam Since the Fall of Saigon', *Papers in International Studies, Southeast Asia Series*, No. 56, Ohio University Center for International Studies, Athens, Ohio.

—— 1981. *The Communist Road to Power in Vietnam*, Boulder, Colorado, Westview Press.

—— 1983. *Vietnam: Nation in Revolution*, Boulder, Colorado, Westview Press.

—— 1987. 'Vietnam Moves Towards Pragmatism', *Current History*, April.

Education in Vietnam, 1982. Hanoi, Vietnam Courier & Ministry of Education.

Eisen, Arlene, 1984. *Women and Revolution in Vietnam*, London, Zed.

Elliott, David W. P., 1975. 'North Vietnam Since Ho', *Problems of Communism*, July–August.

—— 1976. 'Revolutionary Re-integration: A Comparison of the Foundation of Post-Liberation Political Systems in North Vietnam and China', doctoral thesis, Cornell University.

Fall, Bernard, 1960. 'North Vietnam's Constitution and Government', *Pacific Affairs*, Vol. 33.

—— 1963. *The Two Vietnams: A Political and Military Analysis*, London, Pall Mall Press.

—— 1965. 'North Vietnam: A Profile', *Problems of Communism*, Vol. 14.

Far Eastern Economic Review, 1986. *Asia Yearbook*, Hong Kong.

Fforde, Adam, 1982. 'Problems of Agricultural Development in North Vietnam', doctoral thesis, University of Cambridge.

— 1985. 'Economic Aspects of the Soviet-Vietnamese Relationship' in Robert Cassen (ed.), *Soviet Interests in the Third World*, London, Royal Institute of International Affairs/Sage.

— and Paine, Suzanne H., 1987. *The Limits of National Liberation*, London, Croom Helm.

Fraser, Stewart, 1984. 'Vietnam's Population: Current Notes', *Contemporary Southeast Asia*, Vol. 6.

Funnell, Victor C., 1978. 'Vietnam and the Sino-Soviet Conflict 1965–1976', *Studies in Comparative Communism*, Vol. 11.

General Statistical Office, 1979. *So Lieu Thong Ke 1978* (Statistical Data of the SRV), Hanoi.

— 1980. *So Lieu Thong Ke 1979*, Hanoi.

— 1983. *So Lieu Thong Ke 1982*, Hanoi.

— 1985. *So Lieu Thong Ke 1930–1984*, Hanoi.

Gordon, Alec, 1981. 'North Vietnam's Collectivization Campaigns: Class Struggle, Production and the "Middle Peasant"', *Journal of Contemporary Asia*, Vol. 11.

— n.d. 'Notes on "Subsistence" Agriculture and the Transition to Socialism in Vietnam', mimeo, University of Bielefeld.

Gourou, Pierre, 1965. *Les Paysans du Delta tonkinois*, Paris, Mouton.

Grant, Bruce *et al*., 1979. *The Boat People*, Melbourne, Penguin.

Hanoi, 1986. *On the Eve of the 6th Congress of the Communist Party of Vietnam 1976–1986*, Hanoi, FLPH.

Hill, R. D., 1984. 'Aspects of Land Development in Vietnam', *Contemporary Southeast Asia*, Vol. 5.

Hodgkin, Thomas, 1981. *Vietnam: The Revolutionary Path*, London, Macmillan.

Honey, P. J. (ed.), 1962. *North Vietnam Today: Profile of a Communist Satellite*, New York, Praeger.

Houtart, François, & Lemercinier, Genevière, 1981. *Sociologie d'une Commune vietnamienne*, Louvain-la-Neuve, CRSR, Université catholique de Louvain.

Huynh Kim Khanh, 1982. *Vietnamese Communism 1925–1945*, Ithaca & London, Cornell University Press.

IMF. *International Financial Statistics*, Washington, DC.

— 1982. *Socialist Republic of Vietnam—Recent Economic Developments*, Washington, DC.

— 1983. *Vietnam—Staff Report for the 1983 Article IV Consultation*, Washington, DC.

Jones, Gavin W., 1982. 'Population Trends and Policies in Vietnam', *Population and Development Review*, Vol. 8.

Kahin, George McT. & Lewis, John W., 1967. *The United States in Vietnam*, New York, Dial Press.

Keith, Ronald C. (ed.), 1986. *Energy, Security and Economic Development in East Asia*, London & Sydney, Croom Helm.

Kiernan, Ben, 1985. *How Pol Pot Came to Power: A History of Communism in Kampuchea 1930–1975*, London, Verso.

Kolko, Gabriel, 1969. *The Roots of American Foreign Policy*, Boston, Mass., Beacon Press.

— 1986. *Vietnam: Anatomy of a War 1940–1975*, London & Sydney, Allen & Unwin.

Lacouture, Jean, 1968. *Ho Chi Minh*, London, Allen Lane.

Lam Thanh Liem, 1985. 'Nouvelles réformes et crise persistante de l'économie rurale dans le delta du Mekong de 1981 à 1985', *Annales de Géographie*, No. 524 (94th year).

Lane, David, 1985. *State and Politics in the USSR*, Oxford, Blackwell.

Le Chau, 1966. *Le Vietnam socialiste: une économie de transition*, Paris, Maspero.

Le Duan, 1978. *The Vietnamese Revolution: Fundamental Problems, Essential Tasks*, Hanoi, FLPH.

Le Duan, 1984. 'Get a Good Hold of the Laws and Renovate Economic Management', *Vietnam Social Sciences*, No. 2.

Le Duan, & Pham Van Dong, 1975. *Towards Large-Scale Socialist Agricultural Production*, Hanoi, FLPH.

Le Duc Tho, 1984. 'Improve Agricultural Management', *Southeast Asia Chronicle*, No. 93.

Le Khoa *et al.*, 1979. *Tinh Hinh Kinh Te Mien Nam 1955–75* (Economic Situation in the Southern Region), Ho Chi Minh City, Vien Khoa Hoc Xa Hoi.

Le Thanh Khoi, 1978. *Socialisme et Développement au Vietnam*, Paris, Presses Universitaires de France.

Limqueco, P. & McFarlane, B., 1979. 'Problems of Economic Planning for Underdeveloped Socialist Countries', *Journal of Contemporary Asia*, Vol. 9.

Liu Guoguang, 1986. 'Aspects and Problems of Price Reform in China', Centre for Asian Studies, University of Adelaide.

Maclear, Michael, 1981. *Vietnam: The Ten Thousand Day War*, London, Thames Methuen.

Marr, David, 1971. *Vietnamese Anti-Colonialism 1885–1925*, Berkeley, University of California Press.

— 1981. *Vietnamese Tradition on Trial*, Berkeley, University of California Press.

— 1985. 'Central Vietnam Rebuilds: An Eyewitness Account', *Indochina Issues*, No. 59.

McMichael, Joan K. (ed.), 1976. *Health in the Third World: Studies from Vietnam*, Nottingham, Spokesman.

Moise, E. E., 1976. 'Land Reform and Land Reform Errors in North Vietnam', *Pacific Affairs*, Vol. 49.

Moody, Dale L., 1975. 'The Manufacturing Sector in the Republic of Vietnam', doctoral thesis, University of Florida.

Morrow, Michael, 1979. 'Vietnam's Embargoed Economy: In the US Interest?', *Indochina Issues*, No. 3.

Murray, Martin J., 1980. *The Development of Capitalism in Colonial Indochina (1870–1940)*, Berkeley, University of California Press.

Ngo Vinh Long, 1973. *Before the Revolution*, Cambridge, Mass., MIT Press.

Ngo Vinh Long, 1984. 'Agrarian Differentiation in the Southern Region of Vietnam', *Journal of Contemporary Asia*, Vol. 14.

Nguyen Duc Nhuan, 1982. 'The Damage of Socialist Witchdoctors and Bureaucrats in Vietnam', *Politique d'Aujourdhui*, No. 82, translated in JPRS 80846.

Nguyen Huu Dong, 1980. 'Agriculture collective, agriculture familiale, économie socialiste', *Vietnam*, No. 1.

Nguyen Khac Vien, 1974. *Tradition and Revolution in Vietnam*, Berkeley, Calif., Indochina Resource Centre.

—— 1985. *Southern Vietnam (1975-1985)*, Hanoi, FLPH.

Nguyen Kien, 1985. 'A Survey of Vietnam's External Relations', *Vietnamese Studies*, No. 6 (new series).

Nguyen Tien Hung, G., 1977. *Economic Development of Socialist Vietnam 1955-1980*, New York, Praeger.

Nguyen Xuan Lai, n.d. 'The Family Economy of Co-operative Farmers', *Vietnamese Studies*, No. 13.

Norlund, Irene, 1984. 'The Role of Industry in Vietnam's Development Strategy', *Journal of Contemporary Asia*, Vol. 14.

—— 1986. 'Rice Production in Colonial Vietnam 1900-1930', in Irene Norlund, Sven Cederroth & Ingela Gerdin (eds), *Rice Societies: Asian Problems and Prospects*, London & Riverdale, Curzon/Riverdale.

Nyland, Chris, 1981. 'Vietnam, the Plan/Market Contradiction and the Transition to Socialism', *Journal of Contemporary Asia*, Vol. 11.

Osborne, Milton, 1983. *Southeast Asia: An Introductory History*, Sydney, George Allen & Unwin.

Patti, Archimedes, 1980. *Why Vietnam?*, Berkeley, University of California Press.

Pentagon Papers, 1971. London, Routledge & Kegan Paul (as published by the New York Times).

Pham Cuong & Nguyen Van Ba, 1976. *Revolution in the Village: Nam Hong (1945-1975)*, Hanoi, FLPH.

Pham Van Dong, 1985. 'Education in Vietnam—Fundamental Problems', *Vietnam Social Sciences*, No. 1.

Pike, Douglas, 1969. *War, Peace and the Viet Cong*, Cambridge, Mass., MIT Press.

—— 1986. *PAVN: People's Army of Vietnam*, Novato, Calif., Presidio.

Popkin, Samuel L., 1979. *The Rational Peasant*, Berkeley, University of California Press.

Porter, Gareth, 1976a. 'Imperialism and Social Structure in Twentieth Century Vietnam', doctoral thesis, Cornell University.

—— 1976b. 'Vietnam's Long Road to Socialism', *Current History*, Vol. 71.

Race, Jeffrey, 1972. *War Comes to Long An.*, Berkeley, University of California Press.

Rawski, Thomas, 1980. *China's Transition to Industrialism*, Ann Arbor, University of Michigan Press.

Robequain, Charles, 1944. *The Economic Development of French Indochina*, New York, Oxford University Press.

Rowley, Kelvin & Evans, Grant, 1984. *Red Brotherhood at War: Indochina Since the Fall of Saigon*, London, Verso.

Rubin, Susanne, forthcoming. 'Learning for Life? Glimpses from a Vietnamese School'.

Sansom, Robert L., 1970. *The Economics of Insurgency in the Mekong Delta of Vietnam*, Cambridge, Mass., MIT Press.

Siamwalla, A. & Haykin, S., 1983. *The World Rice Market: Structure, Conduct and Performance*, International Food Policy Research Institute, Research Report No. 39.

SIPRI, 1986. *SIPRI Yearbook*, Stockholm.

— 1987. *SIPRI Yearbook*, Stockholm.

Snepp, Frank, 1980. *Decent Interval: The American Débâcle and the Fall of Saigon*, London, Allen Lane.

Stanford Research Institute, 1968. *Land Reform in Vietnam*, Menlo Park. Calif.

Szajkowski, Bogdan, 1981. *Marxist Governments: A World Survey*, London, Macmillan.

— 1982. *The Establishment of Marxist Regimes*, London, Butterworth.

Thai Quang Trung, 1985. 'Le Décomposition du Pouvoir vietnamien', *Politique Internationale*, No. 28.

Thayer, C.A., 1982. 'Building Socialism in South Vietnam Since the Fall of Saigon', *Research Paper*, No. 20, Griffith University School of Modern Asian Studies, Centre for the Study of Australian-Asian Relations, Brisbane.

The Far East and Australasia 1987, 1986. London, Europa Publications.

Thompson, Virginia, 1937. *French Indo-China*, London, Allen & Unwin.

Thrift, Nigel & Forbes, Dean, 1986. *The Price of War: Urbanization in Vietnam 1954-1985*, London, Allen & Unwin.

Ton That Thien, 1983. 'Vietnam's New Economic Policy: Notes and Comments', *Pacific Affairs*, Vol. 56.

Tran Huu Quang, 1982. 'Nhan dien co cau giai cap o nong thon dong bang song Cuu Long' (Identifying class structure in the rural areas of the Mekong delta), *Nghien Cuu Kinh Te*, No. 128.

Trullinger, James W., 1980. *Village at War*, New York & London, Longman.

Truong Chinh, 1986. 'Political Report', 6th Party Congress, *SWB*, FE/8447, 20 December.

— & Vo Nguyen Giap, 1974. *The Peasant Question (1937-1938)*, Data Paper No. 94, Southeast Asia Program, Department of Asian Studies, Cornell University, Ithaca.

Tsai Maw Kuey, 1968. *Les Chinois au Sud Vietnam*, Paris, Bibliothèque Nationale.

Turley, William, 1975. 'The Political Role and Development of the People's Army of Vietnam' in Joseph Zasloff & MacAlister Brown (eds), *Communism in Indochina: New Perspectives*, Lexington, Mass., Lexington Books.

— 1986. *The Second Indochina War*, Boulder, Colorado, Westview Press.

Vickerman, Andrew, 1985. 'A Note on the Role of Industry in Vietnam's Development Strategy', *Journal of Contemporary Asia*, Vol. 15.

Vickery, Michael, 1984. *Cambodia 1975-1978*, London, Allen & Unwin.

Vickery, Michael, 1986. *Kampuchea: Politics, Economics and Society*, London, Frances Pinter.

Vien Kinh Te Hoc, 1980. *35 Nam Kinh Te Viet Nam* (35 Years of the Vietnamese Economy), Hanoi, Nha Xuat Ban Khoa Hoc Xa Hoi.

Vietnam Courier, 1980. *Against Maoism: Beijing's Expansionism and Hegemonism*, Hanoi.

—— 1983. *Herbicides and Defoliants in War: the long-term effects on man and nature*, Hanoi.

VCP, 1977. *4th National Congress Documents*, Hanoi, FLPH.

—— 1978. *An Outline History of the Vietnam Workers' Party*, 2nd edn, Hanoi, FLPH.

—— 1979. *History of the August Revolution*, Hanoi, FLPH.

—— 1980. *50 Years of Activities of the Communist Party of Vietnam*, Hanoi, FLPH.

—— 1982. *Ve Congrès national: Rapport politique*, Hanoi, Editions en Langues Étrangères.

Vietnam Geographical Data, 1979. Hanoi, FLPH.

Vietnam Women's Union, 1981. *Women of Vietnam: Statistical Data*, Hanoi.

—— 1982. *5th Congress of the Vietnam Women's Union*, Hanoi.

Vietnam Workers' Party, 1960. *Thirty Years of Struggle of the Party*, Hanoi, FLPH.

Vietnamese Studies, n.d. 'Agricultural Problems', No. 51.

—— 1976. 'Economic Policy and National Liberation War', No. 44.

Vo Nguyen Giap, 1964. *Dien Bien Phu*, Hanoi, FLPH.

Vo Nhan Tri, 1967. *Croissance économique de la République démocratique du Vietnam*, Hanoi, Editions en Langues étrangères.

Vo Van Kiet, 1985. Speech in *SWB*, FE/8139, 20 December.

—— 1986. 'Economic Report, 6th Party Congress, *SWB*, FE/8447, 20 December.

Wain, Barry, 1981. *The Refused: The Agony of the Indo-China Refugees*, New York, Simon & Schuster.

Wang, James C. F., 1985. *Contemporary Chinese Politics: An Introduction* (2nd edn), Englewood Cliffs, N.J., Prentice-Hall.

White, Christine P., 1982a. 'Debates in Vietnamese Development Policy', *IDS Discussion Paper*, No. 171.

—— 1982b. 'Socialist Transformation of Agriculture and Gender Relations: The Vietnamese Case', *IDS Bulletin*, Vol. 13.

—— 1983. 'Mass Mobilization and Ideological Transformation in the Vietnamese Land Reform Campaign', *Journal of Contemporary Asia*, Vol. 13.

—— 1985. 'Agricultural Planning, Pricing Policy and Co-operatives in Vietnam', *World Development*, Vol. 13.

—— n.d. 'Reforming Relations of Production: Family and Co-operative in Vietnamese Agricultural Policy', mimeo, Institute of Development Studies, University of Sussex, Brighton.

Wiegersma, Nancy, 1982. 'The Asiatic Mode of Production in Vietnam', *Journal of Contemporary Asia*, Vol. 12.

—— 1985. 'Agrarian Differentiation in the Southern Region of Vietnam: A Comment', *Journal of Contemporary Asia*, Vol. 15.

Woodside, Alexander, 1971. 'Ideology and Integration in Post-Colonial Vietnamese Nationalism', *Pacific Affairs*, Vol. 44.

—— 1976. *Community and Revolution in Modern Vietnam*, Boston, Mass. Houghton Mifflin.
—— 1983. 'The Triumphs and Failures of Mass Education in Vietnam', *Pacific Affairs*, Vol. 56.
World Bank, 1982. *World Tables*, Washington, DC.
—— 1986. *World Development Report 1986*, New York, Oxford University Press.
Yearbook of International Communist Affairs, 1984. Stanford Calif., Hoover Institution.

Newspapers

Far Eastern Economic Review (Hong Kong).
Financial Times (London).

Index